Sile

Don't believe a word they say.

Paulette Ingram

ACKNOWLEDGMENT

My love for the father, God the Almighty, and his son Jesus Christ is strong. When I am in solitude and simplicity, I feel the love more intensely.

There is just something about being alone with God that draws me nearer to Him. So, to revitalise my spiritual journey, I searched for ways to connect with God, methods that are true to who God created me to be.

First, I give a wholehearted thank you to my Lord and saviour, Jesus Christ. I thank them for this beautiful journey I have embarked upon. The people who have been placed to walk alongside me, those that remained, and those no longer here. I have learned a valuable lesson from all.

From a very young age, my late great aunt and uncle, alongside my grandparents, taught me a valuable lesson. Not everyone is rowing your boat. Some may be drilling holes. Even so, they have played a part in my journey to make this book possible.

My Mother, my biggest champion. You are an extraordinary woman full of fight, bravery, courage, and knowledge. Dr Maya Angelou's description of a phenomenal woman is a description of you. I thank you for believing in me, supporting me, encouraging me to push forward. I have had the privilege to be your eldest daughter, and I have watched you at your finest moments; I am so glad that I am no longer too young to appreciate and witness the glory of your accomplishments. You made sure life was the best for us and taught me not to suffer fools. I can look back through the lens of perspective and visualise how truly unique you are. Thank you for teaching me to sing whilst making me lie on my back; thank you for teaching me the catwalk with books placed upon my head; it all paid off in the end. I know I was always a bit different, but you embraced my quirkiness and odd fashion sense. Thank you for loving me, just as I am.

Samantha Harewood, my beautiful trusted sister, superhero, and ultimate gangster, cake-eating sister. You always have my back. Dare anyone to say a bad word against me, and you would take on the world. You make me laugh so hard and never suffer fools lightly. I appreciate how you always go out of your way for me to do all that you can. Thank you for the three-way WhatsApp calls with mum, listening to me go on about the book's progress. I'm surprised you didn't tie me up and hide me somewhere no one would find me. Thank you for your patience and generosity and for not allowing me to give up.

The best gift any girl could ask for is to have a sister like you; you are the most significant gift that I could never replace and would never be the same without. I love you to the moon and back.

Ernest Owusu, twelve years ago, in 2009, I told you I was writing a book; in the early days, you sat patiently, watching and listening to me manifest my dream. Many nights you sat up with me into the early hours whilst I typed away plotting scenes for the book, never really knowing what it was I was inventing. When I entered a chapter of the book for a competition on BBC breakfast, you edited it and made sure it was sent off on time. I think you were more upset than I was when it was turned down. Shortly after that, I locked the book away, suffering from writer's block. You attempted to push me to pick it up again, and years later, here I am. Thank you for your encouragement and support.

Kwame and Oscar Owusu, my two sons, my warriors, my Wakanda men.

Constantly reading the manuscript over my shoulders and questioning my terminology and my whys. You kept me busy drawing me back into your lives, reminding me I was still your mum. You gave me peace to write, but never let me forget that the food was more important than my writing. You both make me laugh every day; you kept me sane with sweets and chocolate and being your taxi, telling me I needed a break. At times I wonder who the adult is. You are both very different; I love you both so much. More than Beyonce, now that is true love. Thank you for choosing me to parent you.

Kenneth Black, you came into my life and took on the role of a stepdad. I thank you for your gratitude, humbleness, and advice. For the talks and the wisdom you shined upon me. Your class and dignity are one to be admired. Thank you for believing in me and telling us jokes from your own childhood.

Gregory Francis, the number one brother-in-law, is a true warrior. Nothing stands in your way. Your boldness and valid words are to be admired. Thank you for your patience and spiritual guidance.

Jahmaan, Marshall, and Amharic Francis (my nephews). Thank you for your outstanding patience in waiting for the book to emerge. I know this was done with pure love and dedication. Now you're all old enough to read it.

Dean, my brother, is full of laughter, mischief, and maturity at such a young age.

Thank you for the antics that created some of the stories in my mind. So free-spirited I could write a whole book on you. The love and empathy you showed towards us as children will always remain securely in my heart.

My McEachron family, I am amazed I was graced to spend my early days with you all. It was a true adventure.

Margorie McEachron- Thank you for your guidance, support, conversations, and prayers that spur me on. I feel the in-depth feelings you have for me. You are like my second mum, so devoted and caring. You taught me how to be brave and stand up for myself. You are such a fighter and an inspirational queen. I'm honoured to have you as part of my raising and rising. Thank you.

Sharon McEachron- Thank you for your understanding, honesty, prayers, and positive words of encouragement for me to keep going. The big sister I never had. You helped me with my school work and taught me how to spell, primarily your surname and Hawaii 5 O. I will never forget your kindness and fairness. You are a powerhouse; your inner strength is somewhat to be admired. Thank you for leaving me with memories that sparked my creativity.

Danny McEachron- Always so genuine and waiting patiently for the book to be revealed. Always joking around and making me laugh ever since we were children. You always told me I shouldn't forget you as you used to change my nappy. You have always been my big brother. I am honoured to have you as part of my life and part of my memories. Thank you for looking after me.

Richard McEachron- Waiting patiently in the wings, as children, we were always in trouble; it was your schoolboy antics that made me into the athletic child my mum tried so desperately to clear me of (tomboy). No two days were ever the same; mischief should have been our second name.

George McEachron- Thank you for turning me into the tough nut I am today; your strict and bold nature paid off.

Stacia McEachron- Thank you for being so calm with me as a youngster; thank you for your patience and motivation. Your compliments and inspiration did not go a miss. And from that, my aspirations grew. Your quiet words of encouragement were a true gift. Another big sister to me. Thank you

Maxine Hinds-Thank you for always being there, even when you were not expected. Thank you for keeping me out of trouble, well, attempting to anyway. You are like a big sister to me; I can always pick up the phone with you and talk about anything, especially on Saturday mornings. Thank you for your dedication and belief in me to begin this chapter of my life. Thank you for checking on me and catching me when I was falling.

My childhood days with you all inspired my imagination to run wild and invest in writing this book. Thank you, my Catford crew, for the best Robin Hood childhood we had.

My Croydon Family-Thank you to the whole of my Croydon family, past and present. Without you, I would not have experienced many fun memories and magical moments that influenced my imagination. You taught me how to survive and wear my crown like a queen.

My four heartbeats, Mr R, Sanchez, Si'rese, Kelly. Need I say anymore? I could write a whole chapter on each of you.

You made this book what it Is today and will always be. Without our journey and your energy, this fictional life would never have been lived. Thank you for being more than friends; you are my genies, butterflies, and fairy godmothers. Your friendship has been a true gift, and I love you all. You have been my light in the darkness, the inspiration behind this new journey. I am humbled to have you as part of my world.

Denise Hart- my long-standing friend, thank you for your proudness in me and the journey I embarked upon with you as young sassy teenage girls. The world was our oyster, and we lived it as best we could. We were inseparable and always had each other's backs. No man or beast would mess with us. We laughed and cried together. Drank and ate good food together. We didn't need to say a word to one other. We knew what the other was thinking. Although it's fictional, I know you will find a piece of us within the walls of this book. That's because it's created from a journey of fundamental memories. Thank you.

Chyrel Baptiste- my friend and confidant. You are my biggest cheerleader; you walked beside me for twelve years and never gave up on me. You called me out and held me accountable for putting the book on hold; you even paused reading other books in anticipation of owning a copy of mine. Twelve years is a long time. Never did you drop that baton or allow my crown to fall. Instead, you dug your heels in and continued to pestered me for years. Thank you for your perseverance, dedication, and your steadfast belief in me. It's here, girl!

Pam- my dear friend. Thank you for your guidance and your philosophical views. Your great maturity that covered me in my darkest hour allowed me to create plots and scenes for my manuscript. Thank you for being a true friend and keeping me in check when needed. Thank you for listening to me ramble on about life and its lemons. You always had another view that made me see sense. I appreciate our deep conversations and putting the world to rights.

Angela pascal, thank you for your enthusiasm, interest, and patience in waiting for the book. For calling me constantly and being there for me, and for being a true friend.

Jackie Morrison-AKA-Mama Adjua- My dear friend, your genuine heartfelt drive; thank you for your encouragement and checking in on me to make sure I was still on target. I felt your positive energy around me, even from far away in Ghana. Your spiritual air of grace. The difference in the way you think and feel releases positive energy to keep me driving. When I was unsure of my vision. You asked me, "How many people make bread." That will always stay with me.

Thank you for introducing me to Dr Ava Brown.

Tracey Rowe- My dear friend. My spiritual guidance. God placed you back into my life for gifted reasons. The minute you returned, it was as though you never really left. You have been instrumental in the completion of this book. You have transferred nothing, but genuine love, enthusiasm, and encouragement into this chapter of my life. You make me laugh when you check on me, and I know secretly you are telling me off. You have claimed my trust in you, believed in me and pushed me to my limits. I appreciate your opinions, honesty, and time. Your genuine concern and how you turn serious times into a joke. It's an honour to call you my friend. I have confidence in your abilities.

Thank you for not shying away from taking on this massive project and its contents to turn this book into a play. You have stepped up to the mark and conquered it in true champion style. Hakuna Matata my friend.

Karen Burchill- Thank you for your ears and heartfelt suggestions whenever I felt unsure. Your eager interest. You were genuinely invested in my success to complete this manuscript. You have been a trusted friend throughout the years, one I can rely upon. You and your beautiful family have never changed who you indeed are. Who said neighbours can't be friends?

Veronika Slegrova-Thank you for being an excellent, funny, and inspiring friend. You have been very supportive and kind. You have waited patiently for the book to emerge. You go out of your way to help others.

The understanding between us is right on point.

Elaine Okorefe-Thank you for taking the time out of your busy schedule to read some of the manuscripts and return valuable feedback. Your advice to complete a creative writing course was highly resourceful and beneficial. Your encouragement allowed me to rethink and rewrite characters. Your honesty and direction were truly appreciated.

Vee Roberts (@insight2marketing)

Thank you for consistently checking in on me. You are a genius marketing coach, even when I was not on task or consistent with the job at hand. You understood the book had taken over my life for a short while, but you continued to gently remind me that I had this. Your questions and reasoning always generated new ideas. Your interest and care in people go above and beyond. Thank you

Andrea Graham, (andreaagraham.com, andreagrahamjewellery.com) My fantastic coach. Thank you for recognising my creative skills and coaching me even when I didn't think I needed coaching.

After twelve years, you were one of the first people I spoke to when I decided to restart my journey with Silent River. Your passion, drive, vision, belief, and enthusiasm allowed me to step out of my comfort zone and onto the path God created for me. I was overwhelmed with your unique gift to spot my abilities. You are filled with such spiritual grace. You think on the spot and explode with ideas. You taught me the art of recognising good energy and negative energy.

You taught me to feel the fear and do it anyway. Thank you.

Dr Patrick Clarke OBE- My fantastic mentor. You have known me since I was sixteen; I have always looked up to you. Thank you for your devoted time in mentoring me; you saw the dream and didn't stop pushing me to create this journey and get it out into the limelight. Thank you for your flexibility and for paying attention to my new way of living. I appreciate your drive, direction, and exceptional advice.

Dr Ava Eagle Brown (The Mango Girl)

Last but by no means least, my book coach and publisher. If you have ever met a woman with a prominent, warm, bubbly, and genuine personality, it's Dr Ava Brown. As soon as I met Ava, I took to her straight away. I joined her book for a business course, and I have learnt so much. If you ever wondered what those little numbers in a book meant, this is the place to find out.

I promise from now on, I will read every prologue, epilogue, and book content. Ava taught me how intricate and time-consuming it is to write the book and put it together. Ava, you were always on top of me, spurring me on to take my time but get it finished. You have held my hand throughout the whole process. Your easy nature has been inviting. Ava, you are a great teacher. I love your referral to the contents of a book as soft furnishings. You are an amazing, caring coach who goes above and beyond.

Thank you to everyone who purchases and reads this book. Should you happen to illuminate a piece of yourself in here, I pray it's a positive vibe and that you can find peace and happiness from it.

DEDICATION

Romans 8- verse 31

What shall we say about such wonderful things as these? If God is for us, who can ever be against us?

I dedicate this book to Herbert Delroy McEachron and Louise Miriam McEachron. My great aunt and uncle. Samuel Augustus Ingram and Hilda Maud Ingram. My grandparents, whose shoulders I stand upon.

In memory of a River that runs so deep and still.

A NOTE FROM THE AUTHOR

I have had some strange conversations with myself in public, acting out the role of the characters in the streets, unaware I was staring at people, avoiding near altercations. I have secretly listened to your conversations, searching for inspiration. So, if you recognise a discussion here that you may have had with your closest friend that suddenly stops you in your tracks, and you think, "I say those things. That happened to me," then nine times out of ten, it's probably you.

I watched you laugh out loud and wide as I counted the gaps between your teeth and the pleats of curtains around your eyes. I observed the smoothness of your face, the cracks in your lips. All for the sake of my own selfish pleasure. I have observed your face etched in pain whilst your brows knitted in confusion from the torment. Yet, as sordid as it remains, I was too involved with my feelings to produce a book.

Think back to that time in the shopping centre when you held back the tears whilst telling your friend about your unruly daughter falling pregnant; I was the person standing next to you, checking the date on the milk. You know the one that bumped into you and smiled warmly as she released the bottle from her grip? It bounced over the floor, splashing up your legs whilst your feet were drowned in a white sea. Think back to the time you were having a picnic out with friends and family. You secretly revealed you had met a new man; although you knew he was married, you couldn't help yourself, and one thing led to another. Now he was leaving his wife for you, but you weren't ready for the commitment. I was the person lying on the bench nearby, crunching loudly on my apple whilst taking notes.

Remember when your wallet fell out of your back pocket, I tapped you on the shoulder and handed it back to you. I paused my hold for a while so I could study the grooves of your hand, witness life's hardship. Your fingers were quite feminine but strong. I guessed you worked in an office as your nails were clean and cut short. Not grimy and jagged. I sussed you were in your middle forties or thereabouts as your veins were not prominent and your skin masked only a few aged lines. I rubbed your hand for a while as you stared at me in disbelief. Finally, you stole your hand back, squinted your eyes at me, and walked quickly away. Yes, that was me.

Remember when you sat in the cinema, and the person next to you spilt popcorn into your lap. You laughed so hard together, relieved it was not Coca-Cola. Yes, that was me; I wanted to see your reaction.

I have laughed, cried, lost sleep over this book.

I have shouted at the pages, developed an unhealthy relationship with coffee, and spilt mocha on it. Deliberately had arguments with friends and family just so I could pick out the reality. So, the ideas in my story were not too farfetched. First, I have become a hermit and starved myself because I would forget to eat. Food had no meaning. Then, I missed social appointments because I didn't know what day it was. I developed fictional emotions, and life became one big movie.

The hardest part about writing this book was creating characters disloyal to my almighty God; believe me, prayer played a massive role in this chapter of my life, even more so than it already does. I felt like such a traitor.

But I know God favours me, and these are fictional characters.

I've written this fiction story for a few reasons.

It's by no means a self-help book; however, should you find yourself within its walls and it triggers an idea, a thought, a memory, a notion, a need, a feeling, comfort, to help yourself or others, then, I shall be truly humbled.

My most stirring hope is that every single person who reads Silent River places it upon their bookshelves with an understanding of the feelings and events. So, they may be able to help others or become a listening ear.

I love storytelling; I love the shock factor. My teacher always told me I had a vivid imagination and write best when I dabble in dark stories. The strange thing is I hate horror movies or anything frightening. Of course, this is far from horror, but it's still scenarios I would flinch at.

I have so many stories travelling around in my brain. I needed to release them.

I wanted to take on a new challenge. I wanted to take the risk to trust myself.

I want to feel the adrenalin of being at the edge of what is possible.

The drive of a challenge so big, where I will put my skills on show, is intoxicating.

Paulette Ingram

AUTHORS NOTES

This is a work of fiction. Contents of the book may cause triggers for some readers; this is not the intention. Names, places, characters, events, and incidents are the product of the author's imagination; if any parts are genuine, they have been used fictitiously, researched, or given permission by persons to use parallel realities as fiction. Existing named places are intended to provide the book with a feel of reality and authenticity.

REVIEWS

I have been waiting for so long for this book, and I am happy to say it did not disappoint! If you have any plans, cancel them as this book is too good to put down. You are taken into the lives of five friends and watch them go through trials and tribulations of the life handed to them. There are secrets, lies, deception, highs, and lows. The author really brought the characters to life, which sets it apart from many other fictional books I have read. My only issue is that I needed more; I'm now so invested in finding out what happens next. So please don't make me wait too long for part 2.

Chyrel-Louise-Baptiste (Pediatric nurse)

Written in true fiction style. Gripping from start to finish. I'm impressed by Paulette's writing style and ability to draw readers in for a first-time author. I could taste and smell every description. I feel a Netflix movie coming on

Sanchez McKenzie (Traffic signals engineer)

Spine chilling, it made me think of my own friends. Five friends hang out together for years, never really knowing each other. Then, they throw one another under the bus to get themselves off the hook. Paulette's imagination is dynamic and skilful. I dare you to put it down before the last chapter.

Si'rese (correctional treatment specialist)

Paulette has written a colourful fictitious tale; her witty, dark, and outrageous imagination gleams with engagement and dynamic skill. Paulette has created believable characters that have you uttering profanity. Depicts a harsh reality in which women's lives can be fragmented in an instance. I was hooked from the first sentence, sensitive, disturbing, invigorating, believable content.

I'm looking forward to parts 2 and 3.

DR Malawi (COH)

TABLE OF CONTENTS

FOREWARD

Silent River has managed to grip me on every page with Paulette's attention to detail. Her precise descriptions of Paige's childhood home catapulted me back to great memories of my own childhood house that I grew up in with my parents and siblings.

Paulette has cleverly plotted twists and turns in Silent River that will have you questioning the characters and your own experiences. You will also find yourself eager to find out the answer to every question presented page by page.

Five friends with their individual stories and how they all merge into one. The truth, lies, deceit, and secrets, the plot twists presented in this book within every chapter will have you wanting more!

I have not been captured by a book in a very long time, not wanting to put it down; I'm sure I recognise quite a few characters I have encountered throughout my life; this book is gripping, intriguing, and quite comical in parts.

Silent River will enlighten you into how people's lives can take sudden directions in a moment. It highlights how the decisions we make can lead us to places and experiences we encounter.

Some will be shocked, tickled, intrigued, horrified even, but you will learn to appreciate your life and those around you.

I cannot wait for the sequels of this book, and I am so excited to be turning this book into a play and mini-series real soon.

Tray-Ann Rowe

Creative director/playwright

T.V Presenter
Presenter & Content Acquisition associate at Rep Dat T.V.

Health practitioner

Co-owner of I Am Echo fashion & Confidence platform
Trayannsworld@gmail.com

www.trayannsworld.com
Instagram: Insideouthealth2

Traann2

Iamechofashionshows

Iamechofashionplatorm
F.B.: Tray-Ann

FB: I Am Echo

WICKED ECHOES

The shadow fades, the first hour draws near

I beg for forgiveness, not even a prayer!

Save me from torture.

Save me from pain.

A mass rejection

Drove me insane.

CHAPTER 1

WICKED ECHOES

I will never forgive them for burying me in this dark hole. It was supposed to be a secret that I held onto for life. Ironically, I didn't even know what the secret was.

That's the part that they forgot to fill me in on. But I went along with it because she told me to.

In the smoke-filled, cluttered room, a young girl had been stripped of her clothing. To her left hung a scraggly white translucent nightdress sprayed with a rose scent in preparation for her exorcism. Her emaciated bare feet were bound together with parcel tape. A stream of blood flowed down her bony arms, painting her malnourished fingers red before descending to the floor in droplets.

She forcefully hugged her upper body to suffocate the violent shaking caused by the bitter cold air in the room. Her teeth chattered profusely in the silence as she sniffed back the juices streaming from her nostrils and seeping into her mouth. Her reddish-brown hair hung loose to her shoulders, parted into four sections. The plaits had adopted the appearance of frizzy coils. The oil cascading from the centre of her head caused her eyes to sting, blinding her as it undulated down her flushed cheeks.

The young girl pursed her full lips as she stubbornly clenched her jaw to stifle the cry threatening to erupt from within her.

She drew her legs in hard, pressing them against her chest; she buried her head into her knees, afraid to touch the salt sprinkled on the cold stone floor in a circle around her.

He tried to whisper her name; The young girl didn't dare move towards the singing character. There it was again, the croaky, Jamaican voice echoing in the back of her head. The voice she loved to hear. She managed to slowly lift her head out of the warm pool she had created with her arms and opened one eye to peep at him.

For a minute, she believed in him; she felt the comfort of his voice. She thought it was all over; he was going to save her. But he didn't. He just stood there, by the old washroom door, his body taut and face painted in a whirlpool of torturous emotions, disgust, regret, anger, fear.

The young girl couldn't figure it out; was he blaming her or himself?

His once warm eyes now resembled icy stone. White fuzz, twin to the colour of his eyes, replaced the healthy black beard.

The young girl knew she had caused his pain, but she wasn't sure how or when.

But she did know, whatever this was, had grown enormous, way bigger than him, more significant than his beliefs, which he preached every Sunday. No judge or jury would ever declare him sane. They would have him sectioned, burnt at stake for telling such an absurd story.

The young girl recognised those confusing reflections, those ridged reactions in the man she loved. Old memories held her hostage in her head, swirling around, causing a numbing pain throughout her body. What was he doing?

He just stood there, grumbling something in the background.

He just stood there.

Why did he not come to her rescue? Why did he watch her in that devilish state and do nothing? He should have bolted in there like a warhorse and stamped his authority; he was supposed to be her saviour, there to protect her. He should have put a stop to this ludicrous scene unfolding before him in his very own home.

A man of God, a highly respected preacher, a

family-oriented person, he had changed; he had become party to a brutal murder. Yet, he held that glare in his face, the one the doctor gives you before he injects awful news.

She loved him with all her heart, but it was too late. She would never forgive him for this. And in the end, his betrayal of her would be the death of him.

The older man shook his head and rubbed his hand across his distinguished beard. The tremble in his hands jingled the keys he held. He closed the rickety washroom door and locked it behind him; stumbling back to his creaky rocking chair, he took his place. A genuine tear danced down his crumpled face as he rocked himself back and forth, smoking his pipe.

The eight women stomped sternly into the dimly lit room. The sound of their steps on the stone floor was sharp and deliberate. The young girl could hear the sound, and with that, she abandoned her thoughts of blacking out. Instead, she directed her body to fall unsupported. Her cheek punched the floor as blood filled her mouth from the impact. The child's monotone whimper was an annoyance to the women; her deliberate act of self-destruction was limiting their actions.

The women appeared, armed with strange odd-shaped bottles; they knelt before her arms outstretched before they bowed in unison.

The young girl became hypnotised by the fluid as she watched them swirl it around within its enclosure.

The women's long white cotton dresses stood out against the variations of their multicoloured dark skin tones; the matching head wraps seemed to twirl on forever, and the young girl thought they resembled those of Rastafarian wives. Their faces were filled with an array of emotions painted in a hardcore stance; they were not ones to be ignored.

She flinched at the warm sticky hand placed on her shoulder

"Come, child, it's time." The voice was deep, husky, and bore a strong Jamaican accent.

The poor child frantically shook her head, pressing her bloody hands against the floor, clawing at the stone.

The smell of urine and vinegar filled the air overpowering her senses, causing her to heave up green phlegm from her chest. It surfaced into her mouth and backed down again.

"Come, child, let us do our job. Don't let them come for you. Come, baby."

"Bring the pickney and stop messing," a more authoritative voice called from behind her.

"Bring the devil pickney, and let's get to it."

The young girl's head turned towards the voice; for a moment, she held eye contact with the gruesome features that hovered above. Her brows knitted in confusion as sweat sprang from every pore on her frail body. A sweep of tiredness dances over her.

One of the women began wrenching her arm to heave her up; she appeared so light in complexion she was almost transparent. Her eyes were set so closely together it was making the young girl dizzy. She had the flattest nose the young girl had ever seen, her eyebrows were missing, and it was apparent they had been carefully painted. She resembled a scary clown. A faintly visible moustache rested in a thin line above her lip with a mole to its left; one silver hair spiralled out of it.

The young girl thought she was the ugliest thing she had ever seen.

Another two women gazed at her with sympathetic eyes, but the others were rough, showering her with no concern. They had come to perform a task, and no man or beast would stand in their way. They had blamed the young girl for the family sins; no one cared that she was only thirteen, petrified and alone.

The young girl's chest heaved high as her breathing became deep and heavy. It felt as if it would explode out of her throat. Her body was being pulled off the ground; at first, she thought she was floating. She closed her eyes to imagine herself in a beautiful place filled with colourful cotton wool clouds. But her heart drummed in her chest as her body was viciously ripped from the cold floor and tossed into the air.

The child's head collided with the ceiling in time with her piercing scream.

Immediately, she became dizzy and limp, scrambling in thin air to stop the motion of falling.

The young girl placed her arms across her face to cradle it against the subsequent impact. Her elbows bounced off the ceiling before she realised what was happening. She was being thrown into the air again. What the hell was going on?

Grabbing at anything she could, like a wild cat, she began to fight.

"Hold her." She heard the frustrated voices.

"Get her, hold her tight, take her legs, grab her arms, let's finish this."

She could feel her arms been pulled to her sides as though they were being yanked out the sockets, she winced at the pain, and her legs were held outstretched as if forced into a split. Then, with a sudden jolt, her body was being thrown up again, and she began to cry, heart-wrenching sobs.

"Hush child, we are nearly done." The voice was husky, calm, but irritating to the young girl.

"PLEASE." Her torturing pleas were ignored.

"STOP, LET ME GO!" But her mouth was taped, and the words were just mumbles. Her eyes bulged out of their sockets, tears spilt down her face, spraying all around her.

Then there was calm. Her body stiffened as it was laid to rest on the stone-cold floor back into the circle of salt placed around her. Laying on her side, cramped in a foetal position, she trembled from fear and cold.

A menthol liquid began raining down on her goose-bumped skin. She tried to look around at what was going on, but the fluid stung her eyes, forcing her to keep them shut tight.

Her cry escalated into the dampen walls; her best attempts to stifle them were feeble.

The chanting cranked up a gear, and fear licked her entire body. She writhed in pain as exhaustion becomes entrenched in her body.

"Umm, rangy shinga hum, umm rengay shinga umm".

Chanting in unison, the women were splashing the various ointments over her. It settled in her hair, ran down her neck; a burning sensation covered her body. The smell was overpowering, and she could make out anise seed, banana, and a vinegar aroma.

The young girl felt her body jolt to an upright position. She was too weak to sit up alone, so one of the ladies knelt behind her to allow her to lean against her hardened knees.

She attempted to stroke the girl's head, but the

rough blistered hand-pulled strands of her hair from the roots to calm her. For a short moment, the young girl might have felt a little comfort.

The young girl managed to drag her eyes open to view the women abusing her body in a quest to save her soul and empty her of all the wickedness she had apparently brought upon herself.

The ladies were polished with irritation; they didn't care about her innocence. The young girl was to blame for the embarrassment upon the family; as she referred to them, the witches wanted to inflict pain to make her understand her misconduct and beg them for mercy. But she would die first.

The ugly woman who sat to the left had adjusted her intolerant level towards the girl. She had even tried to reason with her.

Then there was Butch Cassidy, a large lump of a woman; she was probably bought to control any ill behaviour, there to restrain her.

The girl wasn't sure what the whole ceremony was about; all her aunt and uncle had told her was that these women would help her, cure her, wash away her sins, and make her pure. She wasn't sure what she had done to become so unholy.

The young girl was warned to adhere to the rules and show no lousy attitude. They would be here when she got back and make her favourite dinner, akee and salted fish. They said it as if she was going on a beautiful seaside trip with her favourite aunties.

Where was her aunt? Her uncle was of no use.

Why was this happening just to her and not the others? Where were her cousins?

All the people she loved had vanished.

The women continued their eery chant whilst they continued to unplug the tops of the oddly shaped bottles and, one by one, poured the contents over her frail body. They rubbed the oil into her limbs, already stinging from the menthol liquid sprinkled over her earlier. The party was careful not to touch the salt on the floor around her.

The oil penetrated her skin; the girl began to relax to the firm rub on her body. The women eyed one another, the lady with the warm eyes and friendly smile turned to them with a nod,

"It's time", her voice was tearful, and this panicked the young girl.

Then, out of nowhere, she could hear what sounded like the crowing of a rooster; her body wriggled in fear as the tape across her mouth made her hyperventilate.

"HUM RENGAY SHINGA HUM, HUM RENGAY SHINGA HUM".

"Purify her, purify her, take this oil and the blood of new life and purify her."

"Unveil her of her sins, unveil the darkness that

travels with her, rip out the devil within her, and tell him he has no place."

"Cast it to one side, and purify her, Ohllalalalalal, open the grounds great one, hear me and save this young baby's soul."

The girl froze, staring at the man dressed in a long black, gold, and red robe. His large saucer eyes matched his round chubby face accentuating his chocolate skin. A faint scar ran the length of his right cheek. His hair was shaven low, he wore a black and gold beanie cap that covered the middle of his head.

The fingernail on his right pinkie resembled the claw of an animal; around his index finger, he wore a chunky gold ring engraved with a black star. The young girl recognised the symbol, and she remembered the meaning. Something her uncle had taught her about the attendees of the free masons

she wanted to lean over and bite his bare feet to make him shut up.

This would not happen to her cousins; they would not stand for such torture, they would fight with her all their might, and they would win. But she just didn't have it in her.

Abruptly, the man straddled her and produced a clucking chicken, flapping upside down above her head. The women simultaneously bowed their heads and began to speak in tongues, something she recognised from hearing her elders speak this foreign language on many occasions.

The young girl was petrified beyond belief; she attempted to free her hands from the women restraining her so she could rip the tape from her mouth and breathe.

The bizarre priest teased the clucking chicken that was probably more petrified than the girl; he lowered it down onto her body, allowing it to peck around her hair, lips, neck, stomach, and then down in between her thighs and up to her private parts.

The girl's young eyes stayed wide and glazed; cold sweat poured from her, too terrified to scream from the excruciating pain. She held her breath in the hope of passing out. Instead, the ghostly-looking man revealed a long machete from behind his back. He swung it high into the air, holding it there for a second as if judging his direction for a precise swing. His hand came down at speed, chopping the head off the clucking chicken. The girl screeched as she heard the crack of the bone. It hit the floor with a thud, its head still clucking in pain; without any realisation, it had been parted from its body.

The blood escaping from the chicken splashed onto her face into her eyes, blinding her vision as the tape was viciously ripped away from her mouth.

The young girl gagged from the furry and scaly

texture shoved in between her lips as a foul-smelling warm liquid filled her throat. She could hardly breathe as the blood from the dead chicken combined with the vomit building up inside her escaped from her mouth. She projectile vomited like an alien across the room, hitting the old man's robe as he knelt in between her propped-apart legs. The strange man was unphased by this scene. He wiped his brow with an old cloth he pulled out from his large pocket and continued the process.

The rest of the stale chicken blood was inserted inside her, and a raw metallic stench emerged, filling the air. The young girl briefly looked to the old man for help, but he was still sitting in the other room, rocking in his chair.

That's when she saw the priest throw the chicken to one side, wipe his mouth, and pull out a shiny silver probe from a black velvet bag.

He held eye contact with her for a few moments, and the chanting around her became loud and penetrating; she shook her head frantically side to side, attempting to wiggle free.

"Don't fight it, child; it will only hurt more", the ugly woman informed her.

Just then, she saw the probe disappear between her legs. Her ability to blackout did not let her down.

For a moment, she couldn't breathe, fear,

paralysing every inch of her body, then the will to survive took over. The pain was unbearable. Her body gave up as she witnessed something significant being wrenched from between her young groin. As she passed out, she was sure she heard the faint cry of a baby.

Whilst I sat, eagerly listening, her hands trembled as she spoke to me. She clenched her fists, a sensation of indescribable oppression seeming to trigger some unfamiliar part of her.

THE MOLE!

I didn't want to hear her answer, but I asked anyway. I prayed God would not associate me with people so deluded. And if he had, what was his purpose? What was I supposed to gain from this?

This was her version of events; this was what she told me. But how could you trust someone who didn't even know what the truth meant?

Her body appeared to be filled with vague anguish; it was like a summertime mist projecting around her. She did not sit there upbraiding her family; she did not pretend she was not a part of it. Fate had bought her footsteps to the path she had followed. I genuinely believe they were clear in their heads that their purposeful ignorance would not catch up with them.

Now here she was, trying to make sense of it all. Trying to persuade me to believe her version. What if they didn't want her to make sense of it? I knew I was pushing her by asking questions, and I knew I had no right to interfere. But didn't I deserve to know the truth? I'm regretting I even asked. Now I might well be fearing for my own life.

PAIGE

Pay close attention to the prayers you are sent

One can promise you forever, like a stone
That cannot bend.

You once promised me a promise

That my life would be content

But only an illusion stands before me

In a puddle of revenge

CHAPTER 2

A TURN IN PAIGE

The houses we grew up in was a four-story house from the 1800s. The term stately home is subject to debate, but my parents referred to it as such. It was their grand splendour, whatever that meant. They told me that when the queen lived in Catford, this was the house of her servants. After she moved, it went up for sale at an affordable price for the locals. They were fortunate to get it. I believed everything they told me. As a child, the house appeared humongous.

The red-stained wooden front door bore a large square stained-glass window that depicted a bible scene. The door squeaked when you opened it, the hinges large and ancient. They sprayed rust onto the ground when it was shut hard. It was a heavy door, so the only way to close it was by giving it a good bang.

My mum and dad would shout in unison in a peppery Jamaican accent, "Don't slam the blasted door, child, Tek time." But I couldn't take time. I was small for my age and skinny; this door was ten times my height. Okay, slight exaggeration, but it was huge.

I had to stand directly behind it, place both my hands on it slowly, and then run with all my might and slam it shut. I would then turn my back against it and slide to a seated position; that was a whole day's work done for me. My dad would always be standing at the end of the long hallway smiling at me whilst I steadied myself for the next task of climbing those long stairs.

The hallway was mass consumption of floral wallpaper; you couldn't tell where it ended or started; I just remember thinking that part of it was upside down. But did not dare tell my uncle that. Hanging wallpaper was his pride and joy; no one could do the job better than him. At least, that was what he told people anyway.

I think people in the eighties designed wallpaper for the masses to project their mood. Looking back, it had a sense of naivety rolled in with confusion, sex, and drugs.

To the right of the long hallway was the lengthy study lounge. It had been divided by a white wall to create more rooms and a space for visitors. The first half of the room was inviting, the oak door was always ajar, and you could feel the heat from the sun protecting the white shagpile carpet. The carpets that would entice you in, daring you to step on it. The great glass cabinet was home to the odd, random, intricate ornaments that somehow had some meaning to their

Caribbean heritage. We had free reign in that room only to clean the objects; extra polish meant visitors were attending. The radiogram held precedence in that room; it was the master blaster of lovers' rock music and Jim Reeves, the white gospel singer that all the black mums loved and cherished. Sunday dinner wasn't cooked without his music blasting through the home.

The unbalanced photo display covered every inch of the striped multi-coloured velvet wallpaper, with the white Jesus Christ and his twelve disciples taking centre stage.

The front room was an essential place of pride and entertainment. It showed you had succeeded. It was a display of love and hard work. For this reason, we were not allowed to enter without permission, only on Sundays for bible studies.

The second half of the front room was covered in a spine-chilling atmosphere; the light was always off, the door was permanently closed, but I could see the darkness through the keyhole. Large barrels lived in that room, waiting to be shipped to Jamaica; the curtains were always ajar, a stream of light always teased its way in through the gap and snuck around the boxes and barrels piled high to the ceiling.

That is where it first happened, right there in that room, behind the barrels where no one could see or hear. His cornflakes breath was always so poignant.

"Don't tell anyone," He would remind me as if it was okay. "It's our secret."

I didn't want to have this as a secret; the only secret I tried to keep was a surprise birthday party or what my siblings were getting for Christmas. But he said I would get into big trouble if I told on him. His hands were always warm and sticky. He told me that it was like when Adam and Eve found out they were naked, and God banished them from the garden of Eden. I didn't want to be banished. So, I just closed my eyes and let it happen.

He said I should try to enjoy it because Eve did; he also said it was my fault because I was pretty like Eve. So, when his Greek friend, who had recently moved in on our road, eight houses down, would come over for dinner after school, I thought it was okay for him to do the same.

At the end of the hallway was our dining room. This was where we watched tv, ate our dinner, and congregated in family time. I found this room quite cold, with its red-stained floors and pale blue walls decorated with images of rivers from around the world. An archway led you into our sizeable kitchen; attached to that was our washroom, where we hand-washed our clothes in a metal tub then hung them out in the garden resembling an orchard. My parents grew all their own fruit and vegetables; we never went without.

At the top of flight one, directly opposite the stairs, was a bedroom tucked far back into the landing. I used to love climbing those giant winding steps, decorated in a dark red carpet with no comparison with the orange and brown floral walls.

There was never a light to accompany the white door; another area of the house that had appeared dark and dismal. I was never allowed into that room, never knew what or who was in it, and never ever saw anyone come from or go into it. I am sure one night I heard a cry in there, not full-on crying, just sobbing and sniffing, I had put my ear close to the door and whispered a polite hello, but the sobbing stopped.

I told my mum and dad, but they said it was my imagination, and it was an attic room only because they could not get into the original attic, as there was no ladder, but Piper said she heard it. So, when Jazz, Storm, Giselle, and Venus came over, we would sit outside the door, but they never heard it.

My parents didn't like Storm and Venus; they said they didn't have enough prayer in their lives and that they would come to no good.

Next door to the room was a kitchen, with what resembled a barn door; it was short, like a half door. I was only slightly taller than it, and I had to tiptoe to reach the lock on the other side.

It was all white, white cupboards, white doors, ceiling, and floors. A tiny space with a window, you could look out and view the side of the large garden.

The kitchen always smelt of cornflakes, and the kettle was always warm as if it had not long ago been boiling. I hated the smell of cornflakes. It reminded me of him whenever he came near me. That was how he smelt, like cornflakes. My whole body would go rigid with fear whilst he ran his hands over me, touching parts of me I am sure was not allowed. If Piper was there, I am sure she would have snapped his fingers in half. Piper promised if she caught him, that would be the end. Piper would punch him hard. But she was not here, so I just had to close my eyes, count to ten, and pray that God would save me instead. Sometimes God got there in time, and sometimes, he just never showed up. Maybe he had banished me from his thoughts. I'm not sure which would be worse, being forsaken by God or my parents. I wanted to ask for forgiveness; it just felt so wrong.

At the top of flight two, opposite the stairs, was the master bedroom where my parents slept. The wallpaper changed as it ventured around the corner to a dark velvet blue, although the carpet stayed the same. I loved their room; I felt safe and happy.

It was bright, inviting; the sun always overtook the

two large windows that overlooked the main road. It was clustered with a sewing machine, and extreme amounts of material my mum always claimed were in use. She once told me that she sewed for the queen, which was why she had so much cloth.

For years I believed her, even told my friends at school.

Their bed was situated directly opposite the window with a rectangular brown velvet ottoman at the end of the bed. This was where I pushed him one day. I didn't mean to lock him in it. I was just so scared of him. But then I couldn't open it, and he couldn't breathe. My dad had to smash the lock open. By then, he was unconscious but still breathing; the ambulance man told me off for playing silly games.

My parents didn't tell me off; they just shook their heads at me in disappointment that I hadn't killed him. Well, that's how I interpreted it anyway.

I had to read the bible and ask for forgiveness for three days.

But I didn't. Instead, I spent three days asking God why he let him live because shortly after that, he threatened me. I had to bring him breakfast and dinner in bed for three days to apologise to him. It was the worst three days of my entire life.

The carpet in my parent's room changed abruptly from the wine red in the hallway to a floral green. The walls were blue floral with curtains they tried to match. Suitcases stacked high on top of one another framed the room, it was confusing, but I felt safe. When they were out, I would lie across their bed and read the Bible.

My bedroom was to the left of their room; I shared this room with Maddison, Sabine, and Piper.

I loved Piper, but she was not always there; sometimes, she stayed with her brother Leandro at her dad's house. I often wished I was like Piper. Sometimes I would stare at her when she came out of the bath and moisturised her curvy body. I would sit next to her, listening to her deep voice rambling on about her friends and the antics they got up to at school that day. I would then help her squeeze into the tightest clothing possible as she admired her tall frame in the long mirror. If the base of her buttock was showing, she was happy. Piper loved the boys, and the boys loved Piper.

Piper was unusual looking; she was light-skinned, considering her dad was dark-skinned. I heard her mum was dark too, so it didn't really add up. Her hair had adventurous large bouncy curls, light brown with blond streaks, escaping to the middle of her back and complimenting her soft brown eyes. Freckles danced over her high cheekbones, matching the complexion of her blond streaks.

Piper was always draped in clothing no one else would wear. She liked to be unique; she didn't care what people thought of her. If they chose to address her, they should be prepared to get a mouthful of her whiplash tongue. That was the part I didn't love about her, the bitchy side

I was tough when I was in my bedroom because I had to be. If I wasn't, Sabine would have me sleeping on the landing.

There were three single beds in this room; it was cosy, with my bed closest to the door.

A large wooden wardrobe blocked out some of the light that poured in through the tall window. We all shared it for school uniforms and other items of clothing. My uniform was somehow always off the hangers and thrown to the bottom of the wardrobe, which meant I would have to iron my clothes again in the morning whilst getting a good cussing from my mum about not taking care of myself.

It also meant that I missed plantain, eggs, and fried dumplings for breakfast.

My siblings were always happy to have my share. I would only have time to slurp a mouthful of grated, Jamaican hot chocolate, that smooth velvety richness of cinnamon and nutmeg warm in my tummy. Until one of my siblings would nudge me deliberately, so I would have to change my crisp white shirt. I am not sure if they were that evil to do that to me intentionally, knowing I would have to change. Knowing what was waiting for me upstairs.

I would tiptoe as quietly as I could, but he always heard me, he would stand in the doorway of my room and watch me undress, then leave me the smallest gap in the door so I would have to squeeze past him so he could rub himself on me. "Yuck, I hated him with every bone in my body." I wished Piper would just bust in and give him a good beating; she was always so brave

God was always my friend. I prayed to him every day to make sure I got out safely. Sometimes, he answered my prayers. But I wondered how long he would continue to hear me.

Occasionally, I would stop at flight one. I was sure I could hear someone moving around in that room, and I felt connected to it for a stupid reason. When I felt scared, I would sit outside it and just talk. I could hear sniffing in there, but no one believed me except Piper, so I never mentioned it again.

Flight three consisted of a small landing with one bedroom and a bathroom situated next to it. Nothing special, really, brown walls and a square patch of royal blue carpet, slightly neglected. The wooden bannister surrounded the landing and boxed it in; the chandelier above creaked as it swung and sent an eery feeling up my spine. This is where it happened again. His first attack after I attempted to suffocate him.

This was Ariel's floor. She had her own room because she was the eldest girl. One day she asked me to go to her room to collect her cardigan. We were going to the cinema to watch Annie, the badger; I loved this programme. It was about a girl who would turn into a badger when she was shy or scared and confidently completed all the tasks. I was so excited because it was the last part, and she would save her best friend from getting run over. The episode before left us with a big cliff-hanger. The car was fast approaching. Would Annie get there in time to save her best friend?

I ran all the way to the top of Ariel's gloomy-looking staircase, spun into her room, tripped over the mess on her floor, grabbed the cardigan laying on her untidy bed, turned around to leave, and bumped straight into him. Where had he come from?

I placed my trembling hand on his chest and pushed him away from me; he shoved me back, and Ariel's clothes on the floor broke my fall. I lay there petrified to move as he kneeled before me with a devilish grin on his face.

"I told you I would get you back, now you've really made me angry." He placed two fingers into his mouth and sucked on them. Still eyeing me, saliva dripped from his hands as he removed his fingers. I heaved at the ugly sight. This display of absolute gross behaviour was followed by a sharp pain in my groin; I winced at the sharpness and demanded, *God, take me now* if he was not going to deal with him. Finally, he answered my prayers. Just then, Piper appeared into the room. That was when I blacked out.

The next thing I know, the ambulance crew was resuscitating him. I was sitting in the living room watching the commotion, covered in blood. Piper sat next to me, cuddling me. She whispered in my ear, "Don't worry, he won't touch you anymore, but you must not tell anyone about what he's being doing, or we will all be taken away." What the hell was she talking about, there he was dying in front of us, and she didn't want to defend herself.

"But, Pip, we have to confess; they will forgive us," I pleaded with her.

"Don't be so stupid, Paige, this is unforgivable. You nearly killed another person".

"Who me? I blacked out. you did this."

"Paige, you wanted me to. I'm the adopted one, and I will be removed forever, so you must take the blame for me. We're in this together."

"You shouldn't have taken it this far Piper, if he dies, that makes you a murderer."

"Oh, so you want me to protect you, but you don't want the consequence?" The bitchiness was leaking out of both of us. "Say you did it, or I will never help you with anything again."

"You want me to go to prison Piper." I was whimpering at her request.

"No, I don't, but it wouldn't be the first time you tried to kill him; they will think you tried to kill him again because this time you have a reason to get rid of him. But still, they won't take you. Your flesh and blood".

Then it all made sense. How come I was covered in blood, and Piper wasn't? Could I have done this to him and not realised that I freaked out from all the pain.

He was close to death. Then again, Piper was right, I had tried to kill him before, but I was aware of it when I did that. So why was Piper being a bitch?

Apparently, he had teeth marks and punctures all over him, he was going to be in hospital for a few months, and they were not sure if he would survive.

However, I did what Piper said and stuck to the story. When I went to get Ariel's cardigan from her room, he was already in there; he had let the dog in from the garden. It followed him upstairs and attacked him. I tried to save him, and that's why I was covered in blood. Did I mention we had a dog? Poor dog, he was given away after that?

Finally, God had answered my prayers. He left me alone after that.

Flight four, the last landing, slightly bigger than flight three, was a bedroom, bathroom, and kitchen.

These two floors were where the older children resided; we never really went up there. When Sabine and I were younger, we used to see the older boy going up there with some girl. We used to sit on the stairs in the middle of the night after raiding the kitchen. That was the only time Sabine loved me. Then we would see the Nile sneaking by, threatening to kill us if we told.

I loved being a part of the family; I just did not like certain people in it. We had fun together, seaside trips, cinema, house parties were constant. At the end of the long corridor in the basement, my mum used to hold shebeens (underground house parties). We weren't allowed to go because we were too young. The music was always thrummed with bass, and strange-smelling smoke evaporated out of the air whilst my mum collected money at the door. I recognised a few people as they entered in with a familiar handshake, a few uncles and aunties, some friends, and other unfamiliar faces.

It was Saturday, December 12th, 1982, during one of my parents' famous parties, when something awful happened. I am not sure exactly what it was or why everyone was so angry with me. But I got the blame, again.

Things changed for me at that house that night. I

was thirteen, and things got terrible.

I asked myself repeatedly, was it because that man came into my room the night of the party and gave me that sweet flavoured drink? Surely my parents could not be upset about that.

I remember that night clearly. A man I had seen in our house came to give me the drink; he said my mum had sent him with it; I gulped it down because it was cold and refreshing. He did not waste time refilling my glass. I told him I should not drink anymore because I might wet my bed, but he said it was fine, my mum said I could have it.

I fell asleep very quickly, but what was so strange is that when I woke up, I had another period, and my private parts were in agony.

Even more strange, my mum was crying that day, and my dad was furious at her. All my cousins were secretly questioned except me. What they were asked, I never found out.

I was in too much pain to even care about their whispers; I just wanted to sleep. I tried to tell my mum how much pain I was in, but she just would not stop crying.

She made me bathe in this strange-smelling ointment that stung when I sat in hot water. She would not look at me, and everyone was behaving strangely. She kept asking me when the last time I had a period was? Every time I said, "Just two weeks ago, it's very early," she would burst into tears again and keep apologising.

I thought it was a good time to tell her perhaps I should go to the doctor as the pain this time was different, unbearable in fact, but then her wailing just got louder and continued well into the night; in fact, she cried for a whole week. Something changed her that night, something changed the entire family, and all eyes pointed at me. Piper was the only one to comfort me.

The room on flight two became my comfort, and one night the voice behind the door spoke to me. "Don't worry," the voice said, "It will all be just fine in the end."

I couldn't work out if it was a female or a male; it sounded disguised somehow.

I never told anyone because I did not know if I imagined it or not. My family already thought I was mad.

The house was always so hot, with all the paraffin heaters dotted around. However, I could not remove my jumper because my arms were covered in scars. I caused the wounds because I deserved them, scars to remind myself not to shame the family again for whatever I had done.

One night I witnessed my mum unlock the room on

flight one. She went in carrying a plate of food. When she emerged, the dish was gone.

She locked the door behind her. When she looked up, her body twinged slightly at the sight of me. We locked eyes for a few seconds before she quickly scurried away. Not a word was spoken.

THE MOLE!

I wondered how much I could trust Paige. She presented as a dizzy fool that believed her own lies. Hiding behind her burka, as she had conveniently decided to turn Muslim. She claimed she no longer knew who she was, and being Muslim had helped her find herself. She sat comfortably, explaining her background to me. It was difficult to tell if she was laughing at me or being serious. I found it hard to believe that she would be so deceiving. Yet, they were all conniving and convincing. How had they survived so long on lie after lie?

EMPTY SHADOWS

All good things must end

There must be an end to the end

For at the end, a new beginning will begin

That will bring you to yet another explosive end

Should you allow your life to plague your
heart with negativity

Then the end in mind will be unearthly, unfruitful,
with

Undeniable disabled energy.

CHAPTER 3

EMPTY SHADOWS

The blistering heat scorching her, Piper scrutinised the time-worn sinister-looking house where she had once claimed residence as a small child battling to grow up.

Shivers gripped her spine nodule by nodule. As she remembered that dejected and wounded child, she swallowed hard, attempting not to devolve into tears.

"Paige," she whispered to herself, "I'm so sorry." Eight years had manifested a slow dance of sorrow.

The old house was still alive, still wearing its 1982 curtains, and the image was unnerving. It belonged in a pop-up storybook. The roof appeared to have sagged inwards like a fallen cake removed from the oven too soon. The windows were boarded up and painted with graffiti. It was a rotting heap still trying to grab at life, to take down all its victims and reveal their pain. There was no laughter ringing from those crumbling walls, no happy memories of childhood mischievousness, and no memories of good cooking wafting through the front door.

Instead – empty shadows screamed from that roof to pool beneath it. Shadows that frequently invaded Piper's thoughts, time and time again. The same vicious shadows that held her captive and imprisoned her within her own messed up world. It was now 1990; Piper, 21 years old, remembered it all like it was yesterday - there was no escaping the demon that reared its ugly head.

Piper flinched at the oversized warm hand placed around her shoulders. "It's time, little Sis." Her thoughts were interrupted by the smooth baritone voice. She turned to face her brother, staring down at her with deep concern in his hazel eyes. Piper managed a fake but warm smile.

"The cars have arrived." Leandro's handsome face was etched with regret.

Piper wasn't his little sister. She was older by fifteen months, but since Leandro stood a lengthy 6 foot 3 inches and Piper was 5 foot 9, he had always referred to her as his "little" Sis. Leandro had a body that women craved, and he knew it. He was much darker than Piper, with a creamy, smooth, cinnamon complexion, a muscular frame surrounded his rugby player shoulders and thick thighs.

He had cut his hair short in the back and sides, with large shiny curls resting on top that revealed his half-Indian heritage. His features were quite chiselled, which always made him look uncommonly animated.

Leandro held his emotions in his face, so it was difficult to hide his feelings in any situation. Piper studied his features for a while before gently patting his face.

"I don't think I'm ready," Piper revealed. "I can't do this. I need more time."

Leandro turned to her, immediately seething. He lowered his voice, so it was just audible enough for Piper to hear the anger in his deep tone. Through gritted teeth, he asked her, "What for Piper? What are you going to do? Ask him why"? Exasperated, Leandro continued, "For God's sake, Piper, get a grip so we can move on with our lives! You have your chance, now. After this, it's too late."

"Easy for you to say," Piper bounced back, annoyed at her brother's anger towards her.

"Stop living in the past, Pip," he retorted. "That murky, dark, gloomy road. Look at me. I steered off that Path a long time ago, and maybe you should do the same." Leandro closed his eyes and took a deep breath. "Look, in the morning, I'll be flying back to China, so stop dragging my last night back to "Never Never-land Sis," he said resigned. "I came to support you, not go to war."

Piper folded her arms across her chest. Sucking her teeth, she looked away from her brother and shrugged his heavy hand off her burdened shoulders.

Leandro could have kicked himself for being so harsh; he loved his sister dearly, and he certainly did not want to be left with the disturbing fact that he had flown so many miles to get into an argument with her.

One of the reasons Leandro had moved so far away, leaving his roots behind, was due to the drama enacted throughout his life with his dysfunctional family. So, when the job opportunity arose for him to go to China and test and trial prototype computer games, Leandro didn't think twice. Within two weeks, he had accepted the offer with a reputable American company with strong links and a global market share in China. The contract was signed and sealed. Things moved swiftly. One week later, he said goodbye - leaving Piper to wallow in the unbalanced scene behind him.

Secretly, the moment he chose to go was the only moment she had ever despised him.

Leandro glared into his sister's light brown eyes and smoothed back her curly blond streaked hair. He held out a hand to his sister. "Come on, Pip, I'm truly sorry. I don't mean to upset you, and you know that" he said, conciliatory. "Bitter is something you have become; it must be said."

He continued, "I came all this way here for you to try and help you through this, so let's not fight." He paused, a mist formed over his eyes, as he reminded his sister, "Mum would have told us to look out for one another."

Piper was simmering too fiercely to hold her whiplash tongue. "Would she Lea?" she demanded. "How do you know? How do you know what Mum would have wanted? You were only fifteen months young when she left, and then your dad took you off to play happy families with his other ready-made family."

Piper was really in full flow now, her tongue lashing out with venom. "And I don't remember him looking back." She spoke slowly and firmly. "So how *do* you know Leandro. Huh? What she would have wanted us to do - none of us knows."

Piper spoke through the mental chains of scars, the suppression of her tears for way too many years. She took a deep breath and calmed herself a little. "None of us know, Lea, because we were babies." Her voice was settled now. "Mum set us up with a rich man, our daddy, who, by the way, should have looked after us –" another sizeable pause "—well, you were, anyway." Piper gripped her stomach and hung her head. Her tears rolled freely onto the heated steps, drying instantly in the sun's piercing rays.

"Why didn't she take me with her"? Piper choked the words out.

"Don't speak like that Pip, that's not fair." A tear cascaded down Leandro's handsome face. They had both exchanged angry words as they battled with their emotions.

"Fair, Lea? Do you want to talk about FAIR? When your dad took you with him and ran off into the richness of the sunset with his baby boy in his arms. I'm sure if mum knew that for one minute that he would separate us, she would have had us adopted." Piper continued, "But one day Leandro, I will become something big, and I'll show him."

Both children missed their mother like crazy, but neither could find the words kind enough to comfort the other.

Piper survived on some false misconception that her mother had been murdered by accident whilst her aunt and uncle practised witchcraft to cast out the evil spirits within her. She believed her dad left her because she possessed the same insane witch powers her mother had.

Leandro shook inside with anger but tried to contain himself. He couldn't believe that Piper had considered that crazy story, still believed in that mumbo jumbo, but then again, why shouldn't she? No one had ever told her any differently. No one had ever said to her that shit did not exist; it was just a way to control them. Their dad had educated him. Leandro's beliefs were different from Piper's. They didn't understand each other; they didn't know each other.

Yes, their dad should have taken Piper. But his reason for not doing so wasn't because he thought she was a witch, or even because she was a girl, or that he thought she was cursed and feared her. No one had threatened him to convince him to leave her, and he didn't dislike her. It just wasn't appropriate to take her. He just wasn't her real dad.

There was so much Piper didn't know but now was not the time, and it was certainly not the place.

"Stop it, Pip, *stop* now," Leandro spoke slowly yet firmly.

"Why, Leandro, is the truth hitting home?"

Leandro breathed in deeply, sucking in every bit of air before releasing it. "He kept us in contact, Pip."

"Oh, don't make me laugh, Lee. Contact? A few trips here and there? A few visits to the home? Whipped you away after an hour because he said you had allergies? Pathetic. "Piper spat the words with pure venom.

"He loves you, Pip." Leandro pleaded with her to hear him and believe, but Piper only saw her father one way - as the man who deserted her.

"He put you through private school, Pip, gave you got the best education any black girl would long for, but you messed that up too. You allowed your friends to lead you in the wrong direction by keeping some big secret. Where are they now Pip, was it worth it?"

Leandro trembled as he spoke his question; he knew he had overstepped the mark. He knew Piper was going to whip him so hard with that tongue of hers there would be no coming back.

Her blond streaks seemed to be set alight by the sun as her light brown eyes grew to meet the sea of freckles spread across her face. Her skin was flawless and sun-kissed. Suddenly, she appeared to be taller than Leandro.

"Really, Lee, you went there, Mr I'm-so-special, my shit doesn't smell, you really went there? Let me tell you something, you're lucky you're my brother, well kind of anyway.

"Those friends, they were there when I needed them, they saved my mind when your cousin had his hands all over Paige; I asked you to help me, to make him stop harming her, my friends helped instead, because you weren't brave enough to stop him. Those friends, Lee, were there when I was a young girl needing her mum. They were there, Lee. They are still here now. Never once did you ask me how I felt about anything because you got your head so far up your dad's arse you can't see what's in front of you."

Piper glowered at her brother. "Good education, my arse, with a bunch of racist cult leading pigs, my life was hell in that school. Every day, Lee, every day I had to fight someone off, and you know what, no one cared, except the five of us," Piper referred her other four friends.

Piper had said enough; she was breathless and too distressed to listen to her brother.

"So, you see, Leandro - your father loves you and himself," stated Piper. "I never fitted into the jigsaw of his life. He couldn't find a place for me. Couldn't see where my piece fit in, so he shoved it to the side like rubbish—" Piper paused "—RUBBISH, Lea." Piper gripped her stomach even tighter and fell to her knees, sobbing.

Leandro slowly knelt, hovering over his sister, and cradled her like a baby. "I just want you to get yourself sorted, Pip; come on, who else would be so honest with you? I know you're upset, but there is always some drama with you. Even now. You're not living your true life; you've got your boyfriend and your bit on the side coming to comfort you at the same funeral. That's the sort of thing I'm talking about. It's wrong."

Piper knew he had a point, but she didn't respond to his last comment.

The sun was stifling, and all this arguing was quickly extinguishing the high spirits Leandro had arrived with. "He's still your dad, too, Pip. Believe it or not, he loves you, always has. He has had to live with the burden of not being allowed—" Leandro quickly corrected himself, hoping Piper didn't pick him up on

71

to his last statement, "of not allowing himself to take you." Leandro knew it was not just because Piper was not his father's child. The family held an even bigger secret that they tried to protect Piper from.

"So, why didn't he, Lee? Why didn't he take me? I'm his flesh and blood. His biological child! What happened to me?"

Leandro wanted to respond. He hated deceiving Piper like this, but he did not want to be responsible for answering that dreaded question, so his reply was just simply, "I don't know, Pip. I don't know." Leandro pulled Piper to her feet. He turned her to face him and kissed her gently on the forehead.

Leandro led her down the blackened slate stairs she had climbed so many times as a child, the same stairs that held so many memories of childhood pain and laughter. Piper looked back at the steps and thought back to when she had tripped on them and cut her knee so badly, she needed a hospital assistant. Her uncle had stamped on those stairs, cursing them, telling the stairs they were terrible and that they shouldn't trip little Pip up and that they needed to behave themselves. These were the same stairs Piper probably would never climb again. Who would have thought, even a simple thing like a small flight of stairs could hold so many memories?

This thought brought a smile to Piper's weary face,

and she was sure that right then and there, she saw him enter through that burgundy stained wood front door. But, then, with a tilt of his hat, he was gone.

Piper and Leandro sat in silence amongst their five cousins as the limousine gently rocked side to side, slowly finding its groove along the rocky road. The blacked-out windows made the sunny outside world appear dark and dismal. Piper was a baby when she came to live with her cousins. They were more like her brothers and sisters. She had never noticed Paige before, but as they grew older, their bond grew tighter. Piper didn't know any other life; this was her family. Her uncle was her saviour, and now they were putting him to rest. Just one year after his wife, her aunt, also passed away.

The siblings were officially recognised as orphans.

Piper rested her head against the black leather seats, her eyelids heavy, closed in unison.

She released a deep sigh and gripped her stomach as a nauseating feeling rushed over her like a tidal wave. Quickly, Piper released her head from the chair and hastily leaned over to whined the window down. As she threw her head out of the window, the warm atmosphere greeted her with a sudden blast of heat. It was as if her head had just been set alight. Piper felt like she was suffocating. Slowly, despite her dizziness, she pulled her neck in, attempting to sit still and appear calm despite her panic that she might projectile vomit across the car. Piper was always ill at funerals and suffered from stomach cramps. "It's nerves," her auntie used to say. "Oh, how she craved her love.

"You good, Pip?" her cousin Sabine eyed her suspiciously. Sabine was a curious individual and second to last of the siblings who had lived together in the earlier days.

"And when describing you, Piper, I've limited my description for fear of offending," was typical of Sabine, who loved opportunities to try and belittle Piper - always up in Piper's cool-aid, was how Piper described her. She might have been able to torment her weak and pathetic sister, Paige, but Piper would not tolerate it.

Piper fascinated sabine. She wanted to know who her artist was. Who had painted Piper's flawless portrait? Why did the rest of the family always act as if they owed her something? Sabine wasn't alone in her thoughts as Piper herself had often wondered the same thing. It just didn't quite make sense. Sabine was only ever jealous of Piper, she was biologically the youngest of the siblings, yet Piper held the youngest child title as she came along by default.

Sabine hated anything that had Piper's name on it. Sabine hated the colouring of Piper's yellow sand complexion, which always appeared to glisten under the sunlight. Sabine hated Piper's long thick coiled hair that blazed the colour of copper, highlighted with random streaks of blond. Sabine hated Piper's curvy body and sexy demeanour. She hated Piper and the men that chased and coveted her, hated how she talked, walked, smiled, ate, slept; yes, she had watched her sleep.

Sabine just hated Piper.

"Why wasn't she adopted?" Sabine had questioned her parents one day. "Why didn't you both lose her somewhere?" Piper was even named after a river, just like the rest of them.

Piper's uncle had a fixed obsession with rivers. During his teenage years in Jamaica, he was fortunate enough to study and travel the island with a group of limnologists, which influenced his sea life knowledge.

Piper raised an eyebrow at her inquisitive cousin and answered with attitude, "I'm good."

"Ooh, just asking, you look a bit peaky peach."

"Well, obviously. It's scorching, and I'm hungry," Piper retorted with sarcasm

"I've got an apple in my bag. Want it?" Sabine grinned, knowing full well Piper detested apples; they always made her sick and gave her a cramping pain in her stomach.

If Piper hadn't been feeling so ill, she would have leaned over and slapped her cousin. But, instead, Piper eyed her with intent. That was enough for her cousin to know to back off. River appeared from the back seat and wrapped her arms around her Aunty Piper, squeezing her tightly. "I love you, Aunty Pip. I got crisps in my bag. You can eat them."

"Oh, my little princess, you're so intuitive," Piper pulled River over the back seat into the front, strapping her in. River was Jazz's daughter. Although Jazz was very protective and didn't let her out of sight, River begged her mum to ride in the big car with her Aunty Pip. Eventually, Jazz gave in to her daughter. River was soon to be eight but was going on eighty-eight. She knew how to get around her mum. Jazz gave birth to River when she was a mere thirteen-year-old girl. Jazz's mum thought it was best that River believed Jazz was her big sister, but we all protected her, and so did her mum. When Jazz's mum passed away, Jazz decided to allow River to call her mum.

The siblings lost themselves in deep thought, all so busy having conversations with their demons that they hadn't noticed they had arrived at their long-awaited destination. The limousine parked at the top of the hill, away from the congregation. The door to the limo swung open, and a warm breeze flooded the inside of the vehicle.

A tall, well-groomed black woman opened the door. She was conservatively dressed in clean, crisply pressed black attire. A top hat, and fitted tuxedo with an appropriate matching tie, hugged by stiff white collars peeping out of the top, with shiny black shoes in which you could see a distorted view of your reflection. She had black leather gloves and greeted them with warm, comforting eyes. They were mesmerising as she extended a large hand to Piper, inviting her to step out of the car. Piper stared into her eyes and could have sworn their paths had crossed before.

The chauffer squeezed Piper's hand and gazed back at her raising an eyebrow. She continued to hold the door open whilst the rest of her siblings unfolded from the limo, all the while never breaking Piper's gaze. Piper felt a cold shiver run down her spine. She peered back at the pretty driver, who was still gazing at her with squinted eyes. She gave Piper another smile; her face was so familiar. Where had she seen her before?

The driver placed her dark glasses over her large green eyes, distracting Piper's thoughts. Then suddenly, all her familiar features diminished.

"Well, Well, Well? if it's not the Sea of Rivers." The drunken voice rang out amongst the tapping of shoes crunching against the pebble path. The siblings halted in their tracks, disgust and worry written all over their faces. Piper was unmoved by the entertainment standing in front of her. On the contrary, she was silently relieved, for Piper loved him to bits as chaotic as he appeared.

Robert was the eldest of the siblings. He was their half-brother and a severe alcoholic. He hadn't always been a drunk; he used to be a lecturer in a university teaching criminal law. Now the only thing unlawful was the way he drunk himself into oblivion. No one knew how he went from extremely high class to extremely low in no category. Some said it was stress; some claimed that it was witchcraft. Either way, Robert's brain wasn't ruined. He had money stashed away, and lots of it too. Piper was the only one aware of this.

Robert had a soft spot for Piper; he had a way of always telling her a story without revealing anything. Piper was always left wondering what the hell he was going on about. Then again, he was always hurried away by the other siblings before he could ever finish a sentence.

"Thought you could have a funeral and not tell me, who's is it this time, or should I say who have you all killed this time?"

Robert let out a disturbing laugh that echoed over the funeral procession. Sabine was taken aback and appeared quite vulnerable, which was a first for her. Piper thought maybe she should set Robert in her company more often. Nile, the eldest of the siblings, approached Robert, swiftly grabbing him by the arm.

He pulled him in close, "You're drunk. Now leave before your little secret gets out."

Robert pulled away from Nile, and with his sweaty palm, he turned to him, quickly managing to stroke his face. "What's up, Nellie? Am I embarrassing you?" he teased with belittling sarcasm.

Nile was now bubbling like lava out of a volcano. Robert, unaware, was raining speckles of saliva all over his face as the offensive smell of stale alcohol became overpowering.

Nile slapped Robert's hand away. You could feel the sting, the sound resembling the explosion of a firecracker

"You're not welcome here. Now leave." Nile's tone was now filled with aggression, but Robert was not fazed.

"But it's free land, my brother. So you got a warrant for my arrest?" Robert's speech was slurred as he became increasingly loud. "Alright, Pip?" he struggled to enunciate.

"Yeah, I'm good, Rob. You?" Piper responded hesitantly

"Yep, I'm tickety, boo." That was Robert's favourite word, the answer he always gave if he liked you.

"How's, erm, how's...." He placed his hand on his head as if trying to remember a name or place. "Let me, 'member, now, Nile you 'member who I'm talking about?"

Nile was becoming increasingly irritated by Robert's presence. Piper didn't think he would be standing for much longer, but he had come to cause trouble, and he didn't care who with.

"Oooh, my brain is so old. Keeps getting stuck in places. Wait a minute, Pip. It's gonna come to me." Nile gave him a look that said, I dare you.

"Nah, it's gone." Robert backed down

Nile boomed, "Leave, now before I make you."

"Ooh, that name is coming to me now." The rest of the siblings quickly stepped in to huddle around him. Some words were shared out of Piper, Paige, and Sabine's earshot; when the siblings dispersed from around him, Robert had resigned and was ready to leave.

"Rob, why don't you go home, and I'll call you later," Piper suggested, trying to lessen the embarrassment everyone was feeling, not for themselves but for Robert.

"You said it, Pip, so I'm doing it. I'll be back," he said with a wicked grin that made Piper giggle. Piper sighed.

As Robert swaggered out of the cemetery gates, he turned to Piper to address her. "Pip, who's funeral, is it?" Robert's ginger hair was glistening under the sun's rays, and his matching freckles appeared highlighted against his hazel eyes.

Piper hesitated. Her palms began to sweat in panic, feeling like she had suddenly become a party to a shipwreck. Her legs buckled like a young horse from under her. The sky was spinning. She hadn't noticed it before; it was such a bright shade of blue.

Piper crashed to the ground like a box of shattering eggs onto the concrete. Her fall was broken by a circle of hands catching her. Instantly she felt the warm embrace of Rasi's arm and his linen scented cologne as he lifted her to her feet

"Is she finally dead?" Sabine inquired sarcastically

Piper leaned against Rasi in the commotion while she decided if she was hurt. She peeped up at the sky through scrunched eyes. The sun's rays hit her retina like a bright torch, and she squinted hard at the impact. She looked towards Robert. "Robert. It's your dad."

Piper pulled herself from Rasi's arms and attempted to approach Robert to touch his hand, but Robert pulled away, whimpering. He didn't deserve this, but he thought he did. "It's my own fault," he mumbled. "Ok, touché, you all win. You got me." He raised his hand, pointing his finger as if he agreed with himself. Fluid dripped from his nose as he smeared it across his face with the back of his hand. The snot instantly dried to a thin white paste.

Robert's eyes suddenly appeared to become lifeless,

and sweat dripped from his forehead, congregating on his upper lip. Pain furrowed his brows as his face showed the expression of a raging bull. He clenched his fists, trying to control the shaking of his left leg. Robert chewed on his bottom lip as he held back the tears. His lips quivered as if to say something, but he was cut off by Nile talking, speaking gently to him for the first time since Robert had appeared.

Nile's threatening behaviour had disappeared, and he was calm and careful with his words.

"You know you need to leave, Robert, and try to stay away. We don't need our lives going backwards. But, come on, man, you understand the last thing we need is to root up old habits, you can't be here, and that's that, it's our pledge to the old man, you know why".

Piper didn't remember much of her childhood. She had pushed most of her memories deep to the back of her mind. So, she couldn't remember why Robert had always been treated so harshly. But she had a connection with Robert. She was never sure why, but she remembered him being close to her as a child.

Robert hung his head and said nothing; the tears fell like a waterfall in slow motion hitting the ground below, creating speckled splashes on his brown unpolished leather shoes. Finally, Robert looked up at Piper and mouthed the word "sorry." Then he turned and walked away, ignoring Piper's pleas to stop. She watched as he vanished beyond the iron gates, his shoulders hunched over, feet dragging behind him. Robert never looked back.

Piper turned to her cousins for an answer but decided she didn't even want to hear it.

"Please, don't try to explain. I get it. I know; it's history. He's caused a lot of upset. However, you want to dress it up, none of it washes with me. I will find out what you are all hiding."

She looked up to the sky and whispered a silent prayer for her cousins for the secrets they constantly hid.

But something triggered Piper as she walked away. Robert smelt of cornflakes.

A SAD FAREWELL

Have you gazed past the sea of loneliness

To value your own worth?

If you are in love with loneliness

Then you won't mind moments of solitude

Some songs dig a hole straight through your heart

Just to remind you

The end is not far away

CHAPTER 4

A SAD FAREWELL

The people's voices rang out across the cemetery in harmony; the older generation commanded the singing. They were robust, fine-tuned, and the admiration of the congregation. Piper's friends, Rasi, Jazz, Storm, Giselle, Venus, and her cousin Paige harmonised throughout the ceremony, giving her uncle an emotional send-off. River entertained the crowd whilst holding her order of service upside down, projecting her best voice and her own words. Piper turned to her and grinned. River gave her the thumbs up. Marcus, Storm's young son, managed to reach over to River and pull her hair. She let out a loud screech as he giggled that cute baby sound. Piper turned back and leaned into Rasi as he kissed the top of her head, whilst her boyfriend watched on in the distance, attempting to adjust his thoughts to the fact that he was the fool that believed Rasi and Piper were simply just friends.

Shall we gather at the river,
Where bright angel feet have trod,

With its crystal tide forever,
Flowing by the throne of God.
Yes, we will gather at the river,
The beautiful, the beautiful river,
Gather with the saints at the river,
That flows by the throne of God.

Written in 1864, by Robert lowry, American
poet and Gospel music composer

Piper and Paige were conditioned to lead the 'church's service alongside the priest, just as their uncle had requested. Paige was uncontrollable with sadness and was forced to decline the offer. Sabine obviously was furious. _There she goes again_, she thought, _getting all the credit_. When Piper began to sing the solo, the favourite family anthem, Paige stood by her side.

Sabine stood boiling in the church, wishing her all sorts of evil thoughts. But, no, she had not been crying at Piper's soulful singing; she was crying because Piper had once again stolen her limelight.

Maddison, one of the older cousins, grinned at Sabine's imperfect behaviour and gave her a nudge in the side to let her know she had witnessed her foul play.

Dressed finely in their Sunday best funeral clothes, as they were called. You only saved that special black attire for a funeral; it was not worn to any other event. It was like going to a wedding but dressed in black.

Women wailed, big men danced with their emotions whilst their tears fell freely, children cried, unsure of what was happening.

Piper and her siblings stood close to one another, holding hands. At times, they became separated by the large crowd who wanted a piece of them, to show their genuine deepest sympathy or to make sure their faces had been seen with fake tears in their eyes so the siblings would remember they were there, even if they never saw them again.

The large shadows snatched the sun out of the day. Finally, the soil hit the pit of the grave with a booming sound as the men filled it through sweat and determination.

Something made the siblings freeze. Piper shivered through her fear as what was approaching had her feet firmly glued to the hard ground. Piper's mouth opened involuntarily. If she was breathing, no one could tell. Her black shoulder-laced Karen Millen dress gradually began to saturate her back. She gasped and wished the ground to open and suck her in.

There they were again, those wicked echoes appearing in the sibling's head and blinding their vision. Piper began to muffle her cries for help as she watched the eight women with the same authoritative stance stomp across the hilly grass towards her uncle's grave.

The words to the song began to fade. Piper wasn't sure if people had stopped singing or the ceremony had moved away from them. Piper grabbed hold of her wrist and dug her nails in quick and profound, the same way she always did when she felt threatened, the same way she always did to prevent herself from crying.

By the time she felt those familiar strong arms around her, a warm kiss planted on top of her forehead, it was too late. Her body was in full tremble mode. Piper attempted to ease back into the embrace, to feel safe, but the drumming in her heart had taken over, and the sweat began to flow from anywhere it could find an outlet.

"I'm assuming that's them." His deep baritone voice vibrated in her ear. The warmth of his breath and the smell of his fresh cologne was enough to take anyone into another zone, but not right now. Piper nodded slowly. She could see Paige shuffling side to side, silently praying. Her eyes were filled with dread as she stared at them like a snake waiting to hiss poison. Her cousins had frozen, waiting for the old women to attack.

"The witches, walking voodoo dollies." Piper could not believe they dared to turn up, but then again, why wouldn't they? After all, they were always present in her aunt and uncle's life.

Piper began to panic; she hadn't seen them for some years. Here they were again, travelling at speed across the rocky grass towards her uncle's grave, come to anoint the casket and send it on its way, to make sure, in their own beastly world, his body would be bound, unable to travel into the spirit world. That's what she was taught as a child. They were indeed bound for Hell.

Their approach slowed at their arrival to the grave; they circled it in unison, keeping their eyes peeled on it, anger ripped across their faces as they began to hum.

Rasi could feel Piper's fear, and for his own selfish reasons, he pulled her in closer; this was his chance to show her that she should welcome his deep dying love for her and just accept him as her man.

Piper wasn't going to give in so easily to a full-time relationship. Plus, her own regular boyfriend stood right there at the cemetery grounds watching the intimacy between them.

"Relax, sweets, I'm here. It's all good." Sweets was the nickname Rasi had given Piper, simply because she was always eating sweets, the only item of food she never made herself regurgitate.

Piper relaxed even more into his thick muscular chest as Rasi slowly moved his hand over her stomach and gently kissed the side of her head just near her eye. Finally, Piper closed her eyes, raised her hand behind her, and stroked his cheek, returning his loving gesture.

The lead woman, who wore a black turban, stomped her staff hard into the ground, immediately the other seven came to a halt: and as if they had choreographed the routine, they swished their heads in the direction of the siblings and eyed them slowly one by one, as if trying to work out who had murdered the old man. There was a bizarre stand-off that the siblings were sure to lose.

The eight women continued to circle the grave as the congregation back away except 'Piper's grandma. All they needed now was a broomstick to complete the scene.

The women moved in slow motion around the grave. Their eyes are peeled to the ground, chanting in monotone voices. It was hard to hear what was said, but Piper's grandma had none of it. Up went her hand as she commanded them to stop; the women halted in their tracks and hissed at her as they faced her squaring up. "This place is not for you. Now leave." Piper's grandma was confident in her stance.

Then one of the witches dared to speak. "You're the last person to make any request, Yolanda."

Did she just call my grandma by her name? 'Piper's thoughts ran around in her head. A big disrespect, only those closest to her heart called her by that name, even adults called her grandma.

Grandma would never back down; she was the only one brave enough to take this evil on.

Grannie arched her eyebrow. "Oh really? No one is interested in your pledge to the old man. It doesn't matter how many times you circle this grave. God had him a long time ago. This is one power, not even you can play with."

"Who do you think you are, after everything you've done, pretending to be innocent" the team leader of the witches, as Piper called her, truly believed in herself.

"I am a child of God," her grandma reacted. The team leader flinched and stepped back as grandma continued to slay. "Anything thing I have done, God knows it is for protection and survival of my family. Anything you lot have performed is for evil and death, now leave and let the good people continue their homecoming for a king."

A burst of laughter pierced the atmosphere, erupting from the team leader whilst the others stood their stony ground. "A good man, ah, he was no good man. He was the devil himself." Her finger pointed firmly to the ground.

Piper's grandma stepped in front of the woman. There was a pain in her grandma's eyes, pain that only Piper recognised. "And you sat at his right hand," her grandma replied with ease.

' "You used your wickedness and killed the poor man. Now he's dead, just like his wife, of heartache. I'll be damned if I let you take anyone else." Pipers' grandma peered behind at her granddaughter, waiting for some release. "Now 'I'll tell you again, leave.'"

"I'm guessing you haven't told the little Jezebel about what she did to her own mother?" the team leader casually dropped.

Piper sprang from Rasi's arms. "How dare you mention my 'mother? Now you leave right now before someone drops a house on you." There was a faint giggle in the background. Piper didn't even need to turn to know who it was.

Piper's grandma eyed the crew until they began to disperse.

The tall, sturdy lady, Piper despised the most, was producing saliva, foaming up at the sides of her mouth as if she was hyperventilating. Then, through gritted teeth, she grumbled, "You will soon find out the truth, Murderer, "she screamed. Piper stumbled back into Rasi and clung to the side of his trouser leg.

"We were raising you to be a warrior, you and your perfect cousins."

Paige jumped backwards as the woman projected towards her, "YOU'RE A MURDERER," the woman spoke breathlessly, her ample chest hitting the bottom of her long chin. She clenched her fists and raised them above her head, beating the air as if she was Tarzan.

She continued, "Sassy, lickle, whore, standing there as if butter wouldn't melt. Well, let me warn you that nothing good will come of you. Any child you breed inside of you won't see daylight. We warned you then, and I'm warning you now. You cursed yourself a long time ago. It would be a sin to try and bring another into this world. Your body is no sanctuary to carry a child. It's a bottomless pit, you remember that."

Paige stood trembling, bewildered before she realised she was covering her face.

With that, the woman bought her hands down quickly, attempting to strike Paige. Rasi coolly caught hold of her extended arm while she hissed at Paige, "You're a wicked child, wicked."

Rasi released her hand, holds it into her chest, and pushes her away.

Leandro stepped in to support his cousin. "My sister and my cousins have suffered enough at your hands. Their whole life has been revolved around you because of your torture and malicious acts. WELL, NO MORE! Now leave. You're not welcome here to perform witchcraft tricks anymore. Is it not enough for you to brainwash people into thinking that this stupidity exists? You may be able to fool them, but the reason we all remained sane is that your Tittle Tattle could never have any effect on us. We are children of God, and you are Satan's followers. Now leave before I hurt you myself."

An uncontrollable giggle followed from Sabine in the background. She was silenced by the stares from her siblings and resorted to twiddling her fingers.

The women's glares pierced into Piper, as each, in turn, fought their way back through the packed funeral procession. Piper and her cousins watched each one leave like ghosts on a dark night haunting the town.

She swore she never saw their feet touch the ground.

Rasi whispered into her ear. "Chill, baby, revenge is best served cold. Your time will come."

Right now, Piper didn't really care about revenge; these women were not to be messed with

Yes, she just wanted them gone forever from her life, she knew exactly who could help her, but Piper and her siblings were more scared of them dead than alive.

In the distance, Piper could feel the presence of her Four friends standing side by side, waiting patiently to attend to her; they smiled at her warmly, and even from a distance, she could feel their hugs. Jazz, Storm, Giselle, and Venus, her four heartbeats.

The crowd continued to sing out while her Rastafarian uncles beat their drums with meaning to an understanding nation in mourning to a great man.

They carried out the traditional tracking, calling the first line to the song whilst the procession followed in harmony until every bit of earth along with the sea of flowers were placed onto the freshly dug grave.

During the funeral, the focus had been on Piper, the extra sibling. How she had grown and survived the hands of the demons. What did she look like? Was she sane?

White rum flowed as it was poured over the burial ground, claiming to call upon the ancestors to accept and direct the new member of their spirit clan. An A-list of superstitions came with preparing a Caribbean funeral, and whether you believed it or not, you found yourself sticking to the old rituals trying to please the dead.

They had held the infamous nine-night or set up, held exactly nine nights after the death, people had travelled everywhere for the event. An ancient and essential Jamaican custom, where family and friends gather at the 'deceased's house, comfort the bereaved, and give the spirit a good send-off. It would be seen as disrespectful, and the dead could be a nuisance to the living if everyone did not partake in an exclusive send-off.

Piper's uncle used to say it was called nine-night, as that's how long it took the spirits to travel back to their homeland in Africa. Some had come to genuinely pay their respect to others; others had come just to gloat and eat free food and drink.

The siblings were overwhelmed and exhausted. It had been a long three weeks with all the funeral processions at hand, the arguing over whether they should follow tradition or not. But, in the end, tradition won. Why? In the end, they did not know any different.

Piper's heart ached from years of silent tears. They had buried their mum, Piper's aunty, and it was almost as if they were doing it again. It seemed like only a month ago that they had put her to rest. Piper's aunty had never been the same since the night of the party, the one where she cried for days after. She became frail and week very quickly. Her eyes were cold, as blank as a white wall. The memory of her seemed quite distant now to the siblings. She went peacefully. They put her death down to heartache.

Piper and Paige attended to most of her needs during her last days. She pleaded with them to not allow her to endure a long, painful death.

When their uncle found her, she had fallen asleep peacefully, but it wasn't as peaceful as they thought. Piper had given her the extra medication that day. Her last breaths were tricky and lengthy. The girls panicked; they thought she would never go. Maybe they had not given her enough of the tablets. They couldn't bear to hear her suffering; Piper whispered a good by in her ear whilst she placed her hand over the old woman's eyes. They both waited a few minutes, then removed the pillows from her face, plumping them up beside her.

PIPER

We beg for forgiveness

Yet we continuously sin

An empty jar on the table, a silver grin

Forgiveness is for a child, shattered from within

No longer for the adult, our chance is very slim,

We shall depart scarred and wounded

Unless we choose to give in.

Forgiveness is forever, until the end of time

Will you forgive me, blindly, even though
I do not shine?

CHAPTER 5

SHE WHO PLAYS THE PIPER

I didn't consider myself a murderer. I liked to think of myself as an opportunist. I see an opportunity, and I take it.

I didn't pre-meditate other people's misfortunes. It was an instinct at that given moment that I react upon.

I guess, really, it's how you view it.

Being called a cold, callous murderer is a brutal thought. To think of oneself in such a way is harmful to the individual.

My motives were for the betterment of others. Therefore, I did this solely with them in mind.

My actions were beneficial to them and myself overall.

Just suppose I didn't help them, then some belligerent bastard came along and finished them off anyway? Now, that's brutal.

I didn't hunt these people down. They didn't need to be pursued. Some of them were good people, you know those who make the silliest mistakes, then they realise it was really a dumb arse thing to do. That it would sooner or later cost them their life.

I awoke exhausted and pissed off. I had not had a decent sleep-in day, and these constant flashbacks of Paige and my other cousins were no benefit to my mental state.

From my uncle's dressing to the nine nights two months ago, the funeral day, my altercation with the wicked old witches, and trying to readjust myself back into the working life, my energy levels were totally buggered.

Each night, sleep was not securely promised.

I was desperate to put a stop to the whirlwind developing in my mind, but right now, alcohol and a long line of cocaine seemed to be my only means of comfort, and even that was wearing thin.

I had woken up again this morning collapsed in a heap on the floor tangled in my sheets. I laid still for a while, staring up at the ceiling, wondering if I was hurt or just severely hungover from the night before. I fought my hands through the tangled sheets and stared at my scarred wrist, massaging it.

My wrists had taken a battering last night. Even in my disrupted sleep, the attacks were becoming brutal.

In some respects, summertime was hard for me. However, it was a redeeming feature that my body always emanated a blanket of cold, which meant that I could get away with wearing long sleeves even in the heat to hide my wrists and arms covered by history.

I had been self-harming for as long as I could remember. Although I never understood the cruelty inflicted upon myself, it took away the mental pain.

Deep down, I truly believed what those witches had told me; I was unworthy, no good, destructive, and a murderer. Now I had lost the two most precious people in my world; now, I felt so alone.

But I wasn't alone, there were my friends, Jazz, Storm, Giselle, Venus. And, of course, Rasi.

I untangled the sheets from my feet, turned onto all fours, pushed myself up, and modelled in my mirror for a body check to make sure I hadn't gained weight whilst sleeping. I pinched the side of my waist, at least half an inch came away in my hand, "No," I whispered to myself. "That will not do."

I pulled back my over-the-top long drapes and smiled at the gorgeous black postal worker looking up at me. My top was transparent. I was not wearing a bra. We held each other's gazes for a while before he blew me a kiss. If he thought he'd get around two this morning, he needed to think again. I had to admit he was much better than the builder the night before.

I made my way into my white kitchen to boil the kettle for a coffee. I carefully placed five chocolate cookies into a yellow bowl, then smashed them to death with a spoon. I poured my coffee over the top of them, just enough for the cookies to soak up and create a thick porridge. I took a deep breath and prayed that I'd get it out of me on time. With that, I shovelled three spoonsful into my mouth I slammed my timer on. As soon as it hit four and a half minutes, I ran to the bathroom. I stuck the bottom half of my toothbrush into my throat with great success to regurgitate everything from the night before. Satisfied with a good job done, I continued to brush my teeth and take a shower.

How discourteous of me, allow me to introduce myself.

I'm Piper, right now I'm aged 21, I'm the fourth out of my group of friends who have had elaborate twenty-first birthday parties. I had it in a wine bar/club, a place called "The Mansion." It's owned by a man, who goes by the name of Royal, he's like a father figure to us, he took us in when we were aged fifteen, we had begged him to let us come in, and he made us a proposition to keep us off the streets. He's the only man I trust, even more than my uncle and my own dad, who can't be trusted anyway. I had one hundred and fifty people at my party. Rasi had some of them removed as he wasn't happy with their interest in me. Rasi is like my hanger-on boyfriend. He's always there. He does everything for me, he never leaves my side, and I trust him as well. He wants to look after me and make me his girlfriend or wife. I really like him; however, I might miss out if I commit to just one person.

So how do I exist? Well, my mum's parents had been killed in a house raid in Jamaica when she was 13. Her aunties in Jamaica complained she had become a troublesome child, they were unable to care for her, and no one else was willing to attempt to control her outlandish behaviour. She had been beaten, thrown out of school, moved from aunty to aunty, involved in vicious fights, a questionable murder attempt, her time was up. So, my aunt and uncle, my great aunt and uncle, decided she should come to England and try it. They weren't afraid of anything. They had taken in friends' unruly children over the years and managed to sort them out, a bit of witchcraft implanted on you, never hurt anyone.

My mum was only in England for a year before she broke the news. She was pregnant with the neighbour's child, my dad.

Now let me just explain, in a Jamaican family, there are rules to abide by.

1. As a girl, don't even look at a boy
2. If you're a boy, only eat from your mother
3. Make sure you can cook
4. Read your books and make sure you are a doctor, lawyer, or nurse.
5. Make sure your shoes are polished

6. Always have manners
7. Do not steal
8. Do not commit a murder

Now your list might be different, and there are plenty more, but these were our rules in my house. Every Jamaican family has similar rules. It depends on which ones are more precious to you.

Do you get my drift? The biggest shame you could bring upon the family is to appear pregnant and unmarried before you were considered a woman. But, usually, by the age of thirty, it may become a consideration? So, I guess it's ok to commit a murder, but always have manners.

Well, my mum had me at a very young age, fifteen, I was told. The pregnancy was kept a secret right up until the last minute to save the family's grave shame. My aunt and uncle refused to have my mum sent away and be surrounded by some strange people with whom she had no relationship. I heard that they had fallen out with lots of friends and family when they found out they were harbouring a fifteen-year-old pregnant child. When I was born, I was so white that my heritage was questionable, to make matters worse. I didn't look anything like my dad or my mum, for that matter. They were both a lot darker than me, so I was told I was a throwback. Of what, I didn't know.

I have only ever seen a picture of my mum, which I

keep with me all the time. By the time Leandro and I had become toddlers, I was two, Leandro was right behind me in the race age of fifteen months, mum had disappeared. The story I know is that someone had cast some witchcraft on her, it sent her a bit crazy, and crazy didn't sit well in a black community. It was said she was nearly taken away by those witches.

When they came to get her, my mum decided she would rather be dead than alive, so she jumped out the window. Her neck snapped instantly, and she didn't survive. I've never been to her grave because she doesn't have one, she was cremated, and her ashes were sprinkled in Jamaica on the grounds of her original home.

I always felt different from my cousins; my uncle and aunt adopted me and changed my name to a river name, just like my cousins.

Paige and I were always so close, but Sabine hated me. She hated everything about me. To this day, I never knew why. Paige said she was jealous because I was lighter-skinned than her. She didn't really have much of a relationship with her either, and they were sisters.

Paige told me that Sabine had annoyed her so much that she nearly catapulted her out of the window. Paige was always so impulsive. At times she scared me.

I never went to the same secondary school as my

cousins, but we all attended the same primary.

By the time I was twelve, I had gone to a private school as that's what my mum wanted for me, so the least my dad could do was to make sure he had carried out her wish and made sure I had the best education, and that is where I met my friends, Jazz, Storm, Giselle, and Venus.

At Whittingdon high, there we were, five black girls in an all-white private school in Clapham.

After coming from a very mixed primary school in the deep southeast of London, this was a real culture shock to the system. It was time to fail or succeed. I chose to thrive.

Succeeding as a black girl came with a consequence. It meant being quiet and missed or popular and labelled as a trouble maker; either way, I would lose. So, I chose to be popular.

You had to be talented to attend Whittingdon high; no one was offered a place unless you had a skill, and mine was dancing and singing. Of course, my aunt and uncle disagreed with this ability, but what choice did they have? It was my dad's decision, after all. My aunt always maintained, "You should dance for the Lord."

I remember I arrived that morning, nervous as hell, watching all the other girls stretch and practise plies and twists and turns. Some of them were sitting in front of the large mirrors attempting to pin their hair into buns and getting frustrated when it kept on falling out. Thank God for my afro texture hair that stayed put. I sat in that back room waiting for my name to be called whilst putting up with bad racist jokes. "The cleaners are out the back." "Whose tutu have you stolen?" "Didn't realise monkeys wore shoes."

But I kept my calm and my focus because I knew their faces. I stretched my legs out into the splits, folding the top half of my body over to one side and then the next, grabbing hold of my toes each time. When I eventually stood, I cricked my neck to one side whilst staring the other girls down. Yep, you guessed I was the only black girl auditioning for dance.

So, there I was, auditioning at one of the best private schools in London.

My heart dropped when I realised I would be performing in front of an audience. "Oh God, please, not those racist girls."

The administrator showed me where to stand, then walked away to leave me standing in front of the board of eight adults. "Shit." I didn't realise there would be so many.

I positioned myself first, hands hanging slightly in front of me. I looked up and offered a glowing smile.

"When you're ready," another administrator informed me.

I exploded with swagger and confidence as I spun,

twirled, sparkled into split jumps. I had no boundaries as I showed off my chasse and tendu. I demonstrated my strength with a grand jete, a familiar pose. It's a beauty across the dance floor when performed correctly.

I could clearly see the administrators shared the same sentiments for my passion. I watched them give nods to one another, and it spurred me on to create a more formidable performance.

My ability was desirable, a perfect, spellbinding art as I continued to pose and point, leap, and bound, covering every inch of the floor. The elegant flair of well-posed arms matching the hold of my outstretched leg whilst standing on point with the other. Then a sudden emergence of an African flare performance was incorporated with ballet.

The music beat is a mash-up of ballet, contemporary and African beats. I land with power and grace at the same time.

The eight administrators stand and applaud me as I gracefully end my second place, arms in first. Never had they seen such a mix of three different genres; even the racists in the changing room had no choice but to clap. Finally, I take my bow and leave the floor.

As I pass the girls, I turn sarcastically to them, "Ever seen a monkey dance like that." I look on as their eager faces turn a bright red.

I had to wait five weeks to hear if I had been given a space, one of three panellists was unsure if my dance genre would fit their school vision. Finally, they made me perform again, this time asking if I could place my imagination in an English country garden setting. I gave them what they wanted; I even lost more weight from my already tiny frame, but they made me wait until the following year before offering me a place.

On the first day, the principal, Mrs Whittaker, spoke to me in a stern voice. "Piper Monterac, I hope your wait has taught you a valuable lesson."

"My wait, Ms?" I answer angelically.

"Yes, young lady, your wait. I hope we won't have another outburst of your jungle performance within these school walls." She leaned in close to me whilst lowering her glasses. "Do I make myself clear?"

"Yes, Mrs Whittaker, very clear. I will not behave like a little monkey again," I answered sarcastically.

"Good, welcome to Whittingdon high. We will make a human out of you yet. Now run along, and make sure you and your other friends understand the rules of contact with the other children."

I courtesy, as I whispered, "Racist bitch",

"I beg your pardon?" Mrs Whittaker's voice was demanding.

"Itch, Ms. I have such an Itch."

Mrs Whittaker was not stupid, but she lets the

comment slide. For the moment.

I only accepted the place because she turned me down the first time. I'm not even sure I would have gotten in the second time if my dad hadn't offered more money.

I met Jazz first. Jazz was a piano player and extremely good; she played about three different instruments, her long elegant fingers glided over the keys with ease. I liked Jazz straight away; she was in control, and she knew what she wanted for someone at such a young age. Some thought she was bossy. I thought she was smart, a bit stuck up, but it paid off in this strange world we had been planted in.

Jazz didn't suffer fools lightly; she was also very opinionated and controlling.

Mrs Whittaker adored Jazz. She always told her she was very well-spoken for a black girl and quite pretty for a dark-skinned girl. Jazz was sensitive to these comments. She was a spoilt child, and no one could just say whatever they wanted to her. Her tolerance was low, but she held her tongue. That's what her mum had taught her.

Jazz told me everything. Out of the group, she was my bestie. We knew each other's secrets more so than the rest. Jazz would never lie to me or hold anything from me. Even if she thought it would hurt me, she would never hide a thing.

Jazz had a daughter called River; at the time we were fifteen, River was two.

But due to the secret fact that Jazz was only thirteen when she gave birth, Jazz's mum said she would take her on as her own. When Jazz got older, they would tell River the truth. We all fussed over River big time. She was so cute, and we all treated her as if she was our daughter.

Storm Underwood was her name, an absolute chancer. The only white Jewish girl in our group, I didn't believe she was totally white; I could see an essence of something lingering within her. The school granted her the privilege of celebrating all the Jewish holidays. Storm seemed to be out of school quite a bit. When the teachers questioned her about her attendance, Storm would produce her praying carpet from her rucksack, spread it in the middle of the floor, and pray in a monotone voice, spilling out Hebrew words. Well, that's what she said it was.

My parents were Jamaican. I can really say the Hebrew language sounded very similar.

They say everyone has a secret to hide, but how long can you hide it for?

I loved Storm straight away. In some ways, she reminded me of myself.

Storm was a great tennis player, footballer, and swimmer, unusual for a black girl, but she was the best, and those children had nothing on her athletic physique. She was also a maths genius, I know you can't audition for maths, but she was badass. I just wish she showed it as much interest as she did the boys.

Storm had no boundaries. She used her best assets to attract men. Then, when they got too close, she would destroy their emotions. Storm was a light-skinned bombshell, with sleepy green eyes framed by thick eyebrows, pretty, athletic build, sandy coloured hair, with a beauty spot to the right of her top lip. She could pass as a white girl, and that's precisely what she did.

Storm was argumentative, aggressive, persistent, and extremely flirtatious. At times she had this weird shake about her, then she would zone out as if she had stopped listening and become a statue. We never said anything.

Every time storm opened her handbag, you could guarantee that none of the objects belonged to her. Of course, you had to be sure to check your pockets once she left you. On the other hand, she was quite a comedian with a kind heart.

Then there was Giselle. She was Storm's bestie within the group. She played the violin and sang opera.

I never really understood that music genre, but she was a different person when she sang, a gift from her grandmother. That was her skill that won her first place at Whittingdon high. She wasn't frowned upon because she played like an African.

She possessed an unbelievable talent that they had never seen inside Whittingdon high. The school wanted to be the first to highlight a black beauty singing opera. Giselle being the clumsy clot that she was, happily taught the school her art, even gave private lessons to students under the observation of the music teacher. But, once they had all her black girl magic, it was ripped away from her and patented under the school's name. "Whittingdon High teaches opera to the uniquely gifted, taught by our very own music teacher, Mrs Potter." That's what the headline said. Giselle was furious. They even had the nerve to say they had taught Giselle.

The dizzy fool had sold herself, and now she was just an ordinary girl with a talent, just like the rest of us. But, although at first, she was playing the fool to catch wise, now I think she was purely foolish.

Giselle and I were ok. We weren't the best of friends, but we had an understanding.

Finally, there was Venus, Venus Akintola. A dark-skinned goddess with a shaved head, Venus injected into us constantly that it was part of her allergies, but it wasn't. She was hiding her half Nigerian heritage. At age twelve, I thought she was stupid to deny any part of you, but most black girls would not admit that they were from any part of Africa. It was a complete denial when we were growing up.

I'm not sure what Venus did; her mum had lots of money, I guess she was still finding herself. Venus had skin colour issues, I thought she was beautiful, but Storm constantly teased her. Venus was tall, thin, with long limbs. We were all similar heights, which scared the white girls. Every time we spoke or got excited about something, they called us aggressive. When we confronted them, they told us we had chips on our shoulders. Venus was called all sorts of names, from rubber lips to monster to chimp.

Venus had full lips, large oriental-shaped eyes, and a round head. As we grew older, I noticed that Venus' complexion was getting patchy, the patches were very pale, but she informed us it was her allergies. I always found Venus quite disloyal, greedy, and malicious. I'm not sure why she hung out with us. But I didn't dislike her, not totally anyway.

I met Rasi much later in life; I was nearly sixteen. But, unfortunately, I didn't let the other girls know that I had already met him before the time at the mansion wine bar.

I knew I was much younger than him, and he knew he was nine years my senior, but he was as sexy as a marathon bar with all the nuts in the right places.

Rasi wasn't my usual bait, but there was just

something about him I couldn't keep my hands off. However, only being half Jamaican, his heritage would not rest well with my friends or family. You were either a fully-fledged Jamaican, or it was nothing at all.

But I kept him in my handbag for my spare time. I wasn't about to give him up just yet. He was very protective of me, and I felt safe with him.

Whittingdon High taught us to outsmart strangers in our world who looked upon us as if we had just dropped out of another planet.

I wasn't fearful of them; neither was Jazz or Storm. They were mesmerised by our outrageous intelligence and thought it was ok to make "Black" jokes, then after a time the nigger jokes came, that's when we clamped down and took charge of their perfected games, stood up for ourselves, and let them know we would no longer tolerate it. I waited for the ring leader outside school; the other girls stood in the background.

"Hey, bigmouth, who's a nigger now?" I demanded calmly.

The big sturdy girl turned in her path to face me. "You talking to me" she retaliated nervously.

"Well, I don't see anyone else around."

"Look, just go home before I report you." Her stance was trembling.

"Nope, not going anywhere. I'm fed up with your tongue, constantly lashing us with your venom, so I'm here to disconnect your poison."

"Oh, please give me a break. Can't you take a joke?" White people are always only joking when they realise you're upset.

"Oh, you think it's funny, belittling our skin colour?" I began to approach her swiftly.

"What do you want" She stepped back suddenly.

"I want you to stop. I want you to respect us. I want you to realise that we are human beings just like you, not the monkeys you keep referring to us as.

The girl snorted and muffled a laugh; she ate her smile when Jazz stepped in behind me.

I want you to stop leaving banana skins in our lockers and inside our desks and scrawling nigger on our desk with your compass pin. I want it gone."

"Make me."

"I'm going to. That's why I'm here waiting for you because I will hurt you if you don't stop." Ok, I wasn't going to hurt the silly cow, but I had enough; we all had, and the teachers were not backing us.

"Ok, you win. I will sort it out tomorrow." Then, just like, the girl walked away.

We all thought I had scared her enough to make her stop, but the next day upon my arrival to school, she was in the corridor with her mum, waiting outside the principal's office. Her long curly blond hair was now scraggily and straight, her face was covered in dirt tears, she was not in uniform but her own clothes a thin navy-blue jumper and blue jeans with off-white trainers. She grinned at me sarcastically as I came down the corridor. Fake tears painted her face.

"That's her mummy, that's the evil brown girl. There she is. Please don't let her come near me."

Oh, hell no, you did not just call me evil, I thought to myself. Her mum towered over me, dressed in her plaid suit, skin-coloured tights, and perfectly polished brown shoes. Her husband was probably off having lots of affairs whilst she is home getting his dinner ready.

"You're going to pay for this, young lady, for what you have done to my daughter. At first, I was worried about your sort, sharing a school with my precious baby. I was right; you should be ashamed. You and your friends have destroyed the colour of this school.".

When Mrs Whittaker's door opened, out came my aunty. Her face was warm and smiling, but it was a sympathetic smile. How did she get here before me? I left the house before her. She walked past the girl's mum shouting abusive language at me. She hugged me then turned me around by the shoulders. "Come, child, let us go."

I had been suspended for fourteen days. My threatening behaviour had earned me a suspension. I was made an example of. It was either fourteen days or expulsion. I even had a police officer come to my house to give me a warning. My aunt and uncle never told me off; they never questioned my behaviour. I tried to explain, but they just said they got it and it was ok. I wasn't sure if they blamed me or felt sorry for me.

I returned to school after my two-week period; it was the longest two weeks of my life. I was made to apologise to the racist cow. Somehow Mrs Girding, our class tutor, didn't move me away from my friends. I think she knew I was right. The desk and lockers with the racist slurs were all gone, with new ones in their place.

So, life went on a Whittingdon high. We kept quiet for a while and behaved to the best of our ability. However, I had Sophie, the ring leader's number, and I wasn't going to let her get away with it. But for now, I would let her think she had won.

By the time we were all fifteen, we were well established in the school. I had somehow become the head of our year. People would think I was a hood, lord.

I was selling fizzy drinks and sweets to the younger years at 10p a pop, which was a lot back then; it was an extra 5p if you want a single, that was a single cigarette. So I was always smoking in the school toilets. I would recruit the younger ones to keep a lookout, and if they did a good job, they got a lollipop for free.

Just when we thought all was settled, and we were making a good name for ourselves, a note appeared early one morning on the principal's desk.

A note that would destroy us and test our friendship.

I gathered my four friends in the canteen. We huddled in our space by the large window that overlooked the school playing field

"So, what's so serious, Pip? Why the drama?" Jazz inquired. I gave a quick sweep of the place before answering.

"They have information on us, given to them by another source. So someone is watching us."

"Someone like who?" Giselle answered nervously.

"Look," Venus piped up. "We don't know what they want, so let's not panic just yet."

"I've been trying to tell myself that whatever it is can't be that serious; they wouldn't leave us sitting here all this time if it was so urgent." I was confident.

"We've been accused of so many things it could be anything." Jazz spoke with regret.

"We seriously need to think about what this could be and have a story prepared for every event; they sound serious, more serious than I've ever known them, and we cannot go in blindly." So I pulled some paper and a pen from my black leather book bag and advised them to do the same.

"Now, write down the worst three things it could be, then we come up with a story for each one; we don't have any time to waste." All five of us put our heads down and got to writing

We wrote down three different scenarios, our stories for each, and what we should say.

When it came to devising a plan, although Jazz was the mummy of the group, this was where I would take control. I knew the girls depended on me to consistently control the last piece of the puzzle. I knew they held a lot of faith in me; they told me so.

I know I could joke around a lot, but when it came to rolling up my sleeves and getting dirty, I believe I was the strongest; the girls often told me I was hard to break. So I just prayed that whatever it was this time, they were right.

Giselle had these big round eyes that always said, 'read me, I'm lying.' Her silky jet-black hair was still dangling over her forehead and obscuring her eyes.

"Is everyone clear?" I checked.

We nodded

"Is this really necessary?" Venus protested. "Here we are conjuring up a plan, and we don't even know what they want. So I say we scrap this and just wait and see; I don't want to lie."

I gave Venus a cold stare; I don't believe I ever really trusted her, it was more of tolerance, but I was always extra nice to Venus because Venus had skin colour issues that she blamed us for. She was sensitive, so I handled her carefully. Plus, I need her agreement to ensure our plan went through safely.

1.15, that's when we were called to Mrs Whittaker's office, with strict instructions to be on time.

We had been blamed for so many school incidents that spending time in the principal's office became a regular occurrence. Only this time, someone had typed a message on a piece of paper with profound information about us. The letter contained each of our names with a personal amount of data. There was the only thing I knew it could be.

We had agreed to risk our futures for the sake of our bond; pass or fail, we would lose either way.

What I do know is that it cost us our place at Whittingdon high.

THE MOLE!

Ok, so they were accused of a secret that cost them their places at Whittingdon high. But that's not the secret I wanted to hear. Instead, there was another one, an even darker one, one I was beginning to get the impression that not all of them were aware of.

I rolled my eyes as Piper spoke to me. I wanted to burst out and shout, "Liar, liar." But I didn't dare, as I needed to hear the rest of her creative story. I knew she was afraid of the dark, so I wanted to put her in darkness. Torture her and make her tell the truth about all the people around her that had suspiciously died. There was always an accident; someone else was always there to save her, but. It wasn't fair. No matter how long she had to endure the darkness, she wouldn't talk. I didn't have the power to make her repent, but I knew who did.

JAZZ

Does music make you shiver, does it?

I listened to the drama

From within the song

Are you upset by the truth of its words

Or the time it's prolonged?

Does it make you mourn the artist

And sing out of tune?

How happy is a tragic song

That echoes from the moon?

Does music make you shiver?

Does it?

CHAPTER 6

ALL THAT JAZZ

I asked the question so many times that I barely listened to the answer anymore. The answer was always the same, consistently accurate, precise, and well thought out. I was not surprised. Some of the words were robust for a young child to comprehend.

When I asked her for the billionth time what she had said on her dying bed, that time it felt different. I wondered If I had heard her correctly.

Twenty-one had caught me so fast. One minute I was sitting on my dad's knee playing horse, then there I was working hard, running my own accounts business, making sure my dad's dirty money was kept a secret.

I believed my parents' every word when I was naive, unable to make my own decisions, just like any child would.

My daddy was an entertainment lawyer, a prominent badass, top-of-the-range lawyer.

Representing and protecting the interests of some big names in the industry.

He had expertise in several areas of law. He was widely used to support larger entities. The scope of work he was involved in was extensive, but most of it was negotiating. So, if you needed to secure a contract in any field, my daddy was the man.

He was hunted high and low by professionals, who craved his pre-eminent expertise, paying outlandish sums to secure his business.

As a child, we never wanted anything. I was the rich kid of the block, always in the latest designer wear, popular with all the kids and their parents—depending on their nationality. My daughter River, who thinks I'" "m her big sister, had all the toys that other children just dreamed of. She didn't appear spoilt. She had a kind nature and always wanted to share everything. River would wipe away our autistic brother's tears when he cried and cuddle him. For such a young child, she had an old head. River had green eyes and long jet-black hair, which was always loose and messy. She was the cutest little sister ever and very articulate. She would mimic everything I did, follow me everywhere, even to the toilet. My friends adored her way too much. I would get annoyed with them when they insisted on holding her hand when we were out. I watched my mum's every move with her so that when it came time for me to tell her the truth, I would already be a good mum.

I always got invited to dinner or tea. The black kids always had dinner when we went home, which usually consisted of jerk chicken, rice, and peas or something substantial like that.

The white kids always had tea. I remember being asked to tea by William. William was a long, lanky, curly-haired white boy.

He never played with the other boys because his lanky legs wouldn't afford him the service of kicking the ball straight, so the other boys teased him until their wicked taunts filled him with shame and embarrassment. I always wished I hadn't said hello to him that day or stuck up for him when he was being pushed around in the alleyway after school. But anyway, William invited me to tea. I didn't want to appear rude, so I said yes. In total, our friendship lasted a whole three and half weeks and fifty-nine hours.

Not because William's house was not as grand as mine or that it smelt of cat piss, a partner to William's constant smell. It wasn't because his dad was clearly an alcoholic, drunk when we arrived at Williams's house and gawped at me as if I was the cherry on his cupcake. No, none of that. It wasn't even because William's idea of tea was cucumber, banana, and butter sandwich. Not that either.

It was because William tried to kiss me, yep, he took it there, and he wanted to kiss me. Leaned in, mouth wide open, waving his tongue. I arched my back so far; I could feel it jam into place whilst he cradled my back to stop me from falling.

His long furry tongue that hadn't been brushed for days, snaking in my direction, those tonsils jigging in the background singing, "I got me some black."

"Oh, hell no." Before my brain could even connect with my body, his impudence provoked me into slapping his face. Damn, I knew that must have stung as the tears sprung to his eyes and sprayed into my mouth. He released his hand at speed from the base of my back and left me to pound onto the ground as he grabbed his once pale cheek.

I sat and stared up at him as he sobbed uncontrollably. Then I felt terrible, not because I slapped him, but because it hurt him. That was the last time we spoke; in a way, I was relieved.

Before our break up, not girlfriend and boyfriend break up, but like friends' breakup when you're still innocent and are not attracted to one another, William came to my house, before the time I'd been to his. He said we had the best-decorated house in Clapham, which in a way was true. His eyes lit up at the glory of it as his unaware, natural, unbalanced racist comments proceeded to fire wounds into my bones. It wasn't until I was older that I realised there were no consequences for his actions because he was just following his parents' own vengeance towards darker-skinned people.

I remember my mum's face when he asked her if my dad had to sell a lot of drugs to get a house like this. My mum stared at him with owl eyes and encouraged him to finish his chicken. That's when he choked on the jerk and retrieved a long piece of thyme from his mouth. After that, my mum said it was time for him to go home. I remember her asking me if I had lots of other friends. She knew I did. That question meant, get rid of him.

My mum was a proud mummy and wife. My mum was well respected by the neighbours. They depended on her for lots of things, things I thought they could educate themselves on. My mum had the final say on the events within our neighbourhood. She wasn't bossy. She was snobby, though, I guess, in charge.

People admired my mum as she glided down the streets, always entirely made up, never a strand of hair out of place, nails to perfection, and good shoes. Always have good shoes. That was important. Life was her stage. Whether she was acting or this resolute behaviour was born, she put on a good show.

I don't really remember seeing my mum and dad in regular company. However, she would always defend his absence by keeping us well versed about his job. "Your dad is the best lawyer in London. Of course, to be the best, my darling, you must always sacrifice a little. But remember to learn everything to look after yourself, educate yourself on monotonous subjects to keep in with the well-educated and be rich."

Why did I want to be bored and rich? But at age 13, that statement had a ring of excitement to it.

Nothing was ever too much for my parents. The house was always wrapped in laughter and events. Of course, I was always allowed to have whoever I wanted to come over. But, without a doubt, it would always be my besties, Piper, Storm, Giselle, and Venus.

We attended the same private school. We got on like we were born out of the same womb. We were inseparable; everything we did was together. Even our lessons were in the same classes. We could sit together so long as we did not talk, except Venus. She would occasionally sit at the front of the class to get help from the teaching assistant.

I was pretty nervous when I heard about the auditions for Whittingdon high. I had passed by the school on many occasions. So, I envisioned myself already there. But, mum said, 'there was no way they would say no because my dad and I had already manifested it. Whatever that meant at age 11.

I liked the look and feel, but mum said it wasn't the right school for me. But after a few visits to the local schools, my dad insisted that it was the school for me.

I remember mum being angry. She blasted him with expletives words I don't think I'd ever heard her use. But in the end, dad always won.

I was eleven, and mum couldn't understand why people put their children through so much stress. Getting into Whittington High was not easy. It came with a high price and talent. My talent was the piano.

On the morning of the audition, I threw up three times. Dad said not to tell my mum as she would not let me go. "You're strong, baby. You got this." My dad was always so positive and encouraging. "Don't let anyone stop you or tell you can't, not even mummy." He stared me deep in the eyes like he always did, told me to fix up and look sharp. That's precisely what I did.

I walked into that large hall with confidence. I didn't give anyone a chance to ask my name.

"Good morning everyone, my name is Miss Bailey, Jazz Bailey." I glanced over at my parents and smiled. Mum was looking proud. "I'm eleven years old, and I'm going to play a piece by Chopin called Nocturne. I will be playing in E-sharp."

I took my seat at the piano and waited for my cue, there was a long silence, and I could see the panel grinning at my advanced demeanour, but I didn't turn around. I waited, and waited, and waited.

I heard the clock ticking hard into my ears. My

mum and dad were sitting wide-eyed as they waited.

"You may begin, Jazz," came the firm voice.

I gently lowered my head as I searched the keys through my tears of the overwhelmed river I had created. Then, I started gently and swiftly, moving my finger elegantly over the keys. My body swayed in time with the music as I was taken away into another world and time. At points, I played abrupt and ridged, quick, and precise.

I finished and kept my head facing the piano. "Jazz."

I heard one of the panellists call my name.

"Yes," I responded without turning.

"Jazz." I still didn't turn.

"That was beautiful." I released a deep sigh, peeled myself off the small stool with a leather seat, then stepped backwards, turned to the panel, curtsied, and started to leave the room. I heard a faint clap as I go. I turned to see who it was and saw the grumpy-looking white-haired man at the end of the long table. I smiled as he stood to address me.

He cleared his throat before he spoke. "Miss Bailey." He paused. "Miss Bailey, that was an outstanding piece of music. Well done. However, your presence is somewhat immature. The other girls that attend here are not like yourself. They are eager with fire in their bones. I don't sense that from you. Perhaps Whittingdon High is not the place for you right now.

I'd like to see you return next year when we can cater to girls of your kind."

I turned to face my parents. My mum's face was saying, "What a waste of my money on all those piano lessons for you to mess it up. My dad's face was saying, "Fight, baby girl. Fight for it."

I turned back towards the white-haired man to address him. "Mr Bowden, I'm not sure what you mean that I'm not like the other girls, but I have the best piano instructor in London. Perhaps the flaw you see is in your own girls and not me. Perhaps you have not witnessed talent such as mine. Perhaps you are blinded by your own prejudices from seeing me clearly. I have trained with Flowered Museum for some years now, and to be turned away from Whittingdon High with my expertise would be detrimental to theirs and your reputation."

Flowered Museum had the best piano instructors in London. You were guaranteed to get into any music school just by mentioning their name. I could see my dad was proud, and so was my mum because I could hold my own, and I had a flair for words. I'd learnt from the best. But I was not expecting the subsequent response.

"Then perhaps, Miss Bailey, next year, you could show us the skills you have accomplished from Flowered Museum. And return with the right attitude and demeanour. I must say Flowered Museum will be truly disappointed with your failures. Good day, Miss Bailey."

My head hung, my body froze, juices trickled from my nose and eyes as I listened to the commotion my parents were causing, making things worse. I turned and ran as fast as I could. I heard my mum screaming at me to keep my head up.

On my way out, the next contender was approaching the room; I turned my head to one side to hide my tears from her; she crept in, clutching her music piece; I heard them ask her name and where she had come from. Her response was a mere, "I haven't been learning the piano for that long, I'm only a grade 3, but I learn fast. I'm from the flowered museum". The response she received from the grumpy white-haired man was, "Wow, flowered museum, just perform what you have, everyone from such a talented school is automatically granted with a unique gift and a place with us. Welcome to Whittingdon high".

I didn't leave my room for two days. That's when I realised being black was not going to be easy. I would either sink or swim; I chose to swim. Then finally, one year later, I was offered a place at Whittingdon High.

My mum liked Piper straight away. She had this hardness about her. People often referred to her as the little hard nut. This seemed to irritate my mum. "She's not a hard nut," mum would retaliate. "She's just misunderstood. Look out for her, Jazz," my mum would often say, with suspicious concern in her eye. I found Piper quite cold and callous, but my mum didn't see that side of her.

Once Piper was out of school for a long time, like six weeks. My mum did the most embarrassing neighbourly. She cooked her best curry goat dish and took it round to Piper's parents' house. Piper blossomed from a large family and had multiple siblings, seven of them altogether. Paige was the youngest; she was very shy; she only ever waved to us from the highest window in the house. The only time I ever saw her out was at her mum and dad's funeral. I wish I had been able to talk to her, but she was so distressed that Piper's older brother escorted her home early. Piper explained that she didn't get on with her older siblings, but she always seemed happy on the odd chance we were invited to her house.

I am not sure why my mum thought she needed loving or why she needed to pry and go to the house. I just know that I heard her whispering to my dad one night. I heard Piper's name mentioned. Mum visited a few times after that. She always painted this distressed front but never ever said what was going on. Shortly after, Piper returned to school. She said she had been diagnosed with arthritis in her back and couldn't walk.

None of us questioned it as we didn't even know what it was.

We grew together through those years, never leaving each other's side. By the time we were fifteen, we soon realised who was who, and it was clear that I was closer to Storm and Piper.

Piper was fearless and never ever shed a tear. She took on anyone, a force to be reckoned with, but a nice one, always kind. There was never a time she would refuse to do anything for anyone. Your secrets would be taken to the grave even if she was tortured. There was never a dull moment with Piper. I often wondered where she got her energy. But like I said before, she had another side to her.

On the other hand, Storm was dangerous; some referred to her as a sassy hoe, mainly girls did really. She did not really seem to mind because if any girl upset her, she would just sleep with their boyfriend to shut them up. It was always difficult to understand why Storm had no code of conduct. Our own boyfriends were never safe from her grasp. I'm pretty sure my dad may have fallen victim. But I'm going to erase that thought from my head.

I never really had an issue with Storm. I loved her. She was like Piper when it came to men. The only difference was, Piper would never cross that line with her friends. They were both outspoken, assertive, flirtatious, intelligent, caring, and loyal. Venus had reservations about both. She always deliberately took them on to show she was fearless, but they always got the better of her. Venus had calmed down somewhat as we grew older, but her disapproval towards her skin colour did not change. She constantly belittled the girls about their complexion and how light-skinned they were, then when they turned on her, she would claim the victim. Deep down, Storm despised her, but she was still part of our group.

Giselle was a fully-fledged Christian by the age of sixteen, she was the softer of the five of us, or so she made out. We all liked Giselle. Although she was quiet, she was also very outspoken in her manner. If there was a confrontation in the group, it would really upset her, to the point that she would stay away for a couple of days and go out with her other friends. But if there was a secret to be revealed, Giselle would be the first to break. So, we made a pact; if anything should ever happen, we would all go down. That pact was to be tested sooner than we thought.

The week after the eerie night, my dad had been arrested whilst we sat eating at our favourite restaurant. Mum had persuaded him to go even though it was a school night and he had business to attend to. It was also the week after my sixteenth birthday. Dad hadn't managed to celebrate with us because, yes, he had business to attend. That's what got him in the end. Mum made him feel guilty. My pitiful face was a treat River, my little sister, and my autistic brother didn't have a clue what was going on. He just sat waving his hands frantically because his routine had been changed, and no one had informed him. River clung to my neck and cried, "Let my Daddy go."

That's when I found out my dad was a gangster, in and out of prison more times than the prison guards themselves. Everyone feared me, or rather what my daddy would do to them. So, he was never this big-time lawyer mum had displayed. No, he was a gangster, leader of the pack, badass gangster. He worked away so much because he was in and out of prison. This time he wasn't coming out for a long time. He had controlled and organised a string of expensive car robberies, cocaine shipments, and so much more, now his time was up. Just like that, he was gone.

Eight months later, so was my mum. Breast cancer took her home to rest.

On the night she passed away, I sat and spoke with her whilst she stroked my hair. She revealed the biggest secret to me, the biggest secret I would have to keep, The biggest secret I would r to my grave. It was dark and heavy, I had to reveal it to my friends. But I knew I could trust them with anything. It was a burden I did not want to carry alone. My aunty from America moved in with us. She couldn't manage my autistic brother and his needs, so he was shortly put into care. My life was crumbling. River had become very quiet by then; she had climbed into herself and didn't speak much to anyone. Then, one night, she finally came into my room and sat on my bed with me. "Jazzy," she called me, "When is mummy coming home?"

"Mummy is not coming back, River." I was irritated by her question, but she was only three at the time. She didn't understand.

"Then I can call you mummy?" I didn't know what to say. She was too young for me to tell her the truth. But I felt terrible for her. All her family disappeared just like that. So, I agreed to her request.

"Yes, my little sister, you can call me Mummy."

River cheered, bounced up and down onto my bed, screaming. My aunt was not happy with the decision, but River would soon learn the truth. She was just going through a phase. She was hurting like the rest of us.

I wanted my mum and dad so badly. Why should she not have the chance to still call someone her mum? I was her blood mum, after all.

As if I didn't have enough to deal with, our principal, Mrs Whittaker, had received some severe information about us. A typed note was left in her office, and we had been summoned to her with two other teachers. The five of us walked in, greeted by horrified, stern, and concerned faces.

Mrs Whittaker signalled her long scrawny hand for us to be seated. They had already worked out what five they would reprimand, and it had to be the five black girls.

In the far-right corner of the room, I suddenly noticed the nurse. Why was she here?

Mrs Whittaker cleared her throat. She pushed her glasses into her creased face and began to address us.

"Girls, a very serious matter has been brought to my attention." She proceeded to clear her throat again, this time a little louder as she glanced at Storm slouched in her chair chewing gum. Not at all concerned by Mrs. Whittaker, Storm blew a bubble before sitting up and wiping the sticky gum into a tissue she pulled from the principal's box.

Mrs. Whittaker paused for a few seconds before eyeing Storm with disgust. "Now, I'm not going to beat around the bush because I would like this—" she paused whilst searching for her words. Her voice was a bit softer now. "Do any of you girls have anything you would like to discuss?" Mrs. Whittaker peered individually at us as we shook our heads in turn without knowing what she was going on about. There it was again, that uncomfortable clearing of the throat.

"We wanted to give you girls a chance to talk to us

before we contact your parents."

Giselle began to fidget nervously in her chair and pick at her quivering lip.

We didn't stand a chance. We couldn't even hide from what was coming our way. So, we would just stick to Piper's plan. But, because of our secure bond with one another, because we would take each other's secrets to the grave because our love would never be broken, we lost our places at Whittingdon high.

THE MOLE!

I was beginning to wonder if the girls liked one another. Sitting here listening to each individual story was not bringing me any closer to what I wanted to know. So here is Jazz with a vast secret her mum revealed to her on her death bed. So what? She doesn't have anything to prove, but she will act like she does, just because she can. That's just her character. I was getting the impression that I would never find out what the secret was should I continue to doubt her. I was exhausted by her chilling ability to not break. Something wasn't right. It was challenging to work out which one of them was the ring leader, which one of them could manage to silence the others in the group. Risk everything, even their lives. But I wasn't backing down. I had to stay alive long enough to find out.

.

STORM

I know the real reason

For my basket of burdens.

One small red rose

I lay by your curtain

I won't sleep alone forever

This, I am certain.

I took the wrong road

And tripped on my reasons

Thorns in one hand

And love in the other

CHAPTER 7

THE CALM BEFORE THE STORM

I managed to reach the ripe old age of twenty, and I was still putting up with his shit.

My face had become his dimmer switch. Every time I shone, he would rotate me back to darkness. But I loved him; if this was safe love, then I was already dead.

I lay in bed many nights hovering over my thoughts at what I did wrong to deserve this abandonment. Every loving look I gave him was laced with a hot punch of anger and annoyance that struck me to the ground.

I prayed he'd leave for good; when the provider becomes a monster, he has failed to love you, and self-control is no longer an option. So instead, you must fight for everything with all your heart, fight for empathy, love, and your position.

Domestic stress abuse surfaces out of a sick form of depression, and before you know it, you are fighting for your life.

The dishes crashed to the ground, escaping like flying saucers as they were swept off the counter. The

143

shrapnel of glass and ceramics flew, spraying the air like a sprinkler watering the flowers in the summertime heat.

Cupboard doors were ripped from the hinges, hurled across the white glossy work surface, smashing against the black and white marble walls, immediate cracks appearing like the parting of the sea.

I could hear his heavy footsteps crunching against the already battered dishes on the floor, smudging the blood that decorated the once immaculate kitchen.

"Now, I asked you a question, are you going to leave me the fuck alone?" His voice boomed throughout the whole house; I could feel his vibrations against the ceramic floor.

The terrified whimpering of my baby, Marcus, could be heard from the corner of the room. He was still strapped into his high chair when it went hurtling to the floor. His food was splattered over his face, mixed in with tears and blood seeping from the side of his head and lip, his sad eyes were reaching out to me, but I couldn't move to get him.

Whilst World War three had broken loose in our house, yet again. I told him I was sorry for allowing him to be a party to this. The withered persona of a tired body whose disorientation was fading fast was courtesy of my jealous vengeance towards my boyfriend, Marlon, earlier.

The distressing cries of my baby were breathtaking as they howled into the destroyed walls.

I gripped the slippery floor but found I was paralysed from the pain; something heavy lay like a burden on my back. As I coughed, blood splattered onto my hands in the form of large speckles. My head was glued to the floor from Marlon's oversized foot that had stomped it to the ground in retaliation. My head had long been spinning from the impact; I pitied myself as my life whizzed around inside my head.

"You're going to leave me alone, say it." His voice struggling to be strong.

"Let me get the baby first," I pleaded.

"You got time to talk bitch."

"Please, please, I will leave you alone; just let me get my baby."

Marlon deliberated, then stomped one leg behind him close to his baby boy strapped in the harness of his high chair flat out on the floor. I stared up at him, pleading. Instead, Marlon glared down at me and lifted his big size elevens above my baby's head; the shattering scream released from within me echoed throughout the whole building.

"Please, Marlon, no, don't do it, Marlon." I was desperate; I could hardly breathe. The pounding of my heart could be felt throughout the house. I closed my eyes as I couldn't watch my baby's head being crushed into the ground.

"Monster," I yelled breathlessly, "You dirty monster."

Marlon placed his foot flat on the ground with a stomp close to baby Marcus's face.

"Monster, did you say. I'll show you what a monster looks like".

With that, Marlon released Marcus from his high chair. He jerked the baby upside down by his tiny feet; I was screaming at him to stop. Marcus was frantic and shrieking.

Marlon kicked the utensils around the floor as if he is searching for something, but my body wouldn't move. I began kicking my legs and banging my fists, bellowing at Marlon, but he was too far gone to hear me.

"There it is." He jumps.

I looked ahead of me, and I saw the small chopper that I used for meat. Marlon scrambled for it on the floor. Then, with Marcus in one hand still upside down, the chopper in the other, he held it high and swung it down towards Marcus's head. My breath is taken from me, and for a moment, everything was in slow motion. There was no sound, just the breeze from the chopper carrying its final swing.

Marlon pulled Marcus out of the way and hooked the chopper into the kitchen work surface. First, I released a loud cry into the cold ceramic floor; now, the only sound is my teeth clawing and crunching against the ceramic tiles in disbelief.

"Now tell me I'm a monster again, bitch."

I lay stiff and breathless. Finally, I released a silent cry, defeated by the pain and Marlon's vicious act. He dropped Marcus onto my back and left without saying a word. I heard Marcus wail, a gut-wrenching, agonising scream.

I had no right to be praying, but I did; I prayed a little prayer, "Dear God, please gives me the strength to poison him." I know I shouldn't ask for such things, especially from God, but I didn't know what else to do.

With the bit of strength I had left, I pushed myself onto all fours. Marcus whimpered as he rolled to the floor from my back, another prayer and hope, as I slowly wrenched myself to my feet, using every muscle in my body to contract through the pain. I searched desperately for something to lean against. Through blood-curdled eyes, I found the edge of what was the kitchen counter. As I reached out my arms, they fell, crashing to the floor, crunching my chin hard on the edge of the granite surface. Again, blood sprayed around me; yet again, I was on my hands and knees, crying in absolute agony.

Much later, here I am   I stood in front of my stage-lit mirror nursing my wounds. My smooth butter complexion was now filled with lumps, bumps, and bruising. What was I going to tell my parents this time? That I got my head stuck in a mill grinder? I was becoming an absolute joke.

My parents had placed me so high on their pedestal, now their baby girl was letting them down, allowing some bully to walk in, shower me with bruises, and petrify a defenceless baby. Little did they know that their precious daughter's illuminated bruising resulted from Marlon's retaliation, the man I tirelessly abused out of my jealous rages.

I knew I was dangerous and out of control. I also knew Marlon believed the only way to stop me would be inevitable. However, I knew Marlon was not prepared to give the word. He still loved me, this violent woman, even if there was a possibility I could kill him first.

I allowed the water to beat down on my already sore body; it travelled into every cut and over every bruise and lump, stinging my tender skin. Then, finally, as my tears mixed in with the hot water from the shower, I allowed a wail to escape my lips.

I had to air dry my body as I was in immense pain.

I checked Marcus over and gently washed him down. Today, I would not drop him at my parents. Instead, I would take him to my sister. I did not want to hear the cruel truth, and although my sister was the biggest traitor, I would instead put up with her brutal words.

Today, my friend had summoned us all to a meeting, and I would be damned if I was going to miss it.

I slipped into a long-sleeved linen top and matching trousers, attempting to hide the bruises that painted my body. I left my hair to hang loosely onto my shoulders, covering the bruises behind my neck. My face welcomed the extra layer of makeup.

I held Marcus in my arms as I exited the door, locking it behind me; I made my way down the spiral staircase.

"Trying to get away before I came back?" The voice made me jump, nearly dropping Marcus. I froze in my tracks. Marlon had popped out earlier to complete a deal; now he was back already.

"Well, did you ask my permission to go out?" I remained quiet. Marlon always had a problem with me going out.

"What, you turned dumb now?" I hated when Marlon leaned his head to one side. Then he grabbed me by the chin. "I said did you ask my permission?"

"No."

Marlon moved around to the right side of me and stuck his tongue into my ear; I cringed, trying not to move too much in case he physically harmed me. I could feel my green eyes squinting at him with fear whilst I stood shaking.

"Where you going?" he asked, with his tongue in my ear. His revolting attempt at turning me on was making me heave. My ear was wet and warm from his hot breath.

"Marcus is not well. He needs some Calpol, and I, I've come on, I need some pads." I spoke, not making eye contact with Marlon.

"Really? Then leave Marcus with me, and you can go and come back." His eyes pierced right through me while gripping at the back of Marcus's top, attempting to pull him off me.

Marcus was now winging from his father's presence.

"Enough, Marlon, we got business to attend to." I instantly looked up; where did he suddenly appear from? Was he standing there all along, undressing me with his mean eyes?

No wonder Marlon had suddenly found his vicious tongue; he had back up.

It was ok. I would let him ride this one to prove his adulthood to his best friend.

"Storm," Cory addressed me, his voice demanding my attention.

"Hi Cory," my response was a mere whisper. Cory's expression remained grim and brutal as he eyed me whilst chewing on a cocktail stick.

Cory was Giselle's boyfriend. Although Cory and I did not agree completely, I felt relieved that he was there to calm Marlon's skanky arse down. First, Marlon released his hand from Marcus's back. Then, keeping his eyes pinned on me, he stepped to the side, allowing me to pass, but not before ramming his fist into my spine. The impact knocked me to the ground, and tears sprang to my eyes as I gripped onto Marcus, screeching from the sudden rollercoaster drop, making sure not to fall onto him.

This show of calculated abuse was a warning of the day's earlier events; as I lethargically struggled to my feet, Marlon giggled at me like some devilish child.

Marlon was a street man well known for his violent behaviour and petty crime. He had tried for years to fit in with the big boys, such as Corey, but they always had him as a runner; he thought he was worth more than that, so he would take his frustrations out on me. Lately, baby Marcus had become one of his defenceless victims.

Marlon was a lanky five foot eleven inches dark-skinned animal; his daddy beat him and his mother when they were younger, so the cycle continued. He wore his hair in cornrows, which framed his thin, gaunt features and large eyes, his back of the lorry clothes hung from his slight frame, and he thought he was the bee's knees. No classy looking girl would give him the time of day, so he verbally beat them to the extreme they would walk away in tears. He'd been beaten up so many times even he had lost count, but in his head, he was a hustler, not even sensible enough to be approved by any other hustler member, but I liked a rude boy, and that is what I got. I was equally violent.

I did not start off violent, I did not mean to be this way, but Marlon always appeared so weak compared to the other men I had dated; they were fearless, real thug love, and brought in the money. So yes, it came with its downfalls, like you were never the only one in the relationship and ended up fighting another woman off, but he always came back to me with lots of cash, and my downfall was I loved money and lots of it.

When I met Marlon, I was barely sixteen, I wasn't a virgin, and I knew how to please a man. He was so sexually attractive, a smooth operator full of promises. However, I soon discovered he was so weak, and it irritated me. At first, it started out with just a playful nudge; my other boyfriends made naughty jokes about not hitting them, so I stopped, but Marlon didn't say anything, so I carried on. Then when I gave him a slap over the head for not putting the washing on, he still didn't say anything, so it carried on. The next thing I know, I was punching him in the face and promising him I would not do it again, but I could not stop myself. I just got carried away. Everything he did irritated me, and I just wanted to hurt him at times. But then a switch went off in him, and he began fighting back; now, the fights were lethal, and very soon, one of us would pay the price.

My friends and family just assumed that Marlon was the perpetrator and I was the victim. They hated him, and their words were often cruel and threatening, but he never told the truth. He always just let them blame him took whatever they had to say. I guess it was an embarrassment. After all, what man really allows his woman to beat him to a pulp like that without defending himself.

I often wondered why he took so much before fighting back, but when he turned, I was the scared one; I knew when he'd had enough, I knew when I was in trouble.

I had begun dating Marlon when I met him in a wine bar in Dulwich, called the Mansion, owned by a man named Royal. Marlon and his friends ventured in all swagged up and draped in gold. My eyes noticed the dollar signs straight away, and I moved in quickly without waiting for his invitation. Unfortunately, I accosted him just as he was about to talk to another sweet cutie pie propped up at the bar.

"I'll get those," I sweet told him as I paid for his drinks.

"A girl that doesn't want my money, or should I say

need it," he retorted sexily.

"I'm independently independent, and I like to look after my man."

"Ooh, you asking me to be your man."

"Not quite; I'm just letting you know that any man I have will be looked after, financially and physically."

"Ok, how about you give me a test drive and see if I fit the profile as your man."

"You asking me out?"

"Maybe"

"Ok, well, let me know if you are. I'll be over there with my friends."

I grinned at him and went over to join my girls at the seat by the window. He didn't come over straight away, but when he did, he bought us all a drink, five rum and blacks. Piper pushed hers out, and right from that moment, she had an instant dislike.

Piper hated Marlon and Corie vigorously; she wouldn't even look at them or acknowledge them except to be spiteful to them. Marlon often promised he was going to hurt her. I know I considered him weak. Still, I knew what he was capable of, and at times I just wished she would back off, but Piper and Jazz were fearless, especially when it came to those two. Jazz knew people that Marlon and Corey knew, people they wouldn't mess with, compliments of her dad.

I first met my friends when I was twelve years old at

Whittington high private school in Clapham. It was right on my doorstep in perfect walking distance. My parents objected to me going to the local schools as they felt I would be better educated in a private school. But really, my dad saw my potential to head in the wrong direction; this was his feeble attempt to keep me on the straight and narrow.

I didn't think I was terrible; I was talented and misunderstood.

You had to be gifted to get into Whittingdon, and that I was. I loved sports, and sports loved me, so training for the football, tennis, and swimming club was my gateway into the school. I possessed speed, stamina, strength, precision, order, focus accuracy. Everything needed to be a sporty person, but it was not easy; they made me do a trial for everything three times over, then they made my dad get me a blood test because it was believed that I could be at age eleven on drugs. They never said it, but my dad informed me that's what they usually look for. My ability to succeed was beyond comparison; they tried in many directions to not offer me a place, but my dad was a powerhouse, and when it came to his baby girl, he wasn't about to give up.

After spending most of my summer training and a near court case, Whittingdon high offered me a place one week before school began. One of the only white

Jewish girls in a private school. Well, that's what I lead them to believe anyway.

The others all came to Whittington at age twelve as they were not offered the places in their first year as they were not as talented. They were forced to attend their local secondary school whilst their parents pretended to fight for a position. They used the black card to get them in, you know, the parents who tell you your racist if something is not offered straight away.

My stupid white friends didn't even know I was black until Piper and the rest showed up, with their lame black arses, bouncing in as if they just arrived from some American gangster movie. Piper was the first person I latched onto. Yes, I like the rest but not straight away. Piper had a fire, she knew how to laugh, and I never felt judged. Even though Piper had some issues, like being afraid of the dark, scoffing her food like a wild animal, and sometimes I saw her digging her nails into her wrist, I could deal with those issues. She was still my favourite.

Piper spotted my blackness first, then took the liberty to talk to me. I also had to admit I wasn't Jewish, didn't even speak Hebrew. It was a mumbled Jamaican accent.

My skin was as light as a white person, and I possessed shoulder-length blond hair that turned into a fully-fledged afro when it was washed. Although my long eyelashes framed my green eyes and complimented my beauty spot on the right side of my nose, my mum always told me those heart-shaped lips would get me into trouble. Later, she was right. I never had a problem exposing my large breast and showing my cleavage. I would wait until I was out of the house to undo a few buttons on my school uniform blouse, pull my jumper into my size four waist, and roll up my skirt to show my muscular netball-playing legs.

We all did it; we all loved to show off our curvy young, groomed bodies, depending on whose class we were in. Like Mr Fin, he was worthy of a bit more thigh and cleavage. Half the time, you could see he found it hard to breathe. Even at age fifteen, when we were even more scantily dressed, Mr Fin would stutter and sweat as we approached his desk, bending over and asking for help with a maths question we clearly already knew, but he was hot, and I attended maths every day. Then one day, we had a message that Mr Fin would be teaching the year ones; instead, my maths lessons were never the same again.

Piper lived in the deep south-east, someplace called Lewisham or Catford; I couldn't remember which one; she would be driven to and from school every day by some black woman who was a family friend. I must admit she was the best dancer the school had seen in years, but marching in here tantalising your bold

African contemporary moves is not for Whittingdon High. Nevertheless, I liked Piper; I knew she would give me a run for my money; she was curvier than I was also. I might have been a little bit jealous of her.

I liked her forever, but as we grew older, she had an issue with my boyfriend, and we started to fall apart. Piper thinks I never saw the marks on her arms, claiming she was always cold to try and hide them. Piper was cold and callous, dangerous even. I could see that madness in her eyes when she flipped, cool, calm, and calculating. I'm not sure if I feared her or if I really liked her.

Jazz lived in Clapham in a five-bedroom house with her dad, mum, sister River, and autistic brother Jerome; I liked him. He was hilarious, but none of us knew what autism was. We just knew he was different. River was the cutest little sister anyone could ask for. When Jazz's mum passed away, River began to call her big sister mum. I understood why but I disagreed with it. Why would a fifteen-year-old girl want her little sister to call her mum? I didn't like it, but I never said a word. Jazz's life was already messed up. Why mess up your sisters? We always made a big fuss over River. She was always giggling like a young child. She had a great sense of humour. She even knew how to keep a secret.

Jazz's mum paid for a cab every day to take her to

school; her mum was a bit stuck up, just like Jazz. I tolerated Jazz, but talking to her every day was always like having therapy. I found her draining.

Jazz was always bossy and continuously corrected my speech; she sounded like the teacher lectured us about not acting too black. She was ok, I guess, but she did take control of everything. She had helped me outcrop a few tricky situations by taking over, like the time I stole a tenner out of the teacher's bag, and she walked in whilst my hand was still in her purse. Jazz jumped in and said, "Miss, we were just coming to find you. Really, you shouldn't leave your bag open." She snatched the bag up and handed it over to the teacher. Who, in turn, took it and glared at us suspiciously? But we were never questioned.

Giselle lived around the corner from me, and once we realised we lived near each other, she would get the bus to mine and then walk around the corner to school. Giselle wasn't as idiotic as she made out to be, she played the jester, but she was far from it.

Giselle had secrets just like the rest of us. Although at times she appeared timid, this was a cover-up, and later it would get her out of some sticky situations.

Yes, of course, she was talented, extraordinarily talented. Everyone believed that she was insane, allowing the school to patent her musical abilities. Still, her family was paid substantial money and a safe space at Whittingdon high if she allowed them to take over her musical gift. Giselle's family was struggling financially; they also needed to maintain her identity. So, the handout was an ideal welcome. Even though something did not quite add up with her story. I got the impression she would become an informant to get herself out of trouble. Time would tell.

Venus lived in Brixton. Her mum was loaded; well, she had to be as Venus didn't have any other talents I recognised. Besides the image of the devil tattooed on her stomach, the fact she burnt incense and believed in witches, her only other talent was that she got the bus to school. On the days she didn't, her mum would drop her off at school and give her the most prolonged kisses on her lips. It always looked a bit weird to me. A bit incestuous.

I couldn't get along with Venus; we always got into some argument; she would still go on about my skin colour as if it was my fault. I was light-skinned. Every time I opened my mouth, she knocked me down if I made a joke, she told me I was directing it at her, Venus had issues with everything I did or issues with herself. It didn't fit right that she needed extra help in class and had to be at the front with the assistance that helped the dunce kids; being a dunce at a private school was a waste of the teacher's time.

Numerous times, they had suggested to her mum

that perhaps a different school might be better suited; in the end, they gave up trying as Venus's mum contributed an enormous amount financially to maintain the old building.

So here we were, five friends, the only five black girls in the heart of Clapham in a private school personally designed for the white hearted.

We did everything together, even each other's homework. When I would bunk off, the girls would always cover for me, sign me into lessons, hand in homework. Teachers would always look quizzically when questioned whether they really saw us or not. This was because we even sat in on each other's lessons covering for one another. I wouldn't mind, but for years they thought I was white. Then, suddenly, I just looked like the others. After all, black girls look the same; so, we got away with it.

My mum taught me that I would never have to worry in life and be granted anything I wished for; because of my complexion, I could have any man I hoped for or any job I pleased. That's what I believed, and that is how I conducted myself as if the world owed me for just being me.

Those of us who found out early that our teacher would be Mrs Whirring would be replacing Mr Fin shuddered to think of having to spend an entire year in her classroom; she was a teacher and the school deputy. It meant being trapped and subjected to months of unending English language. She told the same mundane stories all the time that we had heard a zillion times.

Stories that no one cared about, she laughed at her own jokes and repeated rehearsed quotes which I'm not sure she really understood herself.

During this time, the principal decided to have a school shakeup; the school needed a revamp, including students.

A few of the parents had made a comment that the school was becoming very dark and needed brightening up; I thought it looked glam to me, massive chandeliers hung from every high ceiling along every ornate corridor, white walls with a splash of colour in every classroom, pale blue carpet ran throughout,

I loved the cosy décor of the old building. There was nothing dark about it until I realised they did not mean the building, but clearly talking about the various cultures that had begun to attend the prestigious school. They were talking about us, the black and brown kids.

Things began to spiral out of hand, and many black girls were getting blamed for something they had no hand in, even if they were not in school that day. Then, five weeks before school ended for summer, a list mysteriously surfaced, revealing all five of our names and some personal information about each of us. About our childhood, it had been typed by someone, very clever. We knew it wasn't by us. Or did we?

It didn't matter how it was found or who leaked the information. It was hurtful, cold, and held no proof. Secrets only we knew about. Secrets we would take to our graves. Someone had been watching us, but who?

However, due to our empty promise to one another, to always stick together and never allow any man, beast or foe come between us, the five of us lost our places at Whittingdon high.

THE MOLE!

Somehow, I believed in Storm. She was brutal in her response. She was so matter-of-fact; I think she felt she had nothing to hide. Her deeply held beliefs could never be shaken. She was the truth standing right before my eyes. But how much was she willing to reveal. There was something special about Storm. It's clear to see she had been misunderstood. Storm could be the one to save her friends, save me. It wasn't a matter of when; it was a matter of how. When I slipped out to use the bathroom, upon my return, she had gone.

PART TWO of chapter 7, A spliff With the Devil.

The thin lady with the icy eyes asked us to wait in the visitors' room. I trembled uncontrollably as she asked me if I would like a sweet tea. Her hair was long and blond. She was thin, and her skin was so transparent I could see her veins making a pattern around her pale face. She attempted to exchange a warm smile, but even that came across as cold. I knew she was judging me. I don't really know what I answered, but something came out of my mouth, and I watched her feet as she headed towards the massive metal door. Her scrawny fingers feebly gripped the handle, and she gave it a jerk to pull it open. Before she disappeared through it, she turned to say, "Someone will be in to see you both soon."

Marlon stood, huddled in the back of the clinically smelling room, his trousers loose and hanging, his shirt was creased and hung sloppily around his waist, he was still wearing sliders on his dry feet. He shivered whilst chewing on a cocktail stick. I could still smell the stale weed and alcohol from the night before. Juices fell from his nose and splashed to the floor, but he made no attempt to wipe his nose, and I couldn't be bothered to hand him a tissue.

I'm not sure how long we sat in that visitor's hospital room. It seemed like an eternity before the large door flew open, and in walked my friends. Then, suddenly, I couldn't breathe. I couldn't let the words out; I was so relieved to see them.

Piper was first to ask after they hugged me tightly. I didn't want them to let go. "Babe, what happened?" Piper was always the stern one, never shed a tear in any situation. I think she must have made a pact with herself to never cry, but we all knew why she didn't. Gisselle appeared as if she may pass out and continuously mumbled prayers under her breath. Jazz was stroking my hair and whispering in my ear. I couldn't hear a word, just the feeling of hot hair on my face. They told me they hadn't located Venus yet.

I responded to Piper's question with teary eyes, unable to talk.

There was a long pause before Piper spoke again. "What have the doctors told you?" She cupped my face in her hands, planted a big kiss on my lips as we all did with each other when times get bad. It was a secure kiss of a tight bond, and if any of us displayed that affection to the other one, it meant no matter what, I've got your back. One by one, the other two friends planted the same firm kiss on my lips, and I knew they had me.

The door swung open again, and in walked my dad wheeling my mum in her wheelchair, struggling to get the wheels to manoeuvre on the stiff carpet, followed by my younger brother and older sister. My three friends squeezed my arm and backed away for my family to step in. My dad glared over in Marlon's direction, looked him up and down, and turned to me, his daughter. Then, falling to his knees, he grabbed me tightly and bawled.

"Marlon," my mum called him with authority. He did not respond. He just sniffled in the corner, banging his knuckles into his forehead. My mum wasn't giving up. "If my grandson doesn't make it, I hope you know it's your fault." Like Dracula, Marlon lunged from the corner towards my mum, screaming at her. Piper and Jazz lunged at equal speed and pinned him to the ground. My dad's arm appeared into the scuffle and pulled Marlon up by the neck, his left hand ready to knock him out. At that, the large door swung open. The doctor's face was a sure sight as he witnessed the distressing scene unfolding before him. My dad released Marlon with a shove to the floor. The doctor let the door swing behind him as he cleared his throat and called my name.

"Miss Underwood"

"Yes", I replied shakily.

Marlon and I had shared a spliff that night, I didn't really smoke, but Marlon always insisted when he knew he would probably punish me for something I didn't do or hadn't said. I think he did it to lessen the blow. We were watching a movie. He was chilled for a change. Until he asked me to go to the fridge, but I was cosy with him, and for once, I felt relaxed around him, so I asked him to get the drink. That was it. His whole persona changed as he became angered. The next thing I know, I was hurled across the floor and knocked into the cupboard. Marcus heard the commotion and came into the room crying. I knew he was getting too big for the cot, but I didn't want to buy him a bed yet as I felt the cot was safer.

I scrambled to my hands and knees before Marlon snatched my legs to stop me from reaching Marcus, but I already had a hold of him when Marlon pulled me back across the floor. I was holding onto Marcus, who, by this time, had fallen flat on his back and was being dragged with me. I screamed to Marlon to stop, and he did, but he took hold of Marcus and carried him back to his cot and closed the door to finish his job on me.

I spent the night curled up on the floor in a heap next to Marlon's cot. That's where I slept until the morning. The strangest thing I remembered about that night was I thought I saw my front door close during all the commotion, but that was impossible as it was just myself and Marlon in the flat.

The first year was challenging. First, my legs would buckle underneath me, then every month for three years, my friends and I went to this place to lay a red rose on his tiny grave. Sometimes we would laugh, sometimes we would cry, and sometimes there was complete silence.

Cot death was the verdict. That's what the judge ruled. So, my parents threw me out for a while, and I moved in with Marlon. My sister and brother no longer wanted anything to do with me, but my friends were still my friends. Or so I thought they were.

Marlon was very introverted after Marcus had passed away; I don't think he could even be bothered with beating me anymore.

Corey, Giselle's boyfriend, was feeling guilty and inadequate for Marlon. I guess he did need a friend. Corey made sure Marlon had a good income coming in. I never asked why; I already knew. This was the life I had chosen, the street life of a thug.

Corey made sure we had everything we needed, even paid for holidays for us. I'd never seen this side of him before, but then again, I guess he was making up for his guilt. After all, he was Marcus's real father. Giselle would murder me if she ever found out I was sleeping with her man.

GISELLE

All that glitters does not shine

All that is alert is not aware

All that is happy is not secure

All that is bold is not brave

All that believe are honest

Insane is what you first need to be

CHAPTER 8

THE HOSTAGE AND GISELLE

It's incredible how life can change instantly or how you don't remember your childhood. I have vague images planted in my mind's eye, nothing fantastic, nothing to write home about. Even though something dark appeared, I won't remember it until something in my adulthood triggers me and collapses everything I built.

Why is twenty-one now such a pinnacle age of regret and troublesome memories?

I was five at the time; I remember standing in the street in my pyjamas. The road was cosy; the houses were not like other houses. They had gaps in between, with the access to drives. My aunty lived right opposite us. It was a quiet road, framed by a beautiful park and trees that escaped up the back. I loved it here as a child; it was safe. It was unusual for black people to live in these parts of Clapham, but we did because my mum married a white man that beat her black and blue. So, it was ok if we kept quiet and put up with it. He was my stepdad, but my brother belonged to him.

I remember I clasped the pack of cards in my hands together tightly as I watched the piercing orange flames engulf my home.

Minutes earlier, I sat upstairs in my bedroom playing snap on the bed with my brother and cousin. I held my breath as my heart raced whilst I watched the flames shoot through the letterbox, up through the house, sweeping through the glass like a whirlwind, plumes of black smoke were billowing from the back of the house, painting the sky with black ash. I had never seen smoke like that before in my young life. It was the scariest scene I had ever witnessed.

It all began thirty minutes before, I smelt something strange, my brother began to cough, my cousin started to cry, we often had my cousin over to stay. Her mum and my mum were sisters, they lived opposite us. My cousin, Georgina's mum, was blind, so my mum would look after her a lot to give her mum a break. She was more like my little sister. I loved her dearly. At the time of the accident, I was five. My little brother Jordan, was three and my cousin Georgina was going to be five the week later.

Miraculously I had walked out unscathed. My mum said I stood waiting to see if the rest of her family would be so lucky. I could have been a ghost for all anyone noticed. Chaos erupted around me as firefighters scooted around me, ordering instructions from one another. The piercing sirens were causing the nerves in my head to pulsate. Nausea suddenly set in, pushing me to feel faint. A warm hand on my shoulder and a soothing voice relaxed my mind putting it a piece.

"It's going to be ok, little one. Sit here, and I'll be straight back." The lovely lady assisted my fall, gently guiding me to sit down on the sidewalk. Then, the lady left me for what seemed like an eternity.

A figure appeared with a torched blanket thrown over them out of the gushing flames, running in all directions like a wounded horse. The person was screaming frantically. The figure was wrestled to the ground by the firefighters, who then sprayed it down with the heavy hose.

My heart was beating fast. I could not stand, so I shuffled myself down the pavement, craning my neck around the firefighters to see who had run from the blaze.

"He's good, He's good, no burns on him, the fire must have just caught the blanket, just some small burns on his hands, stay still sir, please so we can examine you properly."

"I'm fine, really I'm fine, just my hands are a bit sore. I'm fine."

"Sir, you have just run from a burning house. You must lie still, please."

"But I'm fine, I tell you, please let me get up."

"You're in shock sir, please lie still."

"But I'm fine, I'm telling you, look, let me stand."

"Sir, please do as you are asked. You have just been in a house fire, you are in shock, now please, lay still. Is anyone else in the house, sir?"?

"Yes," he whimpered, "My family, please get them out before they die."

"How many are in the house, Sir".

"Three, three people. My two children, niece and my wife, I tried to reach them, but the smoke is thick," the man managed to say through coughs and splutter.

"Don't worry, sir, you managed to get out and tell us who is left in there."

At that, there was quick movement from the fire crew as they dispersed into the house with axes and hose pipes, ladders flying up around the property, names being called in desperation, and hope to locate the rest of the family quickly.

There seemed to be scuffling with the man on the ground before he was placed in the back of the ambulance.

Ambulance crew fussed over him, with all these weird instruments that I didn't know the names of, they were putting things in his ear, making him open his mouth, they cut his clothes from him even though he said he was not burnt, only a few burns to his hands and the back of his legs, he was good to go.

My dad, my brave dad, the hero, saved himself.

I sat on the cold pavement watching all the commotion around me. I clutched my teddy bear shivering, but staying put as I was told. Then I heard that all too familiar voice, "GG," my mum called. I turned to face her smiling, a panicked mum who had my brother in one arm and reached out to me with the other. I jumped up from the pavement and ran to my mum. She hurried us along to a car waiting around the corner. Just before we climbed in, I glanced at my mother as she removed a box of matches from her pocket and disperse them into the bushes. I remember asking for my cousin; nothing was said until we arrived in America.

The new paper report read.

In the late hours of October 3rd, a family was startled by the alarming sound of a loud crackling spreading fast throughout the house. Upon investigation, Mr Roberts, the father of the house, realised they were in trouble as he saw a fire starting at the base of the house. Mr Roberts says he started up the stairs to save the others, but thick black smoke, swirling ash, and intense heat forced him to his knees, blinding his vision. Sadly, Mr Roberts could not reach his family to save them. As a result, his partner and three children were lost in the fire.

I was never the same after that day. When I was older, around fifteen, I found God. I prayed every day, even now that I'm twenty-one. I still pray for my cousin Georgina. She got caught in the smoke on our way out. She never made it. I have night terrors where I can still hear her screaming and calling my name. My aunty had to attend a home for the mentally insane. But we couldn't visit as we were hiding our identity from my violent father, who believed we were dead. My aunty didn't even have us there to support her at her daughter's funeral, her sister and niece and nephew. My grandma and aunty had to attend a service for the people they loved dearly, knowing fully well that we were still alive

The phone ringing distracted me from my thoughts. I placed my hot chocolate that was warming my hands back onto the counter. I removed myself from the kitchen table, walked towards the phone, and picked up the receiver.

"Hello."

"Hi, baby, how you doing?"

My dreary persona changed to an upbeat tempo.

"I'm good; how are you?"

"I'm great, just missing your beautiful face."

"Aww, stop, you're going to make me cry and stain my makeup."

"I need to see you, honey. Mama's missing her baby.

175

When are you coming? The summer holidays are coming up soon, can't you take some time off work? Better still, just come and live with me. What's keeping you there except your friends? I know they're like family to you, and they always look after you, but I'm here. I'm your family too".

I released a huge sigh; I loved my mum with all my heart, but America was not a place that I was interested in moving to right now. I loved England, I loved my friends, and I loved my man, Corey, and my lover.

"Mum, we have been through this a million and one times. It's not appropriate. You're not playing ball, contacting me when you know you're not supposed to."

"I know, baby, but I just needed to hear your voice. I'm missing you. It's lonely up here".

"Stop it, mum, you've got so many families and friends up there. Stop making me feel guilty."

"Ok, but you would really love it here. You'll see when you visit me, you won't want to go back, and the guys up here. Mm mm, well, I'll say no more."

I giggled at my mum's persistent measures to get me to leave England again.

"You're not normal, mum, and anyway, I have a man."

"Not like these ones you don't. On a serious note, baby, I am really struggling."

I knew what was coming next. The conversations with my mother were becoming increasingly strained. I knew eventually I would have to face the situation and make that journey. I also knew once I saw my mum after such a long time, I may not want to return home.

It had been a long overdue wait. My feelings to return to America were becoming more robust.

But I had Corey, and I had my friends.

Corey was Marlon's best friend, Storm's boyfriend. We had been on and off for a few years, and I wasn't really feeling the relationship anyway. He wasn't really the one keeping me here. I had my heart set on someone else, but he was already spoken for, so it was forbidden love, but I couldn't help how I was feeling.

Corey was a bit of a thug. I knew that when I began dating him, everyone loves a bad boy, right? Or so I thought, but after a while, I got fed up with fighting off other women. Some of them were even a lot older than me. Did these people have nothing better to do?

He brought in the money, and sex was of a standard level. He didn't believe in foreplay or sex games. Now I was bored, feeling unloved. My lover, on the other hand, gave me everything I wanted, needed, craved. I smoothed my long black spiral curl back over my head, that one piece of hair that constantly interrupted my eyes. I thought to myself, I'm way too young to be stuck with gangsters and thugs. What the hell was I thinking? Maybe I should return to America. Things just seem to be going from one bad thing to the next, Storms 21st birthday was appearing fast. I needed to be here for it.

I met my friends at Whittingdon high private school for white people. So that's how I chose to address it because that's how it was.

I was twelve years old. We never really fit in. We never left with any grades because we were forced to go before our time was indeed up. That's what you get for holding a pact with your friends.

You had to audition for Whittingdon high. You needed to have a developed motion of grace.

Thanks to my grandma, I was musically gifted by nature.

My grandmother was an opera singer in her young days. She had taught me this tranquil skill that I had become so fascinated with. I would sit for endless hours listening to her. At first, I never understood what she was singing. Soon I would sing about my friends in front of them when they irritated me. My own personal joke.

I remember auditioning for my place at Whittingdon high in front of an eight-person panel. People who only liked others that were like themselves, extremely high class. They had no satisfaction in ordinary people that did not share the same interest as themselves, and they certainly had no interest in me. But my grandmother had taught me how to act, ignore those who looked down on me, and claimed they were better.

I was secretly moved back to England to live with my grandmother, under a new identity. It was the happiest time of my life. My grandmother had moved to England from America, opera wasn't really a thing there, and she had been offered a job in the opera house in England.

For years she cleaned that house and kept the stage in good working condition. Then one day, as the owner was about to lock up, he heard her angelic voice. That's how she began her fight for a place on the stage. When she spotted my talent as a musical artist, she persuaded my mum to not allow my life to be a waste.

I am sorry for it now, I put friendship first, and I never completed my dream.

I thought Piper was the prettiest when I met her. She had an unusual look about her; that image permanently changed with the season; I loved her quirky dress sense and her highlighted streaks of blond against her ginger hair, her face painted in freckles highlighted by her light brown eyes. She was sexy, and she had a body to match.

The brightest in the class, they would say. Her work was always on time. Piper was one of the best behaved in class, a distraction from the fact she was selling Cannabis in the toilets. I heard someone say she had even sold some cocaine. That's a lie that I didn't believe. How would she get cocaine?

Piper loved the boys, and the boys loved piper. Although I believed she was a bit on the frivolous side, Piper was always loyal. Nothing scared her. She was devoted.

She seemed to be quite protective over her little cousin Paige. However, although Piper spoke fondly of her cousin, there was a disappointment in her eyes as she suggested that Paige needed to be stronger and stick up for herself.

I prayed hard for Piper when her aunt died. She had been out for the day with Paige. They sensed something wasn't right. When they both returned home, her older siblings said she had already gone. They never got over not being able to say goodbye.

Jazz had the latest bob all the black girls wanted. She was thin, and her skin held a walnut brown complexion. Her light brown eyes were framed by an oriental shape with long, thick eyelashes, she was the mummy of us all, and we let her. We all tried in our different ways to be perfect. Nothing else mattered to us except each other. Every day the wind seemed to sing a song to the Storm, reminding us we were new at this game of friendship. Perhaps we feared that we were all the same, we were scared to change, but we should celebrate the changes. Eventually, we would learn to do this. Jazz covered everything Piper did. No matter how bad it was, Jazz always had a cover-up for her.

A snobby cow is how some of the girls described her. Yes, she was. However, Jazz gave no one her attention. She was brought up like that; to stand on her own and protect those that could harm you later. She looked down on those that were less fortunate to have the intellectual ability she possessed.

A natural teacher's pet, she even held secrets with the teachers.

My relationship with Jazz was edgy.

Storm was my favourite. She was funny, careless, but helpful.

Storm went through school life pretending to be white. Because of this, she was able to gain us the same privileges as our white counterparts. Storm was idle. She was only in school because that was the law. She paid the younger girls to do her homework and keep a lookout whilst blowing some boy off in the toilets for a spliff.

Storm was suspicious of everyone. Even though she trusted us, we didn't trust her. Our own boyfriends were not safe from her, not even our dads, for that matter. Piper was quite sure our English teacher had fallen prey. I chose not to have that thought in my mind.

Storm didn't care much for Venus. She had skin colour issues. Storm would tease her about how she was as black as night, that her eyes were as huge as owls. Venus hated Storm.

I thought they were all beautiful even Venus, who had issues within herself.

Venus struggled in school, so life was not easy for her. You had to have a talent for Whittingdon high, so we believe her mum must have had lots of money.

I noticed Venus' skin was becoming blotchy. I heard her speaking to a few girls once, telling them she hated being black and would love to be like them.

I felt like Venus had so much going against her. To top it off, she only had one breast due to contracting cancer when she was only nine. At the time, she could appear aggressive and malicious. Piper said perhaps she needed someone to help her leave this life. I'm not sure what she meant or whom she thought could help her. Piper often talked about people being given a choice to leave if they wished.

I didn't always like hanging with the girls, especially when they argued. It made me sad. They thought I was the weaker one, they thought I wasn't strong enough to be loyal, but I hated lying. It made me feel so bad, but Piper was an expert at it.

I sometimes wondered if she really believed her own lies. Piper claimed she wasn't a liar, she claimed to be the most honest person anyone knew, but she could conjure up a story to protect herself and us very quickly.

Only on this occasion, her story held no weight; we were in trouble, there was no one to save us, not even Jazz.

Whittingdon high had given us our reds cards, and our time was up; I was going to miss the leather smell of Mrs Whirring's office, the strong coffee smells as the teachers whizzed around from one lesson to the subsequent chugging cup loads of coffee to see them through the day. After the cleaners had been in, I would miss the polished desks, the smartly varnished wood with a smoky aroma. I remember how we squinted at the blackboard that seemed so far away and the windows that grew a vague mist during the autumn seasons. Our desks were chained together with a metal bar placed in rows. Stuck in the corner of every classroom was the British flag high and bold as if it had been ironed by a stern snotty nose old woman that smelt of mothballs. Isn't it funny the sorts of things you think of when you're a child? It was ruined for us; someone was out to get us; someone was watching us.

We could have made a hundred and one guesses who it could have been, and nearly everyone at

Whittingdon High had a reason to want to see the back of us.

We weren't wrong; we just didn't take any bullshit, but we were in the wrong place to be intolerant. "How dare those black girls to speak up and defend themselves?" was a constant conversation we would hear.

Why did we have to put up with being pushed? Having our hair pulled, touched, and even cut.

I had a bag of dog shit put in my locker with a note saying, "You probably don't know the difference between you and this bag." I cried all day. Piper told me to pull myself together. She never cried, she never let things get to her, she just got her own back, no matter the consequence.

Once one of the girls stole Storms' PE kit, and she found it cut up. Storm knew precisely who did it. She and piper marched straight into her classroom during the lesson, dragged her across the school, pinned her down, and cut all her hair off. I'm not sure how they remained in school, but they were in isolation for months, and they had to speak to the school psychiatrist for months. Our parents became regular visitors.

Now Whittington High had had enough of us. Someone had posted a note about us, with information only we would know. I believed that one of us was a mole, but I was shouted down. How else would anyone in that school know so much information none of us had shared?

We never looked outside the box in this situation. Maybe if we did, our places at Whittington high would not have been jeopardised.

THE MOLE!

I guess she is hoping that I don't realise she is not as dizzy as she makes out to be or as Godfearing. God is just something she chose to hide behind. She thinks she believes in him, but she doesn't. She is just lost with nowhere to go. She is lonely even. She owns a great skill over the others, such as praying on the spot, just like reciting poetry. But she doesn't have a genuine belief in him. Giselle has just gotten away with it because her friends have placed her on the pedestal of praying and quoting verses from the bible. Giselle doesn't even own a bible. Piper would slap her back and forth with verses and scriptures. I'm exasperated by their ludicrous imaginations. It's hard to believe a word they say.

Venus

Simplicity is the fine art of a genius

It is the art of positivity

Allowing your mind to focus on the simple things in
life

It enables you to swim in total warm energy

It is the art of focus

Like a mantra seeking its prey

It's simple, never pounce before you witness

The beauty of what simplicity really is.

CHAPTER 9

SIGNS OF LIFE IN VENUS

There were simple things in life that I just could not stand, like the sound of someone tapping their fingers against a desk, heavy breathing close to me, hot and misty. Lies and unearthliness. Perhaps that's why at age twenty-one, I was so lonely. I couldn't relate to anyone more different than me. I was just brave enough to retaliate not to believe in a person that no one could see or scriptures in the bible made up by some clever author who passed it on to other authors to adjust. Only lonely, lazy people believed such nonsense, unfortunate people who couldn't be bothered to search for their destiny and see what was around them. Unanswered questions from my childhood, I'm still waiting for, to sound feasible. I was just left feeling that part of life was inadequate or simply just irrelevant.

A stream of light beckoned through the slightly opened curtains, illuminating the sensuous curves of my well-toned body. I breathed in the beautiful scenery, femininity in the making. How many times had I done this, laid here, watching her sleep, taking in the rise and fall of her succulent breast pleading to me? No, I could not resist the temptation any longer. I leaned over and teased her nipples with my tongue. I smirked as I watched her release a light moan in what seemed to be an intense sleep. I knew I had her in an emotional state of half awareness, half-dreaming. By the time I got to work on her, she would be in absolute ecstasy, involuntary spasms would have her releasing like a running faucet, and I would be completely satisfied my job was done.

I climbed on top of her, slowly lowering myself down and beyond. My expertly trained tongue trailed down her chest along her slightly distended stomach controlling every jerk of her body until I reached her peak of attraction. Then, just as it was too much to muffle her screams, she gripped the sides of the sheets, dug her toes into the hard mattress, arched her back, threw her neck into a backward headlock, she administered the loudest groans of pleasure into the tranquil semi-dim room.

We lay breathless, spent, watching the fog puffs from our mouths disintegrate into the cold air of the room.

"Did I serve well? I breathed into her ear, then kissed her gently.

"As always, my darling, forbidden fruit is always the

best."

"I aim to please, trained by the best you know."

We stared intensely at one another and giggled like two naughty school kids.

Silence fell upon the already gloomy room as our hands crawled along to meet one another as we lay still, pinned to our backs, staring up at the detailed ceiling.

I allow a tear to fall down my cheek as the beats from our hearts drummed out the deafening silence to steal the show.

After a few chilling moments, I was the first to speak.

"I wish things had been different." I fought back the tears of guilt, regret, happiness.

"I know, baby, but it is what it is. It's our moment in time, our TV show, our happiness, our business."

"Our secret," I sobbed. "It's so wrong. This should not be happening, we are deceiving so many people, and the guilt is starting to kill me."

"Venus, baby, you need to stop. You've got to hold it together, for us, for yourself, please, it will work out you'll see."

"How can you be so calm and so sure? Everything is just swept under the carpet with you. Can you not see it's so wrong? It's not natural. We need to put an end to it. We should find our own partners, be normal like normal people."

"I won't hear of it, Venus; we are good together. We just need to be more careful".

"Better at fooling everyone you mean, we have so much to lose if we are found out, so many people will be destroyed, and so will we."

Silence fell again as I lay thinking about the conversation and what to do next.

"We will be fine; we will cross whatever bridge we need to if we come to it."

Her voice was calm and soothing, convincing even. As she turned to embrace me in a bear hug, she gently kisses my forehead whilst stroking my hair, her heart racing into her mouth, she knew I was right, but I was in too deep. It could only end badly.

We had no idea that Marlon had stepped down from the old tin pan that had been carefully positioned outside my bedroom window. We had no idea for the last three and a half weeks he had been straining his eyes through the narrow gap in the curtain to see who my secret lover was.

When he blackmailed me with the information, I imagined him standing there leaning his back against the damp brick wall; shocked but satisfied, placing his disposable camera back into his pocket. Soon he would use this information against me.

I knew I shouldn't be doing what I was doing, but it had begun so long ago, neither one of us could control it any longer. I was in so deep, and I would die first, but I was thirsty for her love and she for mine.

I wonder what my friends would make of it all. Would they be shocked that I liked women? Or more shocked at who it was? Perhaps both.

I never really fitted in with them anyway, not entirely, I was the darker of the five, and I always felt it.

I met my friends at Whittingdon High private school. When I was twelve years old, I didn't want to go to the stupid school in the first place, always being on the show as if we were animals in a cage.

Some of the girls were so malicious. They used to ask how I got in with nothing to offer and suggested I was using my extremely dark skin as my talent. I found out later my mum paid extreme amounts of money to get me in. I just wasn't talented.

Jazz always said I was too sensitive. She told me I should man up and accept my beauty for what it was. But I couldn't. I didn't want to be dark, and I cried every night. I was so depressed. I didn't expect Jazz to understand, she may have been happy with her shell, but I wanted more. I wasn't bright like Jazz or confident. This was one of the reasons I couldn't believe in a God. Why would he give someone such a strange colouring? What a hard knock to live with.

Jazz could do everything. If you couldn't keep up

with her, then she wasn't very tolerant. Maybe secretly, she had her own struggles. She was definitely hiding something. I hated myself sometimes when I often allowed myself to be led by Jazz. She was always making all the decisions for every event as if we were all stupid. I wanted to get my own back with all of them, but I didn't know-how. We all loved Jazz's little sister River. She was so cute. We took her on as our own after Jazz's mum passed away. Jazz was too strict with her. There was something strange about River; some dots didn't quite add up. I knew she was really Jazz's daughter," But there was something else about her.

Piper always told me I was beautiful. Whether she meant it or not, I don't know.

Piper always got away with everything. I was fed up with always covering for her. Miss butter-wouldn't-melt, I didn't believe a word she said. There was always an excuse why Paige couldn't come out with us. I wanted to talk to her to get some dirt on Piper. I knew it would take some work. But Paige was weak, so it wouldn't take long to break her. Piper always kept her away from us. She was intelligent, conniving, and devious. I saw her throwing her food up in the school toilets, sniffing some white stuff to top it off. That's why she was so thin. They all thought she was curvy. I thought she resembled a broomstick.

Piper always had sweets, brightly coloured ones. I often watched her sitting in the back of the class sucking her thumb and chewing on sweets. In fact, I never saw her really eat food. On the other hand, alongside her sometimes erratic behaviour, she was resourceful, even hilarious. She did make us laugh. When we first started going to the Mansion, Piper pretended she was an amateur pool player. Then, just before she was beaten, she would clean up, upsetting the punters and taking all their money. Once she nearly had us beaten up, Royal and Rasi stepped in to save us. Jazz was so angry.

Giselle, well, she just never understood me as she was in the same boat. I never understood where she got her maturity from. Giselle claimed to be a Christian with a fluffy personality, but she was more devious than Piper. Giselle wasn't as innocent or as God-fearing as she made out. At times she was a fool. I didn't trust her.

Yes, she was musically gifted, could outdo the French teacher in that genre of language. But I wasn't fooled by that sweet smile. Giselle was a spiritual pretender, using religion to cover up her fear of something.

I used to watch her eating her food alone, washing it down with only herbal tea, whilst always remaining oblivious to those around her. So, no, I didn't believe her.

We all attended her baptism, which was supposed to be an emotional time. There was Giselle pretending she was in spirit, looking around to see if everyone was watching her.

Storm used me. She knew I liked girls, and every now and then, when we were older, she would get her fix off me if you get what I mean. Storm would sleep with just about anyone or anything. She had no boundaries, but I liked her. I liked all of them really, but I wasn't really like them. Storm was a let-down, pretending to be white, thinking she could fool us. We saw the black in her. Eventually, when we visited her house, we realised her parents were black from St Elizabeth, Jamaica. Storm showed no shame in her game, she just laughed, and so did the others, but I was fuming. Here I was, wanting to be lighter-skinned, and here she was taking the piss out of fooling white people.

Storm was so pretty. Everyone thought Piper was the best looking. For me, it was Storm, with her sandy coloured European textured hair, her fringe hovering above her green eyes, and her sexy athletic build. I found her irresistible and hard to say no to. She smelt nice in her revealing clothes. She was argumentative, violent sometimes, her body was often covered in bruises. The night I snuck out of her house, the night

Marcus, her son, was murdered, that's when I realised Marlon was beating her.

I tried to get out quickly before she realised I had slept with her man, but Marcus began to cry. I panicked as I was hiding behind the door. I thought she might come in and spot me, so I put my hand over Marcus's mouth just to hush him up. I'm not sure how long I stood there or how hard I squeezed, but he fell asleep shortly after. I kissed him goodnight. I loved Marcus.

I could hear Marlon laying into Storm, she was giving as good as she got, so I slipped out.

I hung out with them through our years at Whittingdon High, none of the white girls would accept me anyway, and the boys always teased me about my colour.

When I was fifteen, there was this one girl who liked me, she asked if she could taste my cheek because it looked like chocolate, so I let her lick my cheek, then every time she saw me, I let her lick my cheek in private. Her hair smelt like strawberries; sometimes, it smelt like she had just got out of bed. Then one day we decided to taste each other's lips, one of the teachers came into the toilets and shouted at us, our parents were called in. I never saw that girl again.

My mum wasn't too mad. She kissed my lips in a way that she never kissed me before and told me not to kiss girls like that. I stared at her as she smiled at my dark face and rubbed her hands over my low-cut hair. She traced her finger down my nose and over my lips.

"Darling, you're so beautiful, and one day someone will love you for you." She breathed slowly whilst she spoke, it was a bit weird, but I felt safe. After all, she was my mum.

Then one day, a note appeared on the principal's desk, typed with our names on it and some personal information regarding our lives. I hadn't sent it, even though I think deep down the girls blamed me. Being with them was so confusing.

We were not prepared for what was about to hit us. We were always so careful with our information, or should I say our lies. I believed there was a mole amongst us. Someone had been watching us. Either way, our carelessness cost us our places at Whittingdon high.

THE MOLE!

Venus possessed so many insecurities it was hard not to feel sorry for her and put her in therapy.

If I believed for one minute, I was going to get a story out of her. I was wrong. Venus wanted Payment; she said her information was worth it. I was at a desperation point. It was almost a consideration. She knew the secret I wanted so desperately to hear.

CHAPTER 10

WHITTINGDON HIGH

Mrs Whittaker could barely keep her eyes open. The sky was an odd misty hue, like a blanket over the dark purple moon she had finally been fortunate to see. Mrs Whittaker had sat up most of the night staring at it, placing each girl within its body, questioning them in her head. She was determined to delve deeper into the secret the girls kept. Mrs Whittaker had received a warning from those above her, the big wigs of the school, the girls were to be dismissed immediately but quietly. They, too, had also received the same anonymous information regarding their secret lives.

The aim was to protect Mrs Whittaker's husband and his invalid interest in the girls of Whittingdon High. They had a duty to the school's reputation. Now, with the girls and their colourful lives, the press would dig deeper and realise the school was not squeaky clean. It would be closed in an instant. The most recognised private school in Clapham. People fought from far and wide to place their children there.

They had allowed five black girls to live up to society's expectations, and they had failed them.

How would she get around this one? Mrs Whittaker needed them to leave quietly, and she would do anything it would take to save her reputation.

Who was the weakest? Who would break first?

Piper would be the last. She was an annoying little brat from a bastard family. It was difficult to see through her vivid imagination. Everything was a show to her. Life should have deleted her a long time ago.

Jazz knew people that could possibly come down hard on Mrs Whittaker and cause problems for the school. But she also knew Jazz held another dark secret that would jeopardise her friendship and life.

Storm could be bribed with one of the male teachers. That would be unforgivable, but she was also a tough nut. There was no way she would reveal anything. Maybe Mrs Whittaker could get her with the fact she suffered from embarrassing epilepsy. She could cause her to go into shock; she would make her talk whilst her body danced a million jolts.

Giselle was weak, or so she claimed, it didn't really matter. She was supposed to be dead in a house fire. Mrs Whittaker would tell her she knew; Giselle would break.

Then there was Venus, from a strict Nigerian background. Her mum would be devastated to know she liked girls and wasn't a virgin. Then again, Venus's relationship with her mother was disturbingly odd. Perhaps she could dig deeper into that and make her speak.

Mrs Whittaker had a job to do. That was to save the school's reputation and keep her husband's secret buried deep within the school's walls.

Her motive was to genuinely help the girls keep their secrets hidden. But unfortunately, they did not trust her. There was no winning them over. Their start at the school had not been a successful one. Mrs Whittaker was very aware of their struggles, being the only black girls in a middle-class private school. She had never been so closely associated with any black people, let alone five young beautiful, sassy young ladies, which was how she saw them. Mrs Whittaker and other non-black staff had become genuinely fascinated by their differences. They had become the school's personal project on how to be inclusive. What made them tick? Train them to behave like clones, to follow suit like all the other girls who attended the school, prove to the world that the little itches could be trained. Elaborate education did not come easy.

Now, Mrs Whittaker didn't care about any of this. She was annoyed they had let her down. They had lived up to the expectations of herself and the others. They had proved to be arrogant, aggressive, disobedient, and damning to the school's name.

Well, they had darkened the school for far too long. Now it was time for them to depart. Unless they agreed to the deal.

The girls sat in the principal's office with good posture, correct grammar, and best behaviour.

Mrs Whittaker had informed them she would alerting their parents. What for now, the girls wondered.

"Miss, why do our parents need to be called? Why is there never anyone to defend us?" Venus questioned with passion in her voice, a clear indication she had enough of this school and its accusations.

"Well, Venus," Mrs Whittaker answered, concerned, "this is a matter that, unfortunately, I cannot let go of. It's also a matter so serious that it is one for your parents to deal with. Should the information be true, I am afraid that whichever one of you it relates to will need to be excluded. We cannot have this disgrace hanging over our school reputation."

The girls were silent. They knew what was coming, and they had prepared themselves for the inevitable. Their friendship was about to be tested, to the core.

"Girls," Mrs Whittaker cleared her throat as she looked around at the other two teachers and nurse in the room. One of the teachers was Mrs Whirring. The girls liked her, and they thought she liked them too. She always had their backs and defended them. That was how they had kept their places for so long. But her face was saying something different right now. It was saying, the games up, girls, you're on your own.

The other teacher, Miss Issacs, was the only black teacher in the school. She had given them a lecture on their first day on how not to be noticed. The girls remembered that speech all too well.

"Young ladies." She eyed each one as she glanced over their faces. "This may be your first day here at Whittingdon High, but I think it only fair that I allow you to have a head start in what may be a race for survival." Survival? The girls thought they'd come here to get an education. Was it going to kill them being here?

"You may not understand what this means right now, but in time it will all make sense. In the meantime, keep your heads down, appear small like a mouse, and do not roar like a lion, even if you are pushed. Your patience will be tested. A skill you will need to develop for the rest of your waking days. After a while, you will come to realise you will never be given any gratitude, justice, or acknowledgement for anything you do. Your dark skin has been a problem since the moment you were born. You will always be invisible to them until the time comes for them to see you."

The girls figured out this was one of those times.

"Walk with your head held high, but not too high, make sure your uniform is pristine at all times, shoes polished, hair tied back, and do not chew gum. Say please and thank you in all the unnecessary places, make sure you are in on time and any homework.

"You will need to work five times as hard, sometimes twenty. If there is ever a chance, you can pass as white in attitude, complexion, or on the phone, then do so. That's it for now. Oh. And don't ask any questions. Black girls are seen as aggressive, and asking questions could appear rude and obstinate. Do I make myself clear?"

The girls nodded in slow surprised unison.

Now here Miss Isaac's was, sitting on the panel of teachers looking sincere and not so stern, just like your nice aunty that your mum would send you to live with if you got into trouble. Her eyes were sad and pleading, her body slumped in the high chair as if she was truly defeated. The girls liked her; they felt a strong bond with her. Not because she was black, but there was something else about her they just couldn't put their finger on.

The nurse in the corner was looking down on the girls with a snooty glare. Storm wanted to punch her.

Mrs Whittaker began to speak again.

"We have not got off to a good start. Ever since you came to this school, it has been one trying event after another. Whilst I am aware that not everything has been your fault, it has been difficult for us here. However, I believe it has added character to the school, your intelligent girls." She glanced across at Venus and smiled. Clearly, she was not talking to her.

"' 'I'm praying that this next adventure is one of untruth, one that is just a cruel joke, and we can move on and put this behind us." The girls were frozen in their seats as Mrs Whittaker rambled on about their time at Whittingdon High. Her flavoured speech was already saying goodbye to them, and they would do what they knew best. They would keep their pact and friendship intact.

"So, girls, ''I'm going to ask you a question. Please do not answer straight away. If you would like to speak to one of us in private, then please do so." With that, she handed each girl a folded piece of paper and pen. "Go ahead, unfold it, read the question, write your answer, and hand the paper back folded to me, please."

One by one, the girls slowly unfolded their papers. They were careful to not show any emotion or shock at the question, and one by one, they wrote their answer, folded the article, and handed it back to Mrs Whittaker.

The clock's ticking overpowered the silence in the

room. It might be the girls' last time seeing those high velvet wallpaper walls with gold strips through the middle. The pungent smell of the leather chairs and classical music in the background they detested, the polished desk you could see the reflection of your face, and the globe that spun every two minutes, giving you information about a country. It wasn't spinning today or talking. It had been switched off.

Mrs Whittaker took a deep breath as she unfolded the papers in turn. Her eyes grew like saucers as she read each answer. Her breathing became more profound as she unfolded the last piece of paper. A bead of sweat rolled down her forehead. She peered at the girls with glassy eyes.

"Ok, so ''I'm assuming the information is true, and this is your only answer. I will give you a chance to answer truthfully. May I reiterate, this is not a game."

The teachers on either side leaned in to read the girl's answers on the paper and slumped back into their seats; Miss Issacs's hung her head in dismay.

"No comment. That is what you all have to say?"

The girls nodded their heads in unison

"Then I will need to call your parents, and perhaps you can reveal to them which one of you —" she paused before her next word, gave birth on the school premises or is still with child. You will be found out, I could keep you here until you grow, but ''I'm guessing your parents will want you to have a termination as soon as possible."

The girls sat and stared coldly at the principal, never saying a word.

Mrs Whittaker slammed her hand onto the table and leaned forward. The panel of teachers jumped at her outburst,

"Which of you is it? I will expel all of you. Never will you return. So, talk now before you all lose your place. One of you is pregnant or has already had it. You can't keep it secret forever, so speak. I warn you now to speak. This will be the end of your life. Some of you are not even sixteen."

"Is it you, Jazz?"

"No comment," was jazz's reply

"Piper, how about you? You like the boys," Mrs Whittaker announced with conviction.

"No comment." Piper's reply was cold.

"It's you Storm, we know you definitely like the boys," she blurted with malice.

"No comment, Miss." Storm answered, matter-of-fact.

"Giselle, talk to me." There was silence for what seemed like an eternity as Giselle quivered in her seat, afraid to look up. She fiddled with her thumbs as the tears fell freely from her face.

"No," she whispered

"Who is it Giselle, you don't want your world at Whittington High to end. Where will you go, Giselle? How disappointed will your mum be?"

More silence as Giselle finally looked up. We held our breath as she replied, "No, comment."

Venus didn't give them a chance to ask. She just boldly replied, "NO, NO, No comment."

"Right, then you will stay here until we call your parents."

The girls were aware their parents were not called straight away as Mrs Whittaker wanted to break them. She was not right to question them without their parents present, which would only make things messy. For once, Giselle did not break. Not yet anyway.

Someone had been watching them, listening to their conversations. They had been so careful with everything they did. Who was it? Who had a one-up on them? They would find out, but not just yet.

Mrs Whittaker hadn't planned for the session to run so abruptly. She had always maintained a calm stature, an upright, stiff upper lip. Yet she was, losing it and frantically clutching at straws, whilst the defiant young ladies, sat and laughed at her.

Giselle appeared petrified as Mrs Whittaker stood up smoothed her navy-blue suit free from the seated creases. Pushing her glasses into the seats of her eyes, she called Giselle's name.

"Giselle, you will be first. Stand and come with me."
Giselle looked side to side at each of the girls as her
shaky legs barely allowed her to rise. Instead, she
gripped the side of the chair as she pushed herself to
an upright position.

Piper caught her eye as she left and placed her hands
in prayer fashion, indicating to her to pray. Giselle
hung her head as she walked out behind Mrs
Whittaker.

The other two teachers and nurse in the corner
stayed put glaring at the girls.

This was it, they were going to try and break them,
and they might succeed with Giselle. The girls
watched in anticipation, waiting for Giselle to return.

"Giselle." Mrs Whittaker tried to appear as if she
gave a toss. "Sweetheart, you're a bright girl, a very
talented one at that. Why on earth would you want to
throw away such a wonderful life? You can tell me. Are
they making you do this?"

Giselle peeped up at her principal but did not
answer.

"It's ok, you can tell me. Whatever you say here is
private. I can help you; let me help you."

Mrs Whittaker had never helped any of those girls
in her life, not with the racist comments, the bullying,
the threats from the boys, nothing, she was only
interested in one thing, and that was her school's

reputation. This damned school. Right now, Giselle wished she never laid eyes on it or her friends.

"I want my mum," Giselle sobbed.

"Oh darling, please don't cry. It's ok. Is it you Giselle, are you the one that's pregnant? I've heard, Giselle, that the baby has already been born. Where is the baby Giselle?

There is no response from Giselle. Mrs Whittaker was becoming impatient.

"Giselle," she said firmly, "I'm going to be straight with you. This dear child will not end well. As you know, you have lots going against you."

Giselle suddenly seemed interested as she looked up at her principal.

"You know what I mean." Mrs Whittaker cleared her throat. "Your dad is not at home. You live with your grandma. How will your grandma cope with two babies? Because that's all you are, a mere baby yourself. You're a black girl, so the odds are already against you." She said this with a sarcastic grin that cut Giselle like a sword.

"How will your grandma cope with prison life?"

Giselle was shocked at her question. What did she mean, prison life?

"Mrs Whittaker, why would my grandma go to prison"?

"Oh, come, come, child, you don't believe that you

have been here all this time without me knowing your identity?" She squinted at Giselle.

"I'm not sure what you mean."

When Mrs Whittaker spoke again, she drew out her name. "Please, Syan, I know everything about everyone in my school."

Giselle's head jerked to an upright position, her eyes bulging, pearls of sweat instantly falling from all the pores of her body. Giselle wiped her forehead with the back of her hand as the tears rained down from her eyes.

Mrs Whittaker had just called her by her birth name. It had been long removed from her birth certificate to hide her identity. That name was dead to her. How did Mrs Whittaker know?

Giselle trembled uncontrollably as the principal giggled at her wickedly.

"So, you see, dear girl, nothing here is a secret to me, so best you tell me the truth, now."

Mrs Whittaker didn't realise she had just started a war.

"You know nothing, you think you do, but you don't." Giselle spat the words with aggression.

"Ah, really, you silly child? You only have your space here because your grandmother needed a hiding place for you. You see, I know you're supposed to be dead, in a house fire with your brother, cousin, and mother. No, your grandmother didn't tell me. I make it my job to find out who is in my school. I will find out which of you was, or is, pregnant and where you are hiding the baby. When I do, I will make sure you are banished from my school. Your life will come to nothing unless you tell me, then I can arrange a termination. That's the least I can do to help you and keep your place here."

Mrs Whittaker released a deep breath as if satisfied with her act.

"Never, I will never tell you. Expel me if you wish, but I won't tell you, NO COMMENT." Giselle mirrored a frame of split personality, which stopped Mrs Whittaker in her tracks.

The principal was not impressed with Giselle's sudden bravery. She banished her from her secondary office. Giselle returned to be with her friends, who were waiting inside the main room. All four girls eagerly stared at her as she arrived. Giselle clasped her hands as she took a concentrated walk back towards them. She shook her head to indicate to them not to ask any questions. She managed to mouth, "They know."

Jazz stood confidently in response to the cold calling of her name. She walked past the girls giving Giselle a concerned glare, and gliding into Mrs Whittaker's smaller office, she shut the door behind her.

"Sit." Mrs Whittaker gestured her hand towards the chair. She tapped her pen on the table as she watched Jazz take her place. She didn't speak straight away, attempting to make Jazz uncomfortable.

"I'm going to cut to the chase. I don't know what idiotic pact you and your girls have sealed between you, but I tell you now, your game is up."

Jazz wondered what Giselle had told her. Did she break in here with this cockroach?

"Game, Miss?" Jazz's tone was questioning.

Mrs Whittaker swung out of her chair and landed on the front of her desk right next to Jazz.

"I know you're pregnant or were. Bringing down the good school's reputation. Let me help you, Jazz. I can arrange an abortion for you."

"Mrs Whittaker, ''I'm not pregnant. You've got the wrong person."

"Really, am I also wrong in thinking your dad is still in prison? Or is he out now. How is your mum managing alone? I understand there's not much money coming in now. I have noticed you're not wearing the high tec shoes the other girls usually wear.

Oh, and whilst we're on the subject, how is your brother doing? Is he still a spastic? Is that the name they use?"

"*Bitch*", Jazz thought to herself, *had Giselle been*

telling the principal about her business?

Jazz breathed heavily, but she didn't answer.

"I'm not really sure how long we can hold your space for here. You see, your mum's payments are behind, and the school is struggling to sub her. I don't want your little secret to get out. If you help me Jazz, then I can help your mum, we both know that she enjoys the nice things in life. Your poor brother, how would she cope with him at home? She would have to go back to work and look after your baby and your little sister River. She's too cute to manage in a home. Oh, how forgetful of me is your poor mum is dead yet." Jazz wanted to lean across and beat her to a pulp, but she prayed for strength to not lower herself to Mrs Whittaker's evil tactics.

"Mrs Whittaker, I told you, "I'm not pregnant, I don't know who is, even if I did, I would never tell you. You can humiliate me as much as you like, but I won't play your silly games. My friendship is more important than your stupid school and the lies it spreads about us. You would be doing me a great favour if you just laid out the punishment."

"You're not going to talk?"

"Talk about what, Mrs Whittaker? I think we are done here."

"I know your secret, Jazz, I know what you are hiding from your friends".

Jazz stood very slowly, and Mrs Whittaker mirrored her praying mantis stance. Jazz tried to hide her wobbly composure as she starred her principal out. Mrs Whittaker was nodding in front of her. "Yes, Jazz, I know."

"Know what, Miss"

Mrs Whittaker grinned as she leaned into Jazz and whispered in her ear. For a moment, the two females held their frozen pose. Jazz slowly pulled away as her tears bounced onto the royal blue carpet, evaporating into the thickness.

"Prove it" was Jazz's response

"I can't, but I know someone who can." Mrs Whittaker knew who had written the anonymous notes. For whatever reason, the girls were about to be taken down.

"I won't betray my friends. I don't care what you say or what lies you tell them. Did Giselle tell you that".

"Oh, darling Jazz, you know I can't reveal what Giselle has told me. It's confidential."

"And so is this, so Mrs Whittaker, we are done."

Mrs Whittaker hung her head in defeat. She was seething. All she could do was order Jazz to leave the room, but not before telling her she would live to regret this.

Storm pulled her skirt high above her knees as she approached Mrs Whittaker's smaller office. She slammed the door shut behind her, swivelled the dark wood chair to face the seat towards her, then straddled it taking her seat. Mrs Whittaker was not fond of Storm, to say the least. She found her obnoxious, slutty, and conniving. She had no doubt it was not Storm who had fallen pregnant, but she wouldn't trust her to not hide a child away.

In fact, she thought talking to Storm was pointless. So, her expression towards her was short and unapologetic.

"Storm."

"Yes, miss?" Storm answered whilst blowing gum.

"I guess I ''m going to ask you if you're pregnant, and you're going to say no." Mrs Whittaker's voice was full of sarcasm.

"Yes, miss, that's correct."

"Do you know who is pregnant, or who has given birth, in my school?"

"Err, no."

"Would you tell me if you did?"

"Err, no."

"Storm, how have you hidden your epilepsy from your friends for so long? I mean, it's one thing that you lied to us about your religion and skin colour, now this? I also know that you snort cocaine in the toilets, and you slept with the male math teacher, enough for me to expel you for good. I also know that you poisoned your mum, which is how she ended up in a wheelchair. A little bit of a Storm, aren't you"? Mrs Whittaker laughed at her own joke. Storm was not all phased. She laughed at the principal. Storm would not be broken. She was a tough cookie.

"Was there anything else, miss? Because I'm bored now. You'll be good to remember about equality in the school. How will this look for you if you release only five black girls? What will the newspaper report say? I'm not scared of you, Mrs Whittaker. You can blackmail me as much as you like. Your threats hold no weight at the end of the day because you don't know who sent that note. And although they appear to know all our secrets, how much do they know about you. Of course, you will have to release us because that's what the letter wants. So, it would be pointless us telling you what truly happened, because in the end whoever is watching us has just won. So, I guess this is goodbye".

"Do you have any morals Storm, does anything mean anything to you, or is life just one big joke."

"No, Miss, I have some morals and beliefs, such as don't trust your principal who doesn't care anything about you or her husband who makes a pass at all the girls. What about you miss, what are your beliefs".

Mrs Whittaker was silent. She sighed a deep breath and shook her head.

"Storm, can I make a deal with you"

"What kind of deal".

"How about you tell me what is going on? Either way, you girls have had your dance, and it's over, but to save the school, I will make sure your families are catered for in your future education".

"A new private school, no way. You know we will not be taken on anywhere else; it's back to our local schools for us".

"I could make sure you are placed elsewhere, with a new identity."

"It's here or nothing; I'm not running, Miss. I've got nothing to hide. You, on the other hand, well, you have plenty."

"So, it's a no-deal then, Storm."

"It's not even a good deal, Miss, quite lame if you ask me."

"What would help Storm?"

"Keep us here and make all our worries go away, find the culprit of the letter, and let's deal with them. We are all in danger here."

"You know I cannot keep you here, even if I wanted to."

"Then I guess we are done here."

The meetings were not going very well, Mrs Whittaker did not want to see them go, but she had pressure from the top.

Mrs Whittaker stood by the door as she opened it

216

for Storm to leave.

Venus strolled into the room with an attitude. She kissed her teeth as she took to the chair and sat down. Mrs Whittaker giggled at her impertinence.

"Venus, how are you?" Mrs Whittaker was genuinely concerned.

"I'm fine, Miss," Venus answered with confusion in her voice at the principal's concern.

"You never really fitted in, did you, with your friends? Do they still give you a hard time with your skin colour?"

"Sometimes, miss?"

"You know they are not really your friends, don't you?"

"Yes, Miss."

"So why do you hang out with them? Why not find some real friends?"

"Because no one else here will accept me, miss. Look how dark I am. No one wants me; no one cares. All the white girls want to do is touch my face and lick my skin to see if I taste like chocolate."

"How does that make you feel, Venus?"

Venus wiped her tears with the back of her hand.

"I want to die."

"Have you been using the bleaching cream I brought you? You must persevere. It will make you feel so much better, soon you will be so white no one will know the difference."

"I'm trying, Miss. But it's so hard."

"Venus, life is not worth living unless there is a bit of snow-white."

"Yes, I know, Miss; you tell me often."

"Which one of those dirty girls is pregnant, Venus? Tell me, and I will make sure you keep your place. I will make sure your mum doesn't hurt you anymore".

"I can't tell you, Miss, because they didn't tell me. I really don't know."

"Do you think you can find out for me?"

"No, miss."

"Why not Venus?"

"Because I don't want to tell you. I can't betray my friends."

Mrs Whittaker was seething. "But Venus, they hate you."

"No, miss, I don't believe they do. Not as much as you hate me."

"Venus," Mrs Whittaker sang, "don't be so foolish. Why would I buy you bleaching cream? Find out, or it stops, and those lovely white patches coming through will go back to being black." Venus was trembling with fear.

"Ok, I'll find out, but if I don't?"

"Then you will be out the door. Just like your friends."

The meeting with Venus was brisk; the others couldn't understand how fast she was in and out. She's not that thick, they thought; perhaps she didn't understand the questions.

Piper huffed as she heard her name called. She observed her three friends escaping from that room, all of them in distress, looking as though they may have messed up. Piper held her perfect posture as she always did, life was a dance to her, and she was always on stage. Piper entered the room and naturally twirled into the chair to sit with an angry Mrs Whittaker.

Mrs Whittaker enjoyed Piper's company, although she would never admit it.

"Piper."

"Mrs Whittaker." Piper smiled widely.

"This whole session is becoming quite tedious. As much as I like you and your courageous imagination, this secrecy is getting out of hand. I just want to help you girls, but I feel I cannot do so because I understand you are all scared of the consequences and have decided that you would all like to keep this undercover. Let me help you. We don't even need to tell your parents. I will be very discreet and make sure the termination is kept within the school, or, if the baby has already been born, I can help you with adoption arrangements. I know a wealthy couple who have longed for a child. They would take the baby in and give it a good life. It doesn't matter about the skin colour; they are open to all sorts."

"Mrs Whittaker, might I say, I love your curiosity. I love how you pretend to care about us and as if the termination would be so simple. I know we are barely sixteen, but our parents didn't raise us as idiots. Unfortunately, I can't tell you about the pregnancy because I don't know of any, so I suggest you speak to the person in question. Oh, sorry, you don't know who that is, do you?" Piper spoke quite comfortably and with integrity.

Mrs Whittaker cleared her throat as she went in for the kill. "Perhaps it is you that is pregnant. I see the way you solicit yourself, and wasn't your cousin Paige abused whilst you watched? I have also heard you are smoking cannabis in my school toilets."

Pipers' heart dropped, but she refused to appear beaten. How did she know so much? How did she know about Paige? She knew there was a mole amongst them. She would soon find out who.

"Mrs Whittaker, ''I'm glad you are so well informed about my life events. We share a common denominator."

"Sorry?" Mrs Whittaker's voice is inquisitive.

"Men, men are the one thing we have in common. Dirty men."

Mrs Whittaker looked at her quizzically.

"Wasn't your husband also charged with underage sex with a minor? Oh yes, that's right, the plaque at the front of the school. Wasn't that in memory of her? The young girl that jumped from the roof of this very building, carrying your husband's unborn child? Was she fourteen or fifteen?"

Mrs Whittaker could barely swallow. She appeared half awake and halfway to passing out.

"You see, Mrs Whittaker, I too have done my own research. And for your information, ''I'm not pregnant, but I would never tell you if I was. I believe you're concerned in case your husband should be blamed again. Rumour has it you stayed with him for the money."

Mrs Whittaker was bubbling over with fury. Piper had hit her right where it hurt, but she had done the same to Piper. The two females eyed each other deviously, wondering what they could say next. Neither muttered a word.

"I guess we are done here, Mrs Whittaker." Piper stood up to leave.

"Piper," Mrs Whittaker called her as she was about to exit the room.

"Yes?"

"Where did you get that information from? It's extremely private."

"I know. That's why I kept it to myself. My friends

wouldn't keep something like that so private.' 'I'm good at finding things out. Everyone has a story to tell Mrs Whittaker. The best-kept secrets are the ones you keep to yourself. You taught me that!"

Mrs Whittaker nodded her head slowly, keeping Piper in her view. "Touché," she responded.

"Piper, what will you tell your aunt and uncle?"

"Nothing, Miss, because ''I'm not pregnant."

"Who is it, Piper? Come on, you're a bright girl, your friends and you especially have added some spice to this school. I don't want to see you go."

"Then keep us on."

"I cannot. It would not be appropriate. My reputation is at stake. We already put up with enough scandal when my husband did, well, you know what he did. Whittingdon high cannot handle any more drama."

"So, what now."

"I will have to let you all go if you don't own up."

"And, if we do?"

"Then I will help you keep it quiet; no one will have to know. I promise I give you my word."

"Why would you want to help us? You've never helped us. You say you like us, but do you? What's in it for you?"

"I get to keep my reputation and the school. You girls get to keep your dignity. Imagine the embarrassment this will cause your families."

"What will I need to do?"

"Just explain to your friends what the deal is, and I will take care of the rest. I can't afford to lose the school Piper, so you either let me help you, or you go quietly, and no one knows why you all left, I mean no one."

Piper thought for a while. Mrs Whittaker couldn't be trusted to tell the truth, but Piper believed she might just be telling the truth for once. Unfortunately, Mrs Whittaker had no control over this situation. It was the person who had left the note on her desk they needed to find. They would be expelled either way as none of their secrets was safe. Someone was watching them.

"Well, I can give you more time if you need it."

"Your very determined for us to open up. Why are you so bothered?"

"I already told you, Piper, I would be ruined if this got out. Imagine the press headlines."

Pupil falls pregnant whilst in school by a mysterious lover. Unfortunately, Mrs Whittaker's husband strikes again.

"We would be closed immediately."

"I'm not sure we trust you enough to tell you. After all, you don't even know where the note came from."

"Is it a boy from the school, Piper"

"I already told you I'm not pregnant."

"Piper, please stop playing games, you all need help, and I'm that person."

Mrs Whittaker wasn't wrong. They needed help, and as bad as she was, Piper believed she was their only hope. It didn't matter if they told the truth or not. The board of governors had already ordered their exit. This last stunt was just the icing on the cake. The girls could either take this into their own hands, leave, and be publicly destroyed. The press would eat them alive and dig into their history. Their whole families would be unearthed and imprisoned. They had had too much to lose. Or, they allow Mrs Whittaker to help them leave quietly and cover up their past. But who was the masked scriptwriter? They still didn't know. That was still a big issue for them. What if Mrs Whittaker had no say in the matter, and their past was still revealed. It was a risk they would have to take. The last line of instructions on the note read. *Get them out of the school, or we will reveal everything!* Who wanted them to fail at life so badly? They were doing a good job themselves.

"I need to speak to the others."

Mrs Whittaker grinned at Piper, left the room, and signalled for the other girls to enter. The girls crowded her as Mrs Whittaker exists the room.

Jazz was the first to speak. "What is going on? you've been ages?"

"Mrs Whittaker wants to make a deal with us." Piper was confident in her statement.

"What kind of deal?" Venus jumped in.

Jazz raised a hand to silence her. "What kind of deal Piper?"

"We tell her who's pregnant, and she helps us keep it quiet."

Storm appeared confused, "Why would she help us, and who said we needed her help anyway? It's way too late for that."

"Well, it would be for the best; I mean, we are too young to be having babies" Piper glanced at Jazz, and we don't want to mess up our lives any further, but "I'm up for the deal. If, of course, the rest of you are,"

"Not so fast, Piper. She's conniving. I don't trust her. I say we sleep on this."

"Oh Storm, you don't trust anyone. I want to hear her out." Giselle pleads

"Giselle, this really isn't the time to turn against me."

"I don't want to lose my place at this school. But we only have another year, and a bit left. This is getting out of hand." Venus appeared frustrated.

"Venus, in case you didn't realise, we are all in this together. Our promise to one another." Storm was now in total retaliation.

Jazz raised another hand. "What you saying Pip,

You look like you're about to bail on us."

"It's not bailing Jazz. It's called being sensible. You read the note they want us out. Truth or not. But if we don't leave quietly, our business will not be quiet either. Just think about it. We don't have much time".

"How much time do we have, Piper?" Storm eyed her. Piper cleared her throat before she responded.

"One hour."

"Bitch, you sold us out. What did you tell her?" Storm lunged towards Piper, and the other girls jumped in to stop her.

Piper had had enough of them, always being at odds.

"Girls, please, look at us fighting one another. Promises are for fools, but that doesn't mean the old bat is not serious. What we need to decide is if our friendship is stronger than keeping our places at Whittingdon High. We don't know who sent that letter, and neither does Mrs Whittaker, so either way, as always, we lose."

"Piper is right; what do we want?" Jazz peered at each of them. "Do we agree to this? We can't keep our places, but we still have our friendship?"

"I want my mum." Giselle was now in tears and quite distressed. "This is really serious; we need some help. I want my friends, please let someone help us. I don't want to lie anymore."

226

"GG," Piper called her firmly like her mum did. "Pull yourself together; what other choice do we have. Ok, so she helps us, and we are free to live in peace with her money and new education. Our family secrets stay intact."

The girls are silent for a while.

"She blackmailed me with my past," Jazz informed them

"Me too," Giselle whimpered.

"Yeah, I had that as well, but ''I'm here for my friends, willing to risk it all no matter what we choose." Storm hung her head in embarrassment.

"You would do that for me, Storm, risk it all?" Giselle's nose was leaking furiously. Venus handed her a tissue.

"Yep, baby girl, I sure would."

"Then we know what we need to do." Jazz held her hands out towards the other girls, who returned her gesture with a group hug.

"This is it, girls. Are we all in agreement?" Piper questioned.

They all nodded their heads at Piper. She wiped Giselle's tears and told her it's the right decision. Everything will be taken care of.

"I don't want you to lie anymore, Giselle. It's not right for you, so let's do this the right way."

Then jealously attacked Venus. "I hope when I have

to hide a secret, you can all keep it to ruin your lives".

Storm nodded at Piper as she walked to the door to let in the long waiting Mrs Whittaker.

"Mrs Whittaker, I have spoken with all the girls regarding the matter, and we have left our decision folded on that piece of paper on your desk. It's a unanimous vote."

The girls left to return to the larger office as they awaited their principal's response.

Mrs Whittaker would miss the girls. They brought character with a sense of achievement to the school, dipped in a cultural difference. But she was left with no choice but to let them go. Her feeble endeavour to reason with them was beyond pitiable

Mrs Whittaker had no choice but to keep the baby's secret buried deep within the grounds of her beautiful school garden. It was a misfortune that the child had been stillborn. In the girls' panic, they had put the baby to rest, where they thought no one would find her, safe in the garden, under the principal's watch.

Once the girls had departed, Mrs Whittaker shook hands with the accomplice whilst exchanging a large sum of money, the same accomplice who had been watching the girls. She thanked them for the information on the girls and promised the identity of the mother and father would be taken to her grave.

That's not the real secret they are hiding; there is a

bigger one!

However, that's how they lost their places at Whittingdon High.

CHAPTER 11

UNDERSTANDING RASI

The sound of the whistle perforated my auditory perceivers like a pole had been driven through them. I pulled the pillow over my head, but I know the sound would not stop unless I made it. I wasn't sure if this was a game or a genuine act. Either way, I had to move expeditiously. Nothing was ever straightforward in my house. Every inch of movement, every flicker of a limb, was meticulously thought out. There would be no deviation from the morning scenarios.

Expert judgment of where you needed to be present for those excruciating, unfolding hours was no jape.

Ascend or be overcome, stand, or be knocked down, fail, or prosper entirely.

I pulled my arm out of the warm duvet, where the cool air greeted it. The sound of the feathered feet against the wooden floor was soothing. I waited for the eleventh footstep before hitting the shiny black buzzer on my bed head. Damn to a tardy; I hadn't strapped myself in. My bed swivelled upside down as the wooden panels opened beneath me and my body slammed me to the floor.

I was conscious of the giggles as I lay there, ensuring I had no broken bones.

"You're late, boy," he said as he shined the light in my fatigued eyes. "Three minutes and 25 seconds, absolute rubbish."

I rolled onto my back to visually perceive my brother, sister, Mother and Father standing over me.

"Sorry, is it genuine or practice?" I winced.

"Doesn't matter, boy, we are all dead anyway. Get up. We will endeavour again later."

My Mother bent down in consideration and gently rubbed my head; she turned my face towards hers and parked a kiss on my forehead. Her lips were warm and soothing. Remi and Rubin teased me as our Mother cuddled me, but I didn't care. I doted her hugs; she always smelt of talcum powder.

"Come on, baby, don't worry, it will get easier. You're doing well."

It took me three weeks to get my escape route time down to one minute and twenty-five seconds, a "world record" my Father verbally expressed, but Remi's time was still lower than mine at sixty seconds. We were astronomically competitive in my house, but my Father pushed us to it. He pledged for us to feel safe should the inevitable take place.

We moved three times and settled in

Knightsbridge. The games seemed to decelerate marginally, and I realised my Mother wasn't moving as freely as she used to. Something changed in my Father; he was more solemn, more vigilant, and didn't seem to travel as much.

My Mother and Father rarely spoke to us like regular parents. Their English always seemed like another language. They deliberately used words we had to look up in the dictionary, learn the meaning, and spell them. "Always be divergent," they would say, "unique." I guess in some ways, we were.

On our tenth birthday, our Mother gave Remi and me a Bible with a note on the page.

It read.

All you require is pristine love, nothing more. Jubilance is the gratification of life, find it, and all will be well. My comely twins, I profoundly relish you both. God engendered you so differently by nature, yet equipollent. Ps, look after your sister always.

Name: Rasi Genesis Malawi Houston
Age: 24 at the time
Place of birth: Hawaii, Waikiki beach.

The youngest of twins, by three minutes, and the eldest to my sister by two years.

Brought up by our Jamaican father, after the death

of our mother when we were age ten. The other parts of our heritage were a contribution from our late mother, which consisted of a quarter Hawaiian, a quarter Mauritian, Brazilian, and Egyptian. Some would verbalize that was a remarkable coalescence, whether they denoted it by complement or as derogatory.

I inherited blue oriental eyes, framed by the longest lashes women would die for.

My chestnut-brown complexion was an authentic compliment to my full-bodied, long jet-ebony hair, which I always wore loose and shaggy, hence my nickname.

I was often told I was sexually alluring with a well-defined jawline structure, a well-developed physique, matching my frame, standing at a lean and mean six foot five inches. Yes, people consistently ceased in their tracks to examine me visually. I was not fazed by their curiosity. My father always taught me to portray myself as an incredibly well-groomed handsome man to all my spectators.

Women referred to me as "sex on legs". Unfortunately, I was not having the same effect on Piper. Yet, I was supposed to be her lover.

Some would verbalize I was born with a silver spoon in my mouth. Emerging from such a well-maintained family was profoundly strenuous. I was looked upon as having it all, so my entity was already bought long before I was born. I had high prospects to live up to, yet my life had to be kept very discreet due to my father's work role.

Nothing was ever mundane for me; I had to adhere to stringent rules, affecting my convivial life. My friends were handpicked for me; any exhibition of wariness and they would be extinguished.

I only ever wanted to consummate a mundane life, whatever that was.

All my friends and family emanated from the same circle, square, triangle. However, you wanted to canvass it optically, this closed life was all I kenned, and I tried to elude, if only just for a moment.

The flight of incriminations of revealing a profound appreciation for someone on the other side of the window was unheard of; a sheer pretence of enjoyment with the opposite sex from this glass world was becoming tiring.

I'd done it all, had my fair portion of agonising pain, with a picture of a painted world no one on the mundane side cared about. When you lose your mother at the age of ten, and then your twin brother is trawled afore face in a vicious racial attack at age 17, you would relish cerebrating a life that would not efface any more silk curtains, the type you cling to that feels like the cessation of your mother's skirt tail.

That's when I found God, at age ten, curious for some comfort. My mother had left me the Bible and musical composition to recollect her by. Moreover, her passing had injected extreme levels of OCD into me. So, designated that at age eleven, I was sent off to live with my uncle in Canada for five years until I could surmount my issues.

The Bible palliated my most significant inner turmoil. By the age of fifteen, I could recite the Bible and the Quran, word for word.

Even that did not safely arrive without its own prescribed issues. Suddenly I was crazy, I needed assistance, had commenced reading the Bible to puerile, and someone had imprecated it.

So, you see, rich or poor, they still believed in the same mixed herbs.

It didn't avail that I was fluent in mandarin by the age of seventeen. I doted languages, I was privileged to have travelled the world liberatingly. By the time I had escalated to twenty-five, I was verbalizing fourteen different languages fluently. I was shunned for this. I wasn't normal.

My life was a painted picture of extravagance. I attended the best universities in England and Canada. Even if I didn't need the edification or wanted to take up a particular role, I was privileged to have the opportunity to the gift of unnecessary choice. I was influenced to utilize every pathway possible. I suppose ultimately, it had its uses.

My father worked for the secret accommodation services, and that's precisely what it was - a sizably voluminous secret. But we wanted for nothing. I had businesses expanding all over the world.

Two years younger than me, my sister owned her own shoe company, designing and making extravagant shoes for fashion shows and over-privileged, abstinent clients. She was my saviour, always present when I needed her, even when I didn't. She was my confidante in everything.

Our only downfall was my father was a black man, a black Rastafarian man living in Knightsbridge. One who was exceedingly prosperous and resided in such an affluent area amongst his white counterparts. I'm sure you can imagine the struggles he faced.

We had been given information about a few wine bars in Dulwich that were struggling financially. I was never comfortable living the life I lived, always catering to the arrogant affluent. I had a team of staff listing areas with a potential future and would appreciate some financial assistance.

I decided to venture out remotely and take a more proximate view of the canvass of Dulwich. It wasn't the Dulwich I had pictured in my head. I'm not sure what I was expecting, but it was quaint, and I could optically discern its future. That's when I met her and her friends. Piper. What a gem.

I knew Piper was young, but I couldn't take my eyes off her. She was sassy, sultry, flirty, curvy, hysterical, expeditious. Witty. I fell in love with all of her. I visually perceived her and her friends that first night we were there. She did not notice us; They sat by the window on the stage at the front of the bar, we sat at the back, examining the view.

At first, I didn't make it conspicuous to my friends that I had an invested interest in her, but I had done my own investigation on her. She emanated from a colossal family, adopted by her aunt and uncle, transferred to a private school, where their places were terminated after an incident that even I could not discover.

I had persuaded my friends to arrive extra early on this particular night, to sit in those chairs by the window. But, damn, she took her time to appear; they were late that night, casually they sauntered in, casual but glam. They approached the bar and ordered their usuals. I could see them looking over at us, sitting in the seats they had taken residence to over the last few months. I knew as well as the bartender that these adolescent girls should not be in here, but I also knew that Royal was looking out for them, and he would rather have them in here than on the streets. On the rare occasion, they had worked the bar for him, under his supervision.

I was nine years Piper's senior, so I should have known better; I'd never been magnetized to a girl of this age before. Life has a way of turning direction on you, and if you're not meticulous, you get drawn into this winding pathway you can't get off. I didn't have any intentions of falling in love with an underage minor.

Affirmative, I did promise my father I wouldn't frequent anywhere near her and believe me, I endeavoured to.

I was relishing this forbidden fruit I had not been granted the privilege of.

The other half of the world was watching us through a fishbowl. I wanted to have a piece of that normality. I was drained of everything being handed to me. I was feeling like the king in the movie *Coming to America*. My father wasn't small-minded, and I indeed wasn't born that way. My father just had an issue with this fledgling girl I had suddenly taken a good interest in.

I make no apologies for my feelings, and I probably should have detoured and transitioned to my own age group. But fidgeting means you are not comfortable in your own bed. Something needed to change.

I was not about to inscribe a testimonial about my

feelings. They were genuine; it was transpiring.

I felt emotionally connected, but her views were philosophical for such a young spirit. In addition, she was a great conversationalist, so much so that I found myself being comforted by her.

Piper was in demand by other men; I knew it would take time, it would take a while to work on her, but I wasn't giving up any time soon. I had already done the maths. By the time she was in her twenties, she would commence to grow and visually warm to me, or so I hoped.

I fell in love with Piper straight away. I know it sounds mushy, and I shouldn't even have been looking in her direction. I would have criticised my friends for doing such a thing, but it was me, and I let it transpire.

Piper and her friends had procured many designations for themselves, and they had no interest in what others thought of them. No one dared to feud with them for fear of being shut down. So, my friends and I took them on as our little sisters; well, Piper's friends were like my little sisters. Piper and I held an unorthodox bond.

I don't believe it was one-sided; I am sure I held some value to her; she was unsure when to settle. Until then, I would be waiting in the wings.

She had a way of daring herself to be in the most challenging situations as if she believed she was virtually invisible. I kept all their secrets covered for them. Even made some vanish, I didn't hesitate to consider they would leave me in the dark about anything.

Piper was open with me, more so than her friends. I felt she was testing me; she sailed in to see if I could withstand the turbulence.

The girl's conception of a joke was no more comical than being claustrophobic in a submarine.

That's precisely how I felt when they decided to invite me to a venue I had not attended, yet alone visualised. Piper told me to come alone and not with my conventional squad.

My first impressions of the place were classy. Impressions as I entered turned to sleazy, sultry. A strip club, and I was the allurement. My OCD expeditiously fired up and commenced to take control.

I turned to leave as a voice whispered in my ear, "Leaving so soon? Relax"

My body turned 360 degrees to face Piper; she was scantily dressed in a black leather leotard, thigh-high boots. My eyes gradually peeled up her body until our eyes met; I consistently visually examined her through the matching black mask affixed to her face.

I suddenly felt aroused as she pulled me into her with her legs wrapped around my waist. We held our pose for a while before she relinquished me and took her place on the stage — a choreographed, mesmerising, exotic flair performed by herself and her friends, Jazz, Storm, and Giselle.

Our gazes remained locked and final as she handled that pole with sexiness and grace. At the finale of her performance, she lowered herself into the splits, pulled me into her, seductively kissing my lips. I pulled her off the stage into my arms. She grinned at me, and the youth in her shined through.

"You're a great dancer," I whispered into her ear.

"Thank you," she responded.

"Would you like a drink?" I queried.

"Yes, please."

"The usual?"

"Of course," she giggled. I acknowledged the rest of the girls now standing above me on the stage. I signalled for them to step down, turning my attention back to Piper.

"Come on; I will take you all away from here and get you a proper drink."

The way to deal with Piper was never to lose it but remain cool, calm and collected. Otherwise, you would be faced with fiery repudiation.

Classy strip clubs were how they had been making their money, where no one cared about your age or who you were.

That's precisely why I made a deal with Royal to let

them work his bar and keep them off the streets.

And so, our journey began.

CHAPTER 12

THE MANSION

The Mansion was a swanky wine bar situated on the outskirts of Dulwich. The interior decor consisted of blue and red velvet wallpaper, covered by large wooden picture frames containing images of famous reggae artists who had passed through or passed away.

The high ceilings held low-level chandeliers, and the red-stained wooden floor was complemented by the dim lights and the mahogany-coloured bar. The resident DJ was always placed to the bar's right when you walked in, playing all the latest soul and reggae songs. The Mansion was a busy bar, especially on a Friday and Saturday night when people who travelled for miles came in to drink and eat at the unique-looking building before proceeding to the hidden underground nightclub.

It had been a long summer; the girls remained together every day just like they promised. They had made friends with the bartender at the Mansion, who took them on as his daughters. The girls had been

243

cheeky enough to ask if they could work in the bar even though they knew their ages would permit him to allow them. Royal was the owner of the bar and a decent man. He didn't want them hanging out with the loose kids on the streets, so he conditioned them to jobs in the bar. He allowed them to drink there so long as they didn't mix their drinks, leave with any boys, and behaved respectably.

They were fifteen when Royal met them. He was aware they had already messed up their futures to protect a secret between them. The girls were now attending their local school and making new friends. One thing that did remain between them was their bond and love for one another. That was unbreakable.

After some months, Royal decided it was time to give the girls a pep talk.

The girls remembered the speech all too well.

Royal approached the girls taking a seat next to them. He held a very serious daddy look on his face as he sat sideways on the chairs by the window and crossed legs.

He was a good-looking man, maybe in his middle forties. His skin was a sun-kissed complexion, and he had a well-groomed goatee that matched his dark eyes. His clothing was crisp and clean, even his fingernails were cut to taste, and even for an older man, he possessed a lean body. Jazz thought he must have been a player in his younger days.

He cleared his throat before he spoke in a raspy voice that had the girls hot in their seats.

"Ladies," he paused as if thinking carefully about his following words. "Now, I've known you, girls, for a long time. I treat you like you're my own daughters. I even let you come into the bar way before the legal age requirements would allow you because I liked you all, and I wanted to make sure to keep you all off the streets."

Royal knew in his heart, Rasi had already spotted them and made a deal with Royal to have them in the bar.

Royal eyed all the girls thoughtfully, ensuring he had all their attention before he continued. Venus shuffled in her chair; she knew they were about to be lectured by big daddy.

The girls looked up to Royal and had nothing but love and respect for him.

"Now, I don't want to have to get my gun out and shoot no man in his foot for messing with my girls." Royal laughed at his statement, but he meant it. "And I sure as hell don't want to see none of you gets hurt unnecessarily. You're young and beautiful girls. You can have any man in the world, but having any man in the world doesn't mean you need to give up your crown jewels too soon." Royal stopped and stared, making sure the girls understood what he was talking about.

"You're playing with fire that would take a whole fire team to put out. These men are men, real men, but they are at least ten years your senior. They will be old and worn out long before your batteries give up. So, enjoy life, have fun, live, but be careful, I wouldn't waste my time telling you anything wrong. Love is a flower. It needs the sun and the rain, and right now, you girls don't have umbrellas big enough or strong enough to hold off the storm that might be coming your way. A little bit of pleasure comes with a whole lot of pain, the pain you girls can't mend on your own."

The girls stared at him in amazement as he rambled on about crown jewels, rain, black men, and strong black women for well over half an hour.

Giselle was the first to speak. "Royal, we love you. You've always looked out for us, taken care of us, but seriously, these guys are just friends, nothing in it, except for the one who has his eye on Pip."

Royal spoke quizzically, "Friends, you only met these guys a few months ago/ you know nothing about them."

"It's ok, Royal," Storm fired in. "Piper's not about to take up with no Asian man, let alone an Asian gangster." The girls laughed hysterically.

Royal looked even more confused and shook his

head at the girls. "Now, who told you all they were gangsters?"

"Everyone's talking about it; that's the word on the street." Storm looked disappointed.

Royal sighed heavily. "This, young ladies, is off the record. They are not gangsters. They are real businessmen with legal, reputable companies. Well, at least Rasi is anyway. He's an entrepreneur, a businessman, with his daddy, very wealthy men. They invest a lot of money into this place and others here, so I provided them with a spot to conduct business. Gangsters, never, and for your information, little Storm, he's not Asian, his daddy is a Jamaican".

"So, he's a coolie Jamaican then," Storm suggested.

"What's wrong with coolies?" Giselle questioned with attitude. Giselle's parents were a mixture of Jamaican, Indian, and Chinese. Giselle was as dark as night with light brown oriental-shaped eyes, and her jet-black hair reached the middle of her back and glistened under the light. Giselle was beautiful, but men somehow never found her attractive, and women always commented that she wasn't bad looking for a dark-skinned girl.

They never saw through her dark skin; they never saw how it damaged her self-esteem. Her friends always told her how beautiful she was, and those men were just shallow, and girls were jealous of her hair, but Giselle wasn't bothered, not like Venus was. Venus was becoming increasingly depressed. She had secretly been using bleaching cream, which was now leaving blotches over her evenly toned skin.

"Awe, don't get so het up G, G, I'm just playing; you're cool."

"Really, Storm, but you wouldn't lie down with me, though would you."

"No, G, G, I wouldn't because I'm not a lesbian."

"You know what I meant, Storm, if you were a man," Giselle snapped back, irritated at Storm's comment.

Storm could sense Giselle's anger and suddenly felt terrible.

"I didn't mean to upset you G, It wasn't directed at you. I'm sorry if I offended you. Please forgive me. You're beautiful." Giselle smiled and starred at her friend before she gave in. Venus sat quietly, observing Storm's prejudice.

"Your forgiven, even if you wouldn't sleep with me." The girls laughed in unison, then turned their interests back to Royal.

"So, Royal, if they're so rich, why are they coming to conduct business here? I mean, it's not exactly the White House." Piper spoke with sarcasm in her tone.

"He has some business he is interested in here; he will stay until it's finalised." Royal eyed Piper intensely, then shook his head. Piper got the impression that little message was directed at her.

Storm seemed to lose interest. "They're not gangsters. Damn I was looking for a bad boy, but I suppose a sugar daddy will do."

Giselle jumped in, "A gangster Storm? Another hoodlum to beat your arse every night until he kills you and your family?"

Instant silence fell upon the group as Storm eyed her friend with hatred whilst fighting back the tears.

"Thanks, Giselle. Now I know what you really think of me."

"Oh, don't pretend that you never knew what everyone was saying, Storm. Every man you meet gives you a good beating; if he doesn't, then it's one of his bitches that does it."

"Well, it's ok with you, little-miss-rich-kid, my mother doesn't stoop so low to pay for my life to be fixed. So yes, Marlon gets angry and raises his hand, but I know he loves me. He's not just sleeping with me because his mother paid him."

Giselle bolted to her feet. "That's not loving, baby girl. You're dreaming. You're just too weak to tell his lame-ass to skedaddle. You're a fool, Storm. Open your eyes, coz when he's finished with your ass, he's going to come for your family like he already has done. So, before you talk about my mother, check your own.

If she cared, she wouldn't let no amateur gangster beat her baby."

"Giselle," Piper boomed, "that's enough. You're out of order."

Jazz gave Giselle a foul look. "You've overstepped the mark. Now stop."

Giselle returned to her seat and stared out of the window, sucking her teeth. Storm excused herself and disappeared to the bathroom.

Venus sat and gleamed a bright smile at Giselle and her loose mouth.

Giselle and Venus never really agreed ultimately about anything, and Venus loved to gloat whenever Giselle put her foot in it.

Royal shook his head at Giselle in disgust. He knew Storm was always covered in bruises, and he had a feeling that no-good Marlon caused it, but whenever he questioned Storm, she would deny it was him. She would insist she had fallen again.

Royal also knew the real reason why Storm took his blows and stuck up for him. For this reason, he chose not to get heavily involved. The girls were barely sixteen, and their lives were full of way too much drama.

Rasi arrived unannounced with his friends, interrupting the tension. Royal stood and acknowledged the men before they reached their exclusive area of the bar. He turned back to the girls before leaving their company. "What I just said may not make sense right now, but as you grow, you will understand what I was talking about." With that, he turned and went back to the bar.

Piper smiled. She understood precisely what Royal had just said. She had an old head on her young body. She had been taught by the best.

Out of respect for Royal, Rasi and his friends waited for him to pass before they joined the girls.

CHAPTER 13

SINK OR SWIM

If you could change one thing about your life, what would it be? Would you have been nicer to the homeless person living on the dirty streets or read your bible more and believed what you were reading? Would you have married the person of your dreams instead of allowing them to disappear? Would you have taken the plane ticket the random stranger offered you in the streets? Or slept with your boss to move you up the ladder? Admitted you were gay? Whatever you would like to change would have played party to the end of your activity in this world. Every life is unique with its own number. If you feel a change is necessary, then take it to benefit yourself. You have a chance now. What's it going to be?

Rasi and his four friends attended the bar every Friday and Saturday without fail. They had become tired of the place, but he was drawn to its surroundings because of who frequented it.

They had taken residence in the same area of the wine bar, in those chairs by the window, at the same time, on the same days, even if they were late, no man or beast would dare to occupy their seats.

Upon arrival, Royal made sure their drinks were served to them instantly.

They had become the big wigs of the place, highly respected decent young men.

The girls' first encounter with them was at age sixteen when they found themselves at the bar in their usual spot ordering drinks. Piper noticed the seats by the window was empty. She checked her watch. "Looks like the godfathers aren't coming tonight."

"Oh, they'll be here," Storm spoke up, feeling disappointed.

"Yeah, they're coming. They're like clockwork." Giselle spoke, watching the door, sipping on her rum and Coke.

"Well, I say we reclaim our seats." Piper was always so daring.

"I can't take the embarrassment of being asked to move." Jazz giggled through her comment. But it would be fun to see their faces. After all, we did own those seats first before they came along."

The girls waited a bit longer; it was now eight-thirty, which was quite late for the men.

"Right, that's it. I need a seat, the rest are full, and those ones are empty." Piper pouted, hand on her hip whilst pointing to the empty chairs. The girls paused their drinks at their lips, waiting for Piper's next move. She downed her archers and lemonade, swished her sexy hips, raised her hand in the air.

"Ladies." She strutted towards the chairs in the short silver swing skirt that caught her just under her bottom cheek, with a white alter neck belly top.

The girls glanced at one another, quickly placing their glasses on the bar, and followed behind like lost sheep, smiling at the other punters as they moved their way through the crowd.

The girls approached the area with confidence and took to the seats, exposing every leg and cleavage. Royal peered his head over the crowd and smiled at the girls knowing very soon they would no longer be welcome in that hot spot.

Venus fidgeted in her chair, looking around uncomfortably.

"Chill, babe, what's the worst that could happen?" Storm leaned across her giving her a substantial childlike grin. Venus smiled back nervously.

Giselle responded in her best American accent, "Well ladies, we about to find out."

The crowd dispersed, and all eyes turned to the girls sitting in the chairs by the window. They could see the bartender having a conversation, but who was he speaking to.

The pretty young bartender who had served them

their drinks earlier was now approaching them with a cat got the cream expression, armed with a tray full of alcohol. She spoke excitedly as she handed the glasses to the girls.

"I got one rum and black, one rum and Coke, archers and lemonade, straight cherry brandy, and one brandy and baby cham." The young girl giggled at the end of the sentence.

"We didn't order any drinks." Jazz looked on inquisitively.

"No, you didn't, but they did." The young bartender was now almost bursting. She pointed behind at the five men coming up behind her. The young girl grinned at them then quickly disappeared.

Fast approaching in the distance danced the sexy swagger of five fine men. The most delicious, likeable chocolate men the girls had ever seen. Their faces resided in a dominant stare; they were sex on legs, defying all meanings of the word hot.

"So, we hear you ladies have adopted our seats." The deep baritone and blue eyes had the girls frozen in mid-air. No one spoke, except Piper, who was not going to show Mr. 'I want to throw you down and shag you now' eyes, that they could not get the better of them.

"I didn't see a name on them when I sat down, so we adopted them and named them after us."

Piper eyed Rasi seductively as she uncrossed her legs, parting them slightly then crossing them over to the other side; she leaned over, showing part of her cleavage, picked up her drink, and took a sip.

There was a silence as the girls looked back towards Rasi and his friends, waiting for his response.

A smirk appeared across his handsome face as he ran his hand through his thick jet-black shaggy hair. "Then might I suggest we adopt new babies to marry yours."

With that, the men pulled some chairs over and placed them in between the girls.

Rasi and his friends sat down, and the whole wine bar appeared to breathe a choreographed breath.

"So, what name did you sign on the adoption papers?" Rasi grinned. Venus looked at him quizzically.

"What? what adoption papers?" Storm glared at her giving a dumb face look.

"He means what's your name."

"Ooh, sorry." Venus giggled nervously. "Venus. My name is Venus, like the planet." The men starred across at each girl in turn.

"I'm Jazz, like the seductive genre of sound."

"I'm Storm, like the weather. Mess with me, and I'll strike you down." She spoke while eyeing up the dark skin guy that occupied her view. He tried not to grin whilst starring into her green eyes.

"I'm Giselle, like the swan, not the ugly one, well the one that was ugly then turned beautiful, you know the story." Poor Giselle was always a stumbling mess, but she made the group giggle.

Silence fell upon them as Rasi shuffled his chair, turning to Piper. "So, what are you made of?"

"I'm Piper, like—"

Rasi cut her short. "Like the river."

They held a silent glare for a moment, Piper seeming a bit bemused by the fact Rasi seemed to know so much about her name.

"Piper, you're like a sea of colours." The girls turned back to Piper, waiting for her comeback.

Piper cleared her throat, leaned forward, lifted her drink, and took a sip from the sugar-coated rim glass. Folding her arms across her chest, she tilted her head slightly to the side.

"You seem to know so much about my name. Why don't you continue?" she grinned sexily, and it seemed to set Rasi on fire.

"If I've offended you, I apologise, but I like to do my homework on areas of interest." His voice was like smooth milk chocolate, deep, baritone, and soothing. Piper felt drawn in. She shook herself out of his trance and responded.

"Well, eight of ten for the research," Piper

responded slowly.

"What about the other two per cent?" Rasi questioned seductively, leaning toward Piper. She didn't seem put off by his flirting as she leaned in even closer. "When you've earned it, I'll let you know." She placed her index finger onto his lips and paused there for a while.

Time seemed to stop as both Piper and Rasi tangoed with their passion. They could have embraced into a passionate kiss; they were that close.

The deep glance was breathless, entwined. They held it long enough before Piper eased back slowly into her chair, leaving Rasi in his stance. He smiled in satisfaction as he sat up, raising his hand to the bartender ordering more drinks.

Venus interrupted the silence. "So, what are your names then?"

The dark-skinned man with light brown eyes and corn-rowed hair answered first.

"Blue, like the sky, like the deepest sea, that's me." The girls didn't know whether to laugh or cry at the lame rhyme. Rasi shook his head in sheer disappointment at his friend.

"Pier, I'm Blues twin, and I mean rock." He was obviously the more serious of the two.

The twins were from a French background. They had been brought up in France from birth until the age of ten with their father. Their mother had abandoned them as babies, then somehow had reappeared into their lives. Their mum took their father to court and won a long and drawn-out court case. She moved them back to England to live with her for a year, then decided she couldn't cope and sent them back to their father in France, aged thirteen.

When the boys were sixteen, their father was gunned down in front of them in their own home. The boys were again sent back to England to live with their stepmother. This is where they spent the rest of their days.

The last in the group to answer was supposed to be Rasi's closest friend

"Ryan, my name means little king." For some reason, Piper took an instant dislike to his voice and to him. He was supposed to be Rasi sidekick, his closest friend. Piper wasn't too sure.

"And I'm Rasi." All eyes turned to him as he spoke. "Ras, short for Rastafarian, and I, for the highest."

His slightly Canadian accented voice commanded attention. Right there and then, the girls noticed his strong attraction to Piper.

The girls stared at him in amazement. Piper appeared uninterested and looked at her friends, behaving all silly. She shook her head in the hopes her friends would not embarrass themselves for the whole evening.

As the weeks and months progressed, the girls were always excited to see Rasi and his humble crew. They felt safe with him

Especially the night that Marlon, Corey, and their lame friends arrived. The group discussed that they would pick up some clothes from Storm's house to come back to the club when out of nowhere, a huge voice interrupted their flow.

"SORT WHAT OUT? Who's this fool, Storm"?

She looked up with fear in her eyes as her friends instantly grew an attitude.

"Marlon, hi, err, these are some friends of Piper and Jazz. I just came over to say hi to the girls."

"Huh, don't make me laugh. With a drink in your hand? Get up bitch, and get yourself home."

"Oh please, she doesn't live with you, Marlon, she lives with her parents, and if she wants to have a drink with her girlfriends, you don't have a say." Piper wasn't afraid of Marlon.

"Just leave Marlon, and stop making a fool of yourself."

"Quiet yourself, Jazz, before I come over there and shut you and your little army up for good."

That was enough for Rasi. He held women on such a high pedestal his nature would not allow any foul play. Turning his chair to address Marlon, his blue eyes appeared to darken.

"Marlon, that's your name, right. Huh huh, don't say another word. I won't sit here and watch you disrespect any woman like that, especially those in my company. Now I don't know who put your makeup on for you this morning, but it's smudged, so if you want someone to wipe it off for you, I'll gladly assist. So, you can choose to leave here fully intact or in pieces; what's it going to be?"

Marlon starred Rasi dead in the eye and realised he was playing with fire, but he would not be done over like a little boy, so he had to play the big man, especially while his friends were present.

"What are you, their pimp, Asian boy?" Marlon and his friends laughed. "This is my woman, and I will talk to her how I please. You can concentrate on those other slappers and leave them fifty pence in the morning." The men laughed even louder.

"Fifty pence?" Piper seethed. "It's fifty pence more than what you make on the streets, still walking around in your shell suit and scraping cash off your girl coz you can't make your own money, dirty scrub."

"Piper, please, stop. She doesn't mean it, Marlon. She's just angry because you called her a slapper. Look, I'm leaving right now."

Marlon, by this time, was making his way around to where Piper was seated, but Rasi beat him to it.

Stepping in front of Marlon, he sized him over before warning him off.

"I dare you to take another step; I won't waste any time giving you a good whooping."

There was a madness in Rasi's eyes that Marlon recognised. All he could respond with was, "Ok, ok, you'll get yours." He didn't even know what he meant by that statement, but he knew this was out of his depth, so he backed off.

Piper, in the meantime, witnessed Corey, who was Marlon's sidekick and Giselle's boyfriend, acknowledge Ryan, and she became suspicious. Her suspicions were aroused by the fact that Ryan and his friends had always maintained that he had never met Marlon or his friends, yet there he was, making secret eye contact with Corey.

Piper sat quietly as she observed the two men.

Royale had now stepped in to escort Marlon and his friends out. Storm was sure tonight she would collect a beating for embarrassing him.

The night had been interrupted. This was the girls' cue to stop for the day and head home.

Rasi watched as they left, keeping his eye on only one person until he felt a sharp nudge in his arm, which made him turn instantly turn to face Ryan, who was giving him a strange glare.

"What do you want with that little slapper? She's

gonna chew you up and spit out the bits she doesn't like, then your heart is going to be broken and crushed to tiny pieces."

"Watch your mouth Ryan, no woman is deserving of that title. I'm just friendly, and when since did you ever care about my interest in women." Rasi was annoyed at his choice of words regarding Piper.

"Since I've seen you interested in a bird", ''that's going to make you serve time, come on, Rasi, you're ten years her senior. She's going to bleed you dry and share it with her little broke arse friends."

"I'm not sure how much time you invest in your imagination Ryan, but perhaps it would be a great vision if you actually saw past your dick. Yes, of course, she is young, but I find her quite good company."

"You got good company, Rasi. Us, your friends, and don't forget the women that are better suited to your age."

"I speak to whom I choose. I don't believe I've ever needed your permission. I've wanted to talk to Piper for quite some time, see what" ''she's about, find out how her puzzle fits together. I'm not about to have her children or make her my wife. We are just talking. How often do you see me speaking to young people?"

"Never, so I don't know why the hell you're starting now. Just be careful.'" 'I'm talking to you as a friend."

"Thank you, I appreciate your concern, I know

you're just looking out for me, but there is nothing in it, so chill."

"If you say so, don't say I never warned you."

Blue had enough of Ryan's speech; he was acting like he was some angel.

"Maybe, Mr Man over here wants her for himself. That's why he's all up in your Kool-Aid, like some jealous bitch."

"Give it a rest, Blue; I wouldn't go near any of them girls. I like living on the outside. When her big brothers are ready to give Rasi an arse whooping, he can't say I never warned him,"

"How do you know" "she's got, brothers?"

Ryan began to stutter, caught off guard. Rasi stared at him, waiting for an answer.

"I heard her mention it to one of her friends."

Pier sat in the background, quietly eyeing Ryan. He 'didn't trust him as far as he could throw him; he always thought he was a bit dodgy. However, the exchanges had been witnessed between him and Corey. So, as a loyal friend to Rasi, he would keep a close eye on Ryan.

The men knocked back their drinks before heading home.

CHAPTER 14

BEFORE THE PAST

Do you find any of these characters trustworthy yet? I've told you their stories to the best of my knowledge. Each time I get closer to them, the avenue changes; their lives have been filled with gloom and despair. None of their imaginary adventures adds up or amounts to anything. Just a rucksack full of lies to one another. I'm in too deep to pull away from listening to the end. If I could change one thing right now, I would have cut my losses and moved on.

Nothing could stop them from always ending up in their conventional wine bar, seated in the same spot. They were like residents without the slippers. They were conscious of every bartender, waiter, and every traditional punter, new and old faces.

Most Saturday nights, they would attend the nightclub below the bar. Rasi had even done a few rounds of DJ work, rapping on the microphone, upsetting some of the other punters who didn't relish the fact that he was an Asian guy honing in on their music. His Jamaican accent even had a clear acquired victory. Nevertheless, the ladies profoundly appreciated him, and he had the room spinning.

Rasi's dad had described the fatal attraction Rasi had for Piper. He warned Rasi about the age gap, he expressed his concerns, but Rasi had no intentions of sanctioning his heart to slip away. It killed him if Piper dated other guys. It made him exasperated with envy to the point he would warn them off.

It was during a sultry summer's night in early August. Rasi dropped Piper at her home like he always did, only this night was different; something eccentric about that evening had them both on edge. A peculiar atmosphere lingered in the air; both Rasi and Piper could feel it.

The night appeared more dark and eerie; it suppressed the blissful feeling that the friends had been experiencing before they approached Piper's front door.

Piper gasped as she pulled the keys from her pocket; sitting just at the foot of her door were two ebony candles. In between them perched a photograph of her as a baby and ashes sprinkled around it. Piper froze, she could feel the terror and agitation in Rasi, but he immediately bent down, endeavouring to move the ritual. Piper gripped his arm and hauled him.

"No, you're not to physically contact it." Piper verbalized quietly and shakily. "Let me borrow your phone, please."

Rasi immediately handed his mobile phone over to Piper.

Gradually she dialled her grandmother's number. The gruffly Jamaican voice on the other end answered.

"Hey, what's happening, baby girl."

"Granny, I'm apprehensive, I've just got home, and someone's put a ritual outside my door."

There was silence as Piper awaited her grandma's directions.

"Granny, are you there? Her grandmother let out a long sigh.

"Yes, Baby, I'm still here; ok, what is it."

"Two ebony candles, a baby photo of me, and what looks similar to some ashes."

"Have the candles been lit?"

"No, they don't appear to be."

"Are the ashes dry?" Granny sternly questioned.

"They look it, but it's hard to tell it's too dark."

"Ok, don't touch it, but you can't stay there tonight. Are you alone?"

"No, Rasi is with me," Piper shamefully replied

"Ok, can he drop you somewhere? Then in the morning, you can return home, ok?"

"Granny, how will you get it? Should I wait for you?"

"Baby girl, not even your grannie is emerging

tonight. Don't you worry, your pretty head? I will sort this out. I know who this is. No harm will come to you if you leave now."

"Ok, Granny, if you're sure, Rasi will drop me off at Jazz's."

"I will call you in the morning. All is well."

Before Piper could verbalize good night, her grandmother had gone. She never verbally expressed goodbye or goodnight; Piper always found this frustrating.

Piper had a hundred per cent confidence in her grandma. Albeit she was alarmed to find something like that, so brutal on her doorstep, she found comfort in her grandma's words and Rasi's presence. She had witnessed plenty of these witchcraft arts as a child, but never had they been for her.

"I'm sorry," Piper turned to Rasi, "but would you mind taking me to Jazz's, please?"

"Now why do you opt to go back to Jazz? You're more than welcome to come back to my place, and I'm right here; it would make sense".

Piper eyed him deviously. Rasi rephrased his speech quickly, holding both hands up.

"No strings attached. I promise to make you breakfast. Whatever you want."

"I like hot pancakes, with strawberries and cream."

"I cerebrate. I can manage that," Rasi teased, the

sexy grin on his face becoming wider.

"To eat?" Piper queried; Rasi leaned into her.

"Whatever you want," he replied with a sultry grin on his face. Piper creased her eyebrows at him.

So, on that eerie warm August night, the friends took that long journey to Knightsbridge.

Piper acknowledged that Rasi had taken a slightly different route, but she was too tired to question.

They pulled up in front of the elegant detached house that stood behind colossal iron gates activated by the approach of his car. She sat upright in her seat.

"Where are we?" Piper grinned.

"We're home," he answered, grinning, not giving anything else away.

"This isn't your dads' home. When did this happen?"

Rasi coolly turned to Piper, and suddenly, he looked deliciously edible. Piper shook her head out of his trance.

"I've always had my own house, Sweets. I relish getting acquainted with people first before I let them into my life. I've grown fond of you and your girlfriends, especially you. I believe I can manage to reveal marginally more of myself."

Piper ignored his remark of 'especially you' and carried on her amazement. "It's a house, Rasi; there is lots to reveal. And five years later, you think you can trust us now?"

"You'd be surprised," was the sexy whisper that left his suckable lips.

Rasi opened the door to his lush house, and it was like a fairy tale. Piper's jaw dropped to the floor as she spun around in the huge corridor staring at the high ceilings and the unusual design that she couldn't make out. Spotlights began to appear and light up from various parts of the wall and ceiling. The walls, ceiling, and floors were made from white glossy granite material. Piper was in such a dream she didn't even feel when Rasi had removed her coat. For all she knew, he could have removed her clothes. She would have been none the wiser.

"Can I get you a drink?" Piper did hear the question, but it wasn't sinking in.

"Mm mm, hmm."

"Wine, soft drink, or hot drink?"

"Mmmmmm hmmm, that sounds good."

Rasi giggled; he left Piper in the grand hallway and proceeded to the kitchen. He decided to pour Piper an archer and Lemonade, a drink he made sure was always available should he ever have the chance to invite her to his residence.

"Sweets."

Piper jumped as she looked towards the baritone, silky voice; she suddenly became embarrassed at her self-indulged gawping. Piper smiled at Rasi as she swished her hips slowly towards him. Damn, he looked fine in his straight-cut jeans, white fitted t-shirt, and loose, shaggy hair. He held a glass out to her. As she took it from his hands, the two held eye contact that said: "Eat me."

Rasi knew he shouldn't, but he was totally smitten. He couldn't stop watching Piper; he had waited all these years to watch her grow. Yet, in the six years they had all been hanging together, he never claimed the title of a steady boyfriend.

Piper maintained that she did not see Rasi's attraction for her; although she often flirted with him, she was unaware of what this was doing to him. So now here she was alone with this fine sexy-ass man, and she was finding him quite appetising for the first time.

Piper took a sip from her glass, still starring at Rasi, wondering what he was all about.

"Come, let's sit unless, of course, you're tired."

"No, I'm good," she lied. Piper followed Rasi into the vast living room and again found herself gaping at the glass floor section with fish swimming beneath her feet; she stood still. At the same time, they swam around her.

Every room in the house was drowned in white with splashes of colour, all tastefully done. The settees were an unusual design, more extensive than her own bed.

"What black man lives in Knights Bridge, in all this"? When piper heard the answer, it was then she realised her thoughts had rolled right off her tongue.

"A black man whose daddy was a component of the secret service."

Piper giggled at her slippery tongue.

"I'm sorry, it's beautiful, and I can't believe we have never been here."

"That's because you spent the last six years running away from me. Whenever I asked you to come for dinner at my home, you always declined."

"Well, I apologise. I mentally thought you were talking about your dad's house, and I didn't feel it was respectful for me to stay there."

"Oh, so you would have stayed then?"

Piper blushed at his question.

"Sweets, I left my father's house a very long time ago, yes I spend a long duration there, but I would never invite you over to stay. That would be uncourteous of me."

Piper curtseyed to Rasi. "Of course, my lord, an absolute shamble that would be."

They both devolved into loud laughter.

"Now that I have you to myself let me ask you a question."

"Ok."

"You do know how I feel about you, right? No

pretending."

"I've heard."

Rasi grinned at Piper's lie.

"So, you don't know I'm deeply in love with you and would be exceptionally ecstatic if you committed to me?"

"What's in your drink?" Piper giggled

"My drink is impeccably fine, thank you." His grin became more animated as he shook his head.

"Piper, I visualise us being a couple, being together."

"You mean like boyfriend and girlfriend together?"

"Yes, consummately homogeneous to that."

"English, please."

"Commit to me, Piper."

"Oh, but if I commit, will I still be able to date other people?"

Piper slurped her drink deliberately. Rasi laughed and removes her glass from her hand. He places it on the table adjacent to him and moves in extremely close to her. He takes her hand and twiddles her fingers.

"Sweets, this isn't a jest. I love you in more ways than one."

"Yes, but you're old; when I get to fifty, you will approximately be sixty. So, you will always be old, all my life."

"It's only nine years. Does that scare you"?

"Not genuinely; I'm just playing with you. Your age doesn't bother me. But honestly, I'm not sure who I am right now. I've got issues, and I don't believe you're ready to take me on."

"I'll be the judge of that. I profoundly relish you and all your rough edges. I've visually perceived your issues, and I am not afraid to take you on. I opt to look after you, love you, and make love to you."

"That sounds like a charming offer, but don't you need to have love back."

"It's not an offer. It's real. I think you like me. You're just scared. It's not me being big-headed. I just know you. You think I don't, but I do. Probably even better than your friends."

Piper knew he wasn't wrong. They had spent so much time together, alone. He told Piper everything, as did she. He was already like her boyfriend. She just had to treat him like one.

She worried about him when he wasn't around. His birthdays had never been missed. Even for his thirtieth, she went all out. Even his dad included her in preparation for the big day.

What was she so scared of? She was twenty-one, after all.

"I would mess your life up. I would hurt you. I don't think I'm ready for this."

"Stop telling yourself that. If you really want this,

you will let it happen. You have no idea how I feel about you. You will want for nothing. I will make sure you are looked after for the rest of your days with me."

"It's a big ask."

Rasi paused for a while in deep thought.

"Sweets, I am more serious than you think. This is not me asking you to look after my pet dog."

"You're scaring me. How much more serious can this get?"

"Be honest, how do you feel about me?"

"I like you, I love your company, your humour, your energy, your geekiness, the words in your dictionary that I never understand, your honesty, your sexiness, your spiritual views, your intelligence. I think I just love everything about you, but it's fascination, not love."

"Everything about me is what makes me, Sweets, so, therefore, it must be love."

Piper was quiet for a while.

"I guess it is," she faintly answered, "I guess it is."

"Is it enough to marry me?" Her head spun around from the shock of his question.

"What are you saying?"

"I am saying, be with me, marry me but not yet!"

"I'm confused."

"No, you're not. You're just refusing to hear me."

"Oh, I can hear you."

"Sweets, I'm asking you to not marry me."

"What?"

"I'm asking you to not marry me until you are sure that I am everything that you want from me. Whether it be in two years, three years, five even. Let me be your boyfriend, well, fiancé, and when you're ready to commit, you simply tell me, and I will be right here waiting. Sleep on it for a while and listen to what I'm asking you."

"What about children?" Piper questioned hesitantly

"Well, as you know, I am not possessed with that gift. I would do anything in the world to bear a child. God has his reasons. I have learnt to accept it, until now."

"How do you mean?"

"If I could be granted one wish to have a child, it would only be with you."

"Have I totally missed your feelings for me? That's serious, like, that's really deep."

"You have missed lots about me, Sweets. I have watched you, studied you even for so long. I know you better than anyone, even your own self. I've got you printed on my heart."

What did she have to lose? Life wasn't really heading in her direction. Piper's childhood had been a struggle, so had her teenage years. She lost the two most consequential people in her life. Albeit she had her friends and cousins, life was not promising.

Rasi had landed in her world when she was scarcely fifteen; she felt so close to him, which was why she confided in him about everything, even down to her latest smear test results. This wasn't just comity; she wasn't sure what it was. But she knew something in her wanted more.

Perhaps her dismissive self needed to quit the games she played; life had dealt both some wild cards. But, would she be a fool to turn this down?

"Ok, I will sleep on it. How many sleeps do I get?"

Rasi massaged her forehead. "As many as you like, but don't sleep on it for too long."

Dinner was accommodated slightly late, and Piper viciously attacked the food like she hadn't eaten for a while. Rasi observed her and grinned at her. He was satisfied she was happy.

They shared a shower that evening, amongst other things.

Piper believed she may have fallen in profound love that night. She never knew love could feel like that. Had Piper ever authentically experienced it before? What she did know was that she was different with him after that night. Rasi had planted a seed in her head, and now he just had to continue to water it.

Piper rolled over in the sizably voluminous bed, forgetting where she was. Her body ascended promptly. She remained still whilst she adjusted her disorientation, then an interruption from her phone ringing; she dashed her head around, leaned over the side of the bed, and grabbed hold of the phone.

"Hello?" she answered breathlessly.

"Hey, babe, where you at?"

"What?"

"I said, where you at? You still sleeping? I stopped by your house this morning, but you're not in. Where are you? I'll meet you for breakfast."

"No, you can't; I mean, I'm still sleeping. I'm out."

"Girl, you sound crazy. Where are you? I can double back; you're still in bed, aren't you?"

"What's the time, Jazz?"

"Don't sweat. It's only nine-thirty." Piper body slammed herself into the pillow and giggled to herself.

"What's so funny"?

"Nothing, babe."

There was a gentle knock at the door before it opened slowly. In peeped Rasi's head, he tried to whisper, "Breakfast?"

"Yes, please, it smells good."

He smiled and hung around the door for a while before leaving.

"Piper. Where are you?"

"Oh, didn't I say? I'm at Rasi's house."

Jazz released a big screech as if she had just shut her

fingers in the door.

"Oooooooooh girl, you been shagging?" she suggested like a big child.

"Girl, let me tell you that was not a shag. That was love, real love." Piper cupped the mouthpiece of the phone with her hand and whispered into the receiver.

"Ok, I need more information." She was like a child with a new toy.

"Not right now. I need to shower and have breakfast."

"You better call me later."

"I will, I promise."

Piper hung up, grabbed the towel left at the end of the bed for her, and scrambled into the shower. Rasi had left her an oversized white t-shirt for when she had finished. She pulled it on and joined him in the elegant kitchen, where she was greeted by a French chef.

"Good morning. I didn't want to wake you, so I took the liberty of ordering breakfast for you."

"Who's that?" Piper pointed towards the chef.

"That's my chef, Marco."

Marco waved to Piper as he tossed the eggs above a high fire. Piper was so taken in by his skill that she missed his sexy French "Bonjour."

"Ready to eat?" Rasi grinned.

"Yes, please."

"Let's sit. Oh, by the way, I have something for you

for when your finished eating."

Piper was intrigued. What did he have for her already?

Rasi leaned into Piper before leaving the room and whispered in her ear. "Try not to sleep with Marco before I get back."

They both laughed out loudly as Piper returned the joke, "How long have I got?"

Rasi returned with a suit bag into the living room and hung it on the back of the door.

He joined Piper for breakfast at the round table.

"Did you sleep well?" He questioned in a gentlemanly manner.

"Definitely, best night sleep I've had in years." Piper wasn't lying. It was probably the first night she had gone to sleep without a drink and a line of cocaine, no nightmares. Also, the first morning she woke up without a coffee and another line of cocaine.

"I didn't mean to leave you, but I wanted to make sure Marco knew you were here."

"Why, who would you normally have here?" Piper felt a pang of jealousy within her question.

"Very funny. No one. Marco constantly asks about you; he's been wanting to meet you for a while".

"Mmm, he seems nice."

"Yes, he is, he also very interfering with my love life. So right now, he's delighted you're here. My chef believes my future is promising".

"You're very sexy when you speak French."

"Thank you, you're very sexy when you sleep."

Piper felt herself getting hot. "You watched me sleep?"

"Of course."

"What's in the bag?" She changed the subject.

Rasi excused himself from the table, reached for the bag, and handed it to Piper.

She stood up and unzipped it. Inside was a white tennis-style skirt, with a pink t-shirt, on the other hanger was a baby blue tracksuit, light enough for the summer weather they were having. There was another bag hanging inside the bag. Piper pulled it off the hanger and looked inside. She looked at Rasi and grinned.

"Thank you very much. This is so thoughtful. I love sexy underwear, and it's my size."

"I wasn't sure what you had planned for when you left here, and I knew you didn't have spare clothes."

"What time did you go out this morning?"

"I didn't. I had the clothes ordered in."

On their way upstairs to get dressed, Piper questioned Rasi about the photo on his wall.

"Who is that in the painting?"

"It's me."

"Why did you have a double painting of yourself,

wearing the same jumper but in another colour?"

Rasi glared at her behind him. He then stopped and turned to the painting.

"You think I'm that vain that I would have a double painting of myself?" Rasi seemed irritated.

"Well, it's art. Perhaps that's what you wanted/"

Rasi dropped his head. He sucked in a large amount of air. When he held his head up, a tear cascaded from his eye.

"It's my brother. He was my twin."

"Wow, you're a twin?"

"Was, I will tell you the story, but please, not right now. He was murdered. Do you mind if I explain another time?" The wrenching pain was now prominent in his face.

"No, not at all. I apologise if I upset you, I didn't know."

"Please, don't apologise. I know you didn't know; I just find it hard to talk about my brother; I promise, very soon, I will explain it to you."

Piper rubbed his arm as they climbed the stairs to change.

This was a completely different world for Piper, a world she could quickly get used to.

CHAPTER 15

SILENT RIVER

Somewhere in the outskirts of Dulwich town centre around 07.37am, Jazz sat on her leather stool, head in her hands resting on her warm, musty-smelling wooden table. A list of smells ingrained, amongst the faint coffee scent was also stale milk spilt over from soggy cornflakes.

Jazz loathed cornflakes, but River was a huge fan, a splash of milk on a mountain of cornflakes and warmed up in the microwave for 30 seconds. The thought of it made Jazz want to heave. "Who does that? Why not just have dry cornflakes, from her dad's side, odd eating behaviours, gross."

"Who's gross, Mummy?" Jazz looked down at the small warm hand touching her leg. Jazz gave her a warm smile, placed her hand on hers. "Mummy's talking to herself again."

"Cornflakes. Mm mm mm," River replied as if there was no need to give any other answer; her mum knew the drill.

Jazz always stood to attention when it came to

River. She was her little gem, a proper little handbag.

Jazz placed River's cornflakes on the table as she scrambled up onto the high chair and sat awkwardly on the seat. Jazz laughed at her as she stuck the oversized spoon into the soft cornflakes and shovelled the first spoon into her mouth, talking to her mum and spraying every bit over her mum's white top.

Jazz jumped back laughing, picking up a piece of cornflakes and pelting it at her daughter. "That's gross."

River laughed wide, projecting a mouth full of sloppiness. Jazz watched her green-eyed daughter as she attempted to scoff the mangled food back into her mouth. River had the most beautiful eyes for a child, the longest eyelashes you ever did see, and the thickest eyebrows. Her hair was jet black, thick, with the curliest coils. Washing it was a nightmare. It took Giselle and her three friends to help clean and dry it. River was small for her age, and Jazz also thought she was immature. She never seemed as advanced as her friends. Or at the proper milestone for her age. But she was also very babied by her mum and her friends.

It was Rivers eighth birthday today; Jazz was feeling overwhelmed.

"Why are you staring at me, Mummy".

"Because it's your birthday and it's the best day in the whole world"!

" You got big love in your right eye."

Jazz giggled as she always did at River,

"Just my right eye? What about the left one?" Jazz scrunched her left eye and leaned in close to River, so she could take a closer look. She peeled her mum's left eye open with her warm sticky hands. "No, nothing in there. Your eye has fallen out, Mummy." They both giggled. River leaned in closer and kissed her mums' eye.

"Let me see if it came back now."

Jazz opened her left eye and planted a kiss on River's lips. "What do you see now?"

"Cornflakes." They both laughed hysterically, missing the ring of the doorbell until they heard a big bang on the living room window.

Both girls jumped and spun towards the window to see Piper standing with a big grin, waving energetically.

River wriggled from her mum's grasp and bolted to the door screaming, "Aunty Pip!" She stopped in her tracks and looked back at her mum, screeching, "It's Aunty Pip," as if her mum had not seen the ginormous present in one arm of Aunty Pip. Jazz glanced at the clock. 8.17, forty minutes was all she had with her daughter.

Jazz loved her friends, but she loved her daughter more. Jazz reluctantly followed her daughter to the door and unlocked the bolts whilst River danced around her feet, jumping up and down. The latch had barely lifted before the door swung open.

Piper jumped over the threshold, singing happy birthday at the top of her voice. She chased River through the hallway with the gift. Jazz closed the door behind them and took a deep breath before turning to the two girls. Struggling through a forced smile, she offered a coffee to Piper, but not before reminding her of the time.

"Her birthday is for the whole day." There was a bitterness in Jazz's voice.

"It's okay, Mummy," River pipped up, "you say that every year."

Piper gave Jazz a look of confusion. "A coffee would be lovely."

River was curious to find out what her aunty had brought her. It was always something extravagant. All four aunties were always trying to outdo each other, but Aunty Piper always won. This year was River's eighth birthday, so she knew it was something big.

Piper left River in the hallway with the large box ripping at the paper and followed Jazz into the kitchen. "You, okay? You seem on edge."

Jazz didn't turn around. She continued to reach for the coffee in the cupboard. "No edge, Piper."

"You called me Piper. You're angry, mad even."

"It's 8.20 in the morning. It's MY daughter's birthday." Jazz starred Piper in the eye. When she exaggerated the word "my," Piper immediately grew an attitude,

"Some people would be happy that their FRIENDS helped them to bring up their child when there is no daddy around when they are ill and need to go to the hospital. When they need a babysitter. When they need the company to put their child to bed, take them to school on the first day and organise parties.

Well, as a matter-of-fact, Jazz thought Piper had lost the plot. She had never asked her or the others to babysit; they just turned up wherever the babysitter was. Jazz never invited them to accompany her on a lonely night; they just turned up and insisted loneliness was in the air. She never asked them to take River to school; they organised a committee with banners to wave her in. In fact, all four friends were overbearing when it came to River. There was no space, so any milestone for River had constantly been hijacked by her so-called friends.

Jazz glared at Piper in disbelief, pushed her coffee in front of her, and sauntered back out into the hallway to watch her daughter, on her birthday, rip the paper from her first present of the morning.

Her first present should have been from her mum.

River breathed heavily as she snatched at the last

piece of paper. She shoved her bum into the air, pushed herself into a standing position, and stepped away from the box silently. Piper stood by the kitchen doorway, hugging her cup of coffee in both hands. The steam from the cup had made her face glow, and she had a cat that got the cream expression. Piper always appeared beautiful in any situation, her light brown eyes and smooth complexion, her virgin hair. Jazz was sure she slept upright in bed.

"What's up, Princess?" Jazz was hoping that whatever it was, River would absolutely hate it. Then that little voice betrayed her.

"It's beautiful." River turned to her mum, then back to her aunty. She wiped her eyes with the back of her hand.

"I can't believe it, my favourite doll. You're the best aunty in the whole world." At that, she ran and hugged Piper tightly as if her world had just been completed, and there was Jazz, feeling like she'd been dismissed.

River picked the doll out of the box and hugged it tightly, swaying side to side. Piper knelt in front of her and whispered, "There's something else in the bag."

River's eyes grew large Piper stuck her hand into the bag and pulled out a tiny box wrapped in pink velvet. She held the box in her hand before telling River, "This one is exceptional wear it all the time for protection." Jazz leant over and removed the box from

Piper's hand.

"I think she's had enough excitement for one morning. It's time to open Mummy's present."

River screeched with excitement and ran into her bedroom, where her mum always left her presents hidden for her to find. Jazz turned to Piper and firmly placed her hand on her chest, "I would really appreciate it if you let me have this moment alone with her. You know Piper, I wanted to give my present to her first. I'm her mum, not you, not Storm, not Giselle, not Venus. Me, okay? She definitely does not need any pretend Daddies like Rasi and his friends!" As she walked away, Piper heard her mumble under her breath that it wasn't her fault Rasi couldn't have his own children.

Piper swallowed hard and stepped back with her hands raised as if surrendering. "Apologies. I didn't mean to offend. We just love River."

"I can cope. I got this." With that, Jazz followed her daughter into the room and closed the door behind her. River already had the wrapper off all her presents and was dancing around them.

"Oooooh, Mummy, look, you got me the same dolly. Now I got two. Can I keep them both?"

"No point, Princess, we will have to send one back. What's your favourite colour?"

"Oh, Mummy, you know it's red."

"Okay, then the dolly with the sky-blue dress gets returned, and you can pick out something else you wanted."

"Oh, Mummy, aunty Piper will be upset. Please let me keep both."

"I said no, and that's the end of it. One is enough."

River dropped her head in disappointment. Exasperated, Jazz quietly slipped the small pink velvet box into the back of her drawer along with the other small boxes her other four friends had given over the last seven years.

When Jazz finished bathing River, she returned to the kitchen to find the other four friends and Rasi sitting with Piper. Storm leapt from the stall and grabbed River by the waist, swinging her around, singing her a happy birthday rap. Jazz side glanced at her as she viewed the oversized gift on the floor next to the others.

"Want to see what Aunty Storm bought you?"

"Yes, please." River ripped off the wrapper that, for some reason, already had holes in it and was greeted by a moving box, again more holes. River jumped away from the pack and clutched her mum.

"Aunty, what's that?"

"Come, baby, don't be scared; you are going to love it." Storm opened the box and was greeted by a soft bark.

"Oh no, you didn't," Jazz moaned, holding her head, "Please Storm, tell me you didn't."

Storm screeched, "I DID!"

River ran to the box and watched as her Aunty Storm removed the fluffy friend. She handed the puppy to River, who was beside herself and had blocked out whatever other presents she may have received.

"Guess she doesn't want my TV then," Giselle commented.

"Or my electronic car," Venus said loudly enough for River to hear.

She came running back into the kitchen screaming, "A TV? An electronic car? Thank you, all my aunties I love, you all."

River then ran off chasing the noisy, over-excited puppy around the house.

Jazz was not impressed with any of their presents, every year the competition got bigger. This year Storm won first place in the race.

"What are you going to name him Re, Re?"

"River, please, call her River."

"Okay, grump, did you fall out of the bed and bang your head?"

Jazz kissed her teeth as she dodged the puppy, which was causing chaos around her feet.

"Where do you expect this thing to stay? And who

is going to look after it and walk it, get its injections? Really, Storm, have you thought about this?"

Storm ignored Jazz's frustrations. Jazz was always stressed when it was River's birthday or any significant event for that matter. She tried to be grateful for her friends and their overzealous energy towards River, but they just never gave her any time with her. Their presents were always a competition, who could get the biggest one, whose present would River like best, who would take her out the most.

River loved her aunties and held each one of them in high regard. However, she didn't have a favourite, and her relationship with each of them was so different.

The girls always bought out the other side of River, the loud, energetic side. Her silence was always evident with her mum. Jazz often envied Piper and Storm's natural high energy, the wittiness of Giselle, and the nurturing nature of Venus. She felt she should be all these things as a mother. Jazz was often classed as the mummy of the group. So why did being a mother not come naturally to her? Why did she feel this now eight-year-old child would reveal her insecurities and betray her to the core? Why was her relationship so bland with her own child? Jazz portrayed a stringent character. She always had, right from the start.

Was she so strict that River just couldn't relate to

her, she wondered as she stood watching her close buddies make a big fuss of her daughter?

Rasi tapped Jazz out of her thoughts, "It's going to be ok. You're a great mum." As he did every year, he then slipped her an envelope to help pay for River's private schooling and anything else she needed. Piper knew he provided her with financial help as that was just the way Rasi was. But she couldn't help but feel a tinge of jealousy.

"River," Storm called; River didn't respond. "River, River." Jazz tapped River on her shoulder, who in turn spun around to face her mum. "Aunty Storm is calling you, baby."

"Sorry, Mummy, I didn't hear her."

"Of course, you didn't, Princess. Aunty Storm needs to remember to be in front of you when she speaks."

Storm cut her eyes at Jazz and mouthed the words "sorry."

"It's okay, Aunty Storm. I know you forget sometimes."

"I was just asking, have you decided on a name yet."

Giselle pipped in, "Give her a chance; she just got him."

"I have got a name, actually. I'm going to call him Thunder."

Jazz bent down in front of her daughter and turned

her towards her, they shared a private joke which annoyed Storm, whilst the others smirked at her.

"Must you generate negative energy into this house with a name like Thunder? Can we have some peace?"

River laughed aloud.

"What did you say to her"? Storm demanded.

Piper nudged Storm playfully. "It's the art of sign language, my darling. I suggest you learn it like the rest of us".

Storm had promised to learn this magnificent skill, but after'" 'Marcus's death, she had sunk into a deep depression, and although her friends stood by her every day, life had moved on very quickly without her. Although River was able to vocalise very well, she became tired very fast and would prefer to sign. Her hearing impediment did not allow her to hear the beautiful sounds from behind her. For an eight-year-old, she had learnt the art of lip-reading very quickly. Compliments of her Aunty Piper. However, we will know very soon that teaching some skills to children is best left alone.

CHAPTER 16

DISTORTED WINDOW

The world is full of fears that people are afraid of; some people will take on their demons even if they know it would cost them their state of mind. You think you can trust some people with your life; you really shouldn't believe that statement, ever. Don't ever believe you know someone to the core; life and people change every day. Sometimes you are so blinded by what's around you, you may miss what was happening in the middle.

It was the week before Storm's extravagant 21st birthday. The last of the bunch to turn this incredible milestone. Storm knew her day would be grand as she was a princess. That's how she had always been treated by her family and friends, and the following week would be no different. All the girls and their parents would present Storm with luscious gifts, just as they had done for the others. But not before shopping for their outfits.

The girls had been out drinking at the Mansion. Storm had left early because she had an argument with

Marlon. The girls had failed to contact her the following day, so they decided to pay her a visit.

Rasi had become their consistent driver. He never said no to girls, especially if Piper was involved. They made plans for him to park around the corner behind Storm's house. Due to the fact he and Marlon did not get along, it was sensible that he waited outside.

It was one-thirty in the afternoon, and Storm hadn't been home to her parents' house, so they decided to make the trip to Dulwich to her and Marlon's flat.

Storm's curtains were still closed when the girls arrived, and Marlon's silver BMW that Storm had purchased for his 25th birthday was parked outside. Another car was also parked near Marlon's that they recognised as Corey's car.

There was no response to five abrupt rings on the doorbell. Giselle decided to use her fist to bang the black wooden door. Jazz peeped in through the letterbox calling Storm's name. They were about to give up when they heard Storm bellowing, "Hold on, just finding my keys."

Piper had travelled around the side of the property to peer in through the side window. She found a small metal bin to balance on with one foot. Piper spied through the gap in the curtain where they had not been flushed tight. The sun was shining onto the glass, so she placed a hand above her forehead, blocking out the light.

Piper spotted someone in the distance, but the image appeared distorted.

Pressing her head closer to the window to get a better view. Piper witnessed a scene that had her frozen fast in her tracks. She didn't call out because she couldn't. She didn't move because she couldn't. Piper was in shock. All she could do was gawp at what was unfolding before her very eyes.

Piper dropped her head in despair, unsure of whether she felt disgusted, confused, or both. One thing she did know, Storm was ruined, crushed. How had they not noticed? They knew everything about each other.

"Piper, Piper. Where are you?" Piper ran round to the front of the house like a scared child being called by her mother after getting lost.

"I'm here." Storm stood on the porch as she reached the front door with her hand on her hip.

"What were you doing, trying to climb the back gate?"

"No, just wondering why your curtains were closed at one-thirty in the afternoon." Piper retorted.

"It was a late night, you know that. I was absolutely shattered, been sleeping all day, I didn't even hear the doorbell." Piper looked pitiful at her.

"You left long before we did, baby girl, and you only

had one drink."

"What's your name, Inspector Clue? So? Oh, please don't look at me like that, Pip. I am allowed to have a lie-in".

"Mmm, course you are. If that's what you want to call it." Jazz couldn't understand why Piper's attitude had changed so drastically. Maybe she was hot and bothered after all the sun rays were intense this afternoon, and Piper didn't like too much heat.

"Are you coming in, or you going to stand out here sulking?" Giselle rolled her eyes at Piper, who was now well and truly annoyed. Piper kissed her teeth at Storm and walked past her into the flat.

Marlon was sprawled across the red leather settee; inside their plush flat, with all the latest designer gear, he made no effort to acknowledge the girls as they came in, and they barely acknowledged him.

Piper looked around suspiciously whilst side-stepping Marlon and taking the seat opposite him. She sat there glaring at him in disgust. It took all the strength in her to not walk over and punch his skanky arse like a bean bag. Marlon could feel the tense atmosphere between them. He peeped over his shoulder to where Storm was giggling with girls, satisfied they were not in earshot. Marlon turned back to Piper. Locking eyes with her, he grabbed hold of his crutch and whispered, "Want some?"

Piper held her hand over her mouth, imitating a vomiting motion. She leaned into him and whispered back, "You're a joker like you could satisfy me with that little thing. Furthermore, mine is not for sale. Where's your boy, Ryan? Did he slip out through the back door?"

Marlon shot up in his chair as if he was about to pounce on Piper.

"What are you talking about"?

"Oh, don't pretend you don't know, you greasy good for nothing pimp, selling out your girl like she's some prostitute because you're not man enough to make enough money for her."

"Hold your tongue Piper, as that will be your last words. You know, nothing."

"Really, I know you can't satisfy your girlfriend, so you must watch while your friend shows you how it's done, you lame-ass scrub. What kind of a man are you? Maybe I should get someone to pimp your sister."

"You little bitch, now you're stepping out of line." Marlon was trying his best to whisper, but Piper was making him seethe.

"Ooh, did I hurt your feelings? Going to run to mummy? Or have you pimped her out as well"

"Shut up before I make you. You've gone crazy, talking pure foolishness."

"I saw you, Marlon, I saw you take that cash from

Corey after Ryan, who claims he'd never met you before, was going at it with your girlfriend over the kitchen counter while you both stood watching drinking beer like you were in the wine bar having a chat with your friends, I..... Saw......you." Piper was holding the tears back as she was so concerned for her friend.

"You could easily be bumped off for that. How do you think your friend gets her money and all of this?" He waved his hand around, highlighting the elegant furniture in the flat.

"I won't let her continue like this. You're a dog Marlon, I will make sure that my friend comes to her senses. I won't let you do this to her."

"Too late, Ms Universe, nothing you can do. I'm going to make sure you eat every name you just called me."

"You don't scare me, Marlon. You try to act like some gangster, but not even the weasels out there fear you. Why don't you get a real job and stop following other people?"

"What are you two whispering about over there?"

Piper jumped up at the sound of Storm's voice, who was now approaching her with the others.

"Yeah, let us in." Giselle sneered at the closeness between Piper and Marlon.

Marlon sat back in the chair, grinning at Piper.

"Yeah, Pip, it would be better. Why you don't fill them in?"

Piper cleared her throat and turned to the girls. "It was nothing, really. I was just pestering Marlon to make sure he bought you something nice and elaborate for your birthday. I also asked his opinion on the gift we bought you."

Storm smiled like a big child. "I can't wait to see what my surprise is."

Judging by her quick thinking, Marlon thought Piper should have won an Oscar for that performance.

Piper turned back to Marlon and gave him a sarcastic grin. Jazz was feeling uncomfortable, she knew Piper too well, and that performance won no Oscars. Piper was hiding something.

"Now that we know you're ok and not lying in some gutter somewhere, we need to go."

"Oh, stay a bit longer." Storm pouted,

"Babe, we've got to go. We need to pick our outfits up for next week. You have yours. Why not just come with us?"

The door to the kitchen clicked everyone turned to face it.

"Ladies," came the husky voice of Corey. He walked towards the group, and every hair on Piper's body stood on end. Venus immediately stood, indicating to the girls it was time to leave. Where the hell did he come from? Had he been there all along? Corey always appeared just like a ghost.

"Alright, girls."

Everyone except Piper mumbled a quick hello; Corey raised an eyebrow at them. Giselle walked straight into his arms and kissed him directly on the lips. Corey pulled her in and extended the embrace. "You ok, babe?" she questioned sexily.

"Yeah, I'm good. You going to buy me a shirt when you go on your shopping spree?"

"If you behave yourself."

Corey grinned, and with a show for the girls, he handed Giselle a large sum of money. "Here, get yourself something extra. Make sure you don't look like these bunch of target hoes."

Jazz was furious. *Did Giselle just giggle*? she thought to herself.

"I warned you before, Corey, stop referring to us like that."

"I wasn't talking to you."

"Don't talk to any of us like that."

Corey knew he couldn't mess with Jazz. "So, how are your geeky friends?" He changed the subject. "They coming to the party next week?"

"Why do you care"? Venus interrupted whilst heading for the door.

"I'm just interested, bet they don't know how to

party, they too busy sitting in posh offices making calls to the taxman, drinking champagne."

Piper giggled at his comment. "Why, you jealous, Corey? Not everyone makes a living out of crime." Corey crunched hard on his cocktail stick as Jazz finished the emotional battering.

"Maybe you should try buying your girl a bottle of champagne and teach a few life lessons. Maybe one of those geeks can show your girl how a lady is supposed to behave, better still what she is truly worth."

Corey had no come back for Jazz; he knew better than to fight with her. It wasn't because of her dad's position in life. That was just a bonus. Jazz really wasn't scared of him.

"Oh, thanks, Jazz. Nice one. What does that say for me?"

"Just shut up, GG. You're such a traitor when you're with that stupid excuse for a man." Piper was irritated

"Oooh, Pip," Corey stepped in. "You don't think I'm man enough for you?"

"I wouldn't spit on you if you were on fire. You make me sick."

Jazz pulled Piper by the arm and led her out the door.

"It's time, ladies." With that, the girls walked back to the car where Rasi sat waiting.

Rasi's car was a top-of-the-range metallic blue Range Rover. His chair was reclined to a forty-degree angle. The bass pumping from his car was smooth and clear as it bounced the sound into the air.

He was playing if I gave my heart to you, by John Mclean.

A firm tapping on the darkened windows as Rasi turned to find Piper grinning at him with her face pressed up against the glass. He admired her stupidity for a few seconds. Even in her playful moments, she was still as sexy as hell.

He thought about how he'd love to suck those tantalising lips to sudden death. Slowly he unlocked the doors to let the girls in.

"Well, was everything ok, ladies?"

There was a pause from the girls before Piper spoke.

"Yeah, she's good, just letting her stupid boyfriend control her, nothing to write home about, business as usual."

Venus had the urge to peek behind her before they drove off. Sure enough, she had just witnessed Ryan hiding around the corner, waiting for them to pull off. They held eye contact for a few seconds before readjusting herself.

Sighing heavily, she mumbled, "Yeah, business as usual."

CHAPTER 17

A BLIZZARD AT STORM AT MY 21ST PARTY

Now, if there is a party to be celebrated, I must say that I am the champion of all champions, well, alongside Piper anyway. We both knew how to host a good party, and our friends had no issue letting us loose on their events. It so happened to be my birthday, not just any old birthday, but my 21st birthday, and I had all my special friends to do it with.

I had just finished devouring my red pepper burger in a bun and laughing loud and wide with crunched-up food in my mouth. The doorbell rang, and Jazz beat me to it. Venus stood at the door looking as gorgeous as ever, my last friend to complete the pack. Jazz threw her arms around her and welcomed her in.

Upon her arrival, she seemed a bit uncomfortable. She gave us a look as if we had left her out. Truth is, we hadn't, she had only just started a new Saturday job a couple of weeks ago to help pay her way through college, and she couldn't take time off as there was no one to cover her.

It wouldn't have made sense for all of us to not be here to set up for my birthday anyway.

I had managed to wangle the time off, and Piper was good friends with the boss, so he said she and Jazz would be free if someone could cover her. We worked every other Saturday and one day of the week. I thought we were a great team, the boss loved us, and I loved my job. The money was great, and two days a week earned us plenty. We had only just convinced Venus to join, and she couldn't afford to take time off. Her mum had gone all weird on her and stopped paying for all her needs.

"Aww, hey, babe. You look great. You trying to outdo the birthday girl?" I jokingly asked her. She grinned sarcastically, and I was a bit confused.

"No one could ever outdo you, Princess. You look gorgeous."

I gave an overenthusiastic, "Thank you," and hugged her.

"How was work today? What did you think? Will you go back?"

"Would have been nice to have some friends for back up, but I guess today is way too important, but yes, it was different."

"Don't worry," I told her with a warmth in my voice, "it's quite safe there, and next time, we will all be in together."

"Yeah, I know, that will be great. I can't wait to see you in action." She answered me with another sarcastic tone. I didn't want to deal with her attitude today, it was my birthday, and I wasn't letting anyone spoil it.

"Right, come on then. I'll help you get dressed," Venus suggested.

I glanced over at Piper, who had already offered long before Venus arrived. Piper gave a sideways nod of her head to indicate it was ok.

I slipped out of my loungers that I played around in after my shower. Venus already had my dress in her hands and was ready to help me slip into it. I placed my hands onto her shoulders whilst I stepped my feet into the white gap, and Venus pulled the dress up over my muscled legs, my bottle-shaped hips, and my God-sent perky breasts. I watched her as she slowed in that area. Her head was down as Venus slowly glided the dress over me. Finally, she stood before me, face to face, as she pulled it up over my shoulders. We stood for a few seconds without a word, then slowly, she dropped her hands down over my breast, rubbing her thumbs over my nipples whilst moving closer to my mouth. My breathing was heavy and pulsating.

"Venus, what are you doing."

"Anything you want me to do. Happy birthday."

"You need to stop," I commanded.

"I thought you wanted me. I've seen you with that girl at the strip club, and you don't usually say no to me."

"Venus," my voice was firm, "I don't know what you thought you saw, but this isn't it, now stop, and this will never be spoken about again."

"Ok," she responded slyly.

I lowered my voice, just audible enough for her to hear.

"I'm not your mum V."

"What?"

"I know about you and your mum. Marlon showed me the pictures. Don't worry, I haven't told the others. But I'm not her. It's abuse V. You need to speak to someone."

"What photos? What are you talking about?"

"V, Marlon saw you. He watched you through the bedroom window at your mum's house a while back. He saw you and your mum, you know, doing things you don't do with your mum. Marlon photographed you with her. So, I get why you think it's ok to come on to me, but I'm not like you." I starred at Venus as she held back the tears

Venus continued to move behind me and pulled the zip up on my dress, deliberately catching my skin in the zipper. I winced as she whispered in my ear, "Bitch, you dare say a word, and I will slit your throat." My heart raced as I saw Piper, Jazz, and Giselle stood in the doorway. "You look like a real princess," Piper exclaimed whilst eyeing Venus with a quizzical glare. Venus dropped her head in embarrassment.

"She needs a plaster. She's bleeding," Venus replied coldly before walking away.

I held back the tears from the threat I had received. I had never heard; Venus talks like that before.

So, we were all dressed and ready for the ball. The DJ had arrived the party was in full flow.

My parents had stayed a while before they disappeared off to my Auntie's house to spend the night. They warned us to behave but have fun. My younger brother was begging to stay, but my dad wouldn't let him thank goodness. My older sister promised she would stay and keep an eye on us, but I knew once my parents left, she had other plans. After all, why does a twenty-five-year-old want to hang with a bunch of rowdy twenty-one-year-olds? My sister kissed me goodnight and promised she would be back in the morning before mum and dad returned.

It was 10.30pm, and people were still arriving. I told my parents it was only 30 people. I lied. It was more like seventy. Our house was huge, so it's not like we would be squashed. As children, we played hide and seek lots and still found it hard to seek each other out.

I was feeling overwhelmed and truly blessed. My

house was decorated like a palace, and I felt on top of the world.

Someone shouted, "Where's the brandy?" Somehow, Marlon hadn't bought enough brandy. I couldn't find him in the house, so Rasi and his friends offered to go out and get some more. My uncle owned an off licence down the road from our house. He would always have secret opening hours for his regulars, especially on a Friday and Saturday night. Tonight, he knew his favourite niece was hosting her grand event.

Giselle was upset with us. We hadn't prayed; she went on and on, but there just wasn't any time. Everyone had a role in upholding, and everyone was busy doing it.

We would be all right for one night. God had us whichever way. We were pretty sure one night without prayer would be fine. What was going to go wrong?

At around 2am Piper asked for spare towels to put into the bathroom, I told her where to find them, and she disappeared upstairs

The house was busy, bustling people, moving in and out of each other's space. I passed Jazz in the hallway.

"You ok baby, you enjoying yourself," she questioned me in a hurry.

"Oooh yes," I replied excitedly, "the DJ's going to play our song in a moment, so make sure you're all downstairs."

"Will do baby, where's Pip?"

"Upstairs sorting towels for the bathroom"

"Where's your boyfriend and his gang?"

I sighed loudly at her question.

"Ok, ok, I know I don't like them, but he's done well this evening. He's paid for everything, and if your happy, I'm happy to."

"Thank you, babe. They're in the front room with the DJ."

"Your cake has just arrived."

The lady who baked the cake looked so familiar, but I couldn't decide where I knew her from. I think she was an old friend of my mum and dad, perhaps I had seen her when I was younger.

The DJ announced our favourite song. **UP TOWN TOP RANKING** everyone pounced onto the dance floor to begin our ritual skank routine.

Marlon and his friends had disappeared, probably outside smoking. He knew this was my favourite song and I loved dancing with him. I'm sure he could hear it. Anyway, it didn't matter. I had my four favourite friends with me. We had formed a massive crowd as we sang at the chorus. We laughed hard, holding hands, and screaming the words, unaware that one of us was missing. Unaware of what was taking place.

I climbed to the top of my stairs and greeted Venus

with a cat that got the cream expression.

"Hey, girl, what you up to" I slurred. But I do remember Venus ran to the start of the stairs to greet me, "just used your bathroom, running back down for more tracks. The DJ is so cool."

"Isn't he just? Have you seen Pip?" I questioned.

"Er, yes, she just went back down."

"Girl, I think I drank too much; I didn't even see her."

"Come on, let's go find her, ooh my tune." Venus became excited.

We hurried back downstairs and joined in with the dancing.

I never returned upstairs until Rasi returned and questioned Piper's whereabouts.

That's when I realised we hadn't seen her downstairs. I hadn't seen her at all. We had let her down.

CHAPTER 18

JAZZ, STORM'S 21ST PARTY- JAZZ

I'm such a lightweight, two drinks, and I was anybody's. Well, not literally, but I could have been.

I was left to decorate the front room as I was so fussy about what went where and how.

I liked things to look inviting, attractive, and classy. Storm's parents had already warned me about cello tape on their floral wallpaper, so I used string to hang most decorations wherever I could. I stepped back, admiring my handiwork. I would love this if it was mine, so I knew miss fussy-pots would love it too.

Piper stepped up behind me and placed her hands on my shoulders. "It's beautiful. Well done, she's going to love it."

If Piper said it looked good, then it was amazing.

"Thank you, that means a lot."

"Tonight's going to be great," she whispered.

I knew it was going to be great. We always had fun.

I followed Piper and Giselle up the stairs to see Storm in her dress. The image at the door stopped us in our tracks. Venus appearing as though she was ready

313

to lunge in at Storm and kiss her. Although Storm rejected her, she seemed as though she may be enjoying the moment. Did I hear Storm say that Venus' mum was abusing her and Marlon had taken pictures? Piper walked in and broke up the party. I shook my head and swiftly escaped into the spare room to change.

I believe the first person or couple may have arrived around 8.30pm. I remember greeting someone at the door and offering drinks and food. I thought the DJ was playing a bit loud. I asked him to turn it down a little bit, but he just kept saying he couldn't hear me. He laughed and then turned it up. I thought we might get a visit from the police and then be shut down.

I ventured from room to room, making sure everyone was behaving themselves and that no one was sneaking upstairs, only to the toilet. I passed the girls a few times in the hallway. We were all busy doing our jobs. Piper had been in the kitchen serving food before Giselle swapped with her. It was evident we were the hosts of this party, and Storm was the princess.

Venus appeared unusual, as if she was waiting for something to happen, but she always developed some strange attributes when we were out, so I ignored her behaviour. Tonight was about Storm. She would have the best night, just like she had done for us.

I knew most of the people at the party. But I think

to some of them, I was just known as Shakespeare's daughter. That's what they called my dad on the streets. Even though he was serving some valuable time, the mere mention of his name had people stepping back when they saw me. It was always hard to make true friends because people only hung out with me because they were scared.

When my mum passed, they let my dad out on day release to attend the funeral. I couldn't even look at him. I was so angry at him for making me an orphan. He smiled at me curiously. He managed to tell me that I had protection whenever I needed it. I just had to say the word. Was that all he could say after not seeing me for five years? I had visited once or twice with River, but it was too upsetting for us. He always looked at River with a weird kind of pity in his eyes. He made me promise, no matter what, I would always look after her. He also told me I should stop allowing her to call me mum. River was six now; it was too late for that. I had even taken on the mum role. I was her mum, so why was everyone so intent on me not telling her the truth?

Damn, I didn't realise Storm had invited so many people. All the girls were wearing weaves and started with cement makeup. That's what we called it when the makeup is thick.

Every girl in there was showing some part of their

cleavage or baseline of their bum. You could tell the religious, church-going clan from the ones who just went for the babysitting service and to keep them away from the wide-eyed uncles who visited on a Sunday morning after church to eye up their favourite niece. We all had one of those lurking in the background.

"Hey Pip," someone shouted, and I turn to see who is calling my friend by her abbreviated name. Oh damn, it's one of Marlon's hussies. I watched Piper sprint in her direction. I follow swiftly behind as the girl returned Piper's aggressive speed through the crowd. I knew I needed to get to Piper quickly to stop her from being a real menace.

I didn't even see Piper reach her destination, but I did see her hand around the girl's throat. I also watched Marlon circle the two cats, trying to adjust his concern for his whore. Marlon reached for Piper's arm and yanked her away from the girl who had turned a shade of dark red. Piper was not impressed and swung for his face with her free arm, catching him in the eye. Marlon let out a screech and covered his eyes. He attempted to swing back at Piper, but I swiftly stepped in. He lowered his hand and warned Piper she was going to pay for that. I turned to the girl and ordered her to leave.

That was just drama number one.

Drama number two was a white boy spiking drinks

with cocaine, two girls foaming at the mouth, and being rushed to hospital. I don't believe Rasi had ever been to a party like this before. His parties were very controlled and orderly; everyone sat in rows with glasses of champagne, pinkie finger lifted, laughing at ordinary jokes for ordinary people.

I was supposed to be the observant one, always paid attention to detail, but alcohol adds to the fact and makes you hallucinate and imagine events that didn't really occur.

You see, if you asked me where Piper was, after drama number one, I would have told you, she was right there singing, Uptown Top Ranking, with the microphone in her hand, in her two-piece pink outfit. Piper always occupied the microphone. She had a beautiful voice; we always begged her to sing.

Then, I saw Giselle standing in the doorway. The light had turned her body into a silhouette and drawn a frame right around her curvy shape.

It wasn't until I saw her standing there, looking frantic, that I realised something was wrong. I shook my head and tried to sober my vision real fast as I made my way over to her. By this time, I could see her tear-stained face. She could hardly breathe; she was holding the sides of the door for dear life.

Storm dived under her arms and ran three at a time up the stairs. I pushed Giselle to one side. My legs were shaking, buckling underneath me. As I climbed the stairs, I could see Storm crouching on the floor outside her bedroom door, fighting with herself to not projectile vomit.

That's when I realised I hadn't seen Piper at all.

CHAPTER 19

GISELLE, STORM'S 21ˢᵀ PARTY

I didn't come from a god-fearing house, if I was frank, I don't think my mum believed in God, or instead, she thought God didn't believe in her.

My mum was desperate to escape my violent dad and, in doing so, had committed an unforgivable crime, one she felt she was not worthy of being forgiven.

So, she just drifted through life believing that every malfunction was a punishment and deserved what she had coming to her. On the other hand, I wanted to save her, so I prayed for her every day. It must have been working because God hadn't taken her yet. I joined the church when I was 15 with this white girl who convinced me to come along with her and her mum. She had hounded me for weeks to attend. Eventually, I agreed.

After the second visit, I decided it just wasn't for me, you see, I'd been to Sunday school as a child, and it never felt like a funeral every day. These people were quietly praying. They were spaced out, hiding the gaps. I can sing a clear tune, but I didn't recognise any of the songs, and it made me sound as if I was tone-deaf. It was cold.

I felt terrible because I was supposed to be serving God. Instead, all I could see was the priest's mouth moving. I had long switched off before the sermon had even got into its flow.

Catherine was her name. "Will you come again, G?" She smiled at me. G? Did she just call me G?

"Erm, I have to see what my aunty says, we have family coming over, and I need to help cook." So, I signed myself with the cross for lying straight out of the church.

"Oh, do come again. I really love your company. Maybe you could come over to mine one Sunday, stay for dinner. I could comb your hair. It's so curly."

Did she just run her hand through my hair? Before I could respond, I watched her wipe her now greasy hand across the bum of her dress. As she ran to catch up with her mum, she shouted, "See you soon, GG."

Something fell from her pocket. I quickly manoeuvred to pick it up and stood flabbergasted while I held the small cling filmed pouch of weed in my hand. Not who she said she was. I shook my head, pelted the package into my handbag, turned, and walked away.

So, guess what? We never met up again, not because of the weed, but because I know God didn't make church a place for me to fall asleep. I did go to church, just not that one. That is where I learnt to pray, it became warming and comforting, and I had my friends with me. I enjoyed the response I would get from people when I prayed, especially the elders. I believed in this church. I got asked to take on Sunday school and teach the little kids. I never forgot my cousin, Georgina, who didn't make it out of the house fire. She was with us the night the fire began. We thought she was behind us as we came downstairs. Mum had gone back in to save her, but Georgina had been engulfed in flames. They were too much for my mum to take on.

When she realised dad had survived the fire, we had to leave. My aunt was blind, she was missing her daughter, and it broke my mum's heart to see her like this. After that, she was never the same. We escaped to America with the help of some family. Often my aunty would hold my face and cry uncontrollably, sometimes she called me Georgina. Mum would remind her Georgina was dead, but my aunty insisted I sounded so much like her. I guess when you miss someone immensely, you begin to imagine that anyone sounds like them. When we were alone, I would share a song with my aunty that she had made up. I didn't really know how I knew the words, but the music and the warmth of my auntie's voice were so familiar. There wasn't a funeral for any of us, as there were no bodies to bury. Instead, our family over here in England held a massive memorial service. My grandmother was the only one who knew we existed. Once I grew older, and my features changed, my grandmother insisted I come over to live with her, so she could accompany my musical gift.

I began praying for myself and my friends every time we went out and returned. Then we met Rasi and his friends. He eventually revealed that he often took the sermon on a Sunday in his own church. I enjoyed the fact that he prayed with us, usually for us. Sometimes he would giggle after he said, "Dear Lord, bless Piper and her friends and lead them in the right direction towards righteousness."

After a while, it became the norm for me to pray for us. Did you hear that? It was normal. So why in hell, on the day of Storm's birthday, did we decide it was no longer necessary?

I warned them that if anything terrible happened tonight, it would be because we didn't pray.

Oh, dear God, why didn't we listen? Why didn't I insist?

I partied hard that night, everything was going so well, and then the devil decided to dance with us. We had turned our backs on God, and the devil stepped in.

Looking back, Piper had disappeared for a while, strange that each of us could vouch for where we thought we had seen her, in the kitchen, upstairs, going down the stairs, outside talking to Rasi.

Where had I seen her? I saw her in the hallway. The truth was, none of us had seen her since she went upstairs. We told ourselves we had because we didn't want to appear irresponsible, appear as if we were immature.

We had all seen Venus at different times standing at the top of the stairs, but she had managed to distract each one of us.

I was at the bottom of the stairs when I heard the baritone howl. It shook through me like shattered glass, a cry from the mountains and then a faint crying. At first, I couldn't move. I prayed to God to give me the strength to reach the top of the stairs.

At first, I thought Rasi was just over exaggerating when he asked us where Sweets was? And suddenly, we didn't really know, so when he bolted up the stairs like a lion protecting his pride, I realised we hadn't seen her, and something could be wrong, that instinct within him, that cold stare he gave us when we appeared clueless.

We all felt he was overreacting. The others didn't bother to move, just carried on dancing. I followed him to the bottom of the stairs because I wanted to see his sheepish grin when he realised he'd been an ass. I wanted to hear her curse him out and tell him to stop acting like a plum; she was fine. But she wasn't okay.

Her body lay limp on the bed covered in blood, wrapped in Rasi's arms as he sobbed uncontrollably, rocking her back and forth.

"Oh, dear God, no. Please, no."

I stumbled down the stairs to find the others. I stood in the doorway of the front room, unable to hold myself up. Jazz was the first to spot me, then Storm flew under my arm, and Jazz pushed me to one side. No words were spoken.

More cries echoed throughout the house. It all happened so quickly; by the time I got up from off my knees, Storm had gotten everyone out of the house. All that was left were cups and plates, some butt ends, the smell of alcohol, weed, and food stains on the carpet. Even the DJ was taking out the last box.

I turned to go back upstairs and join my friends.

We were huddled around piper on the blood-stained bed. Rasi gripped her so tightly as if he could squeeze the pain away.

We sat there sobbing in the faint light until I said, "Ambulance, we need an ambulance."

There was a firm "No." It came from Pip.

"You need to go to the hospital, Pip." Jazz looked at her with pleading eyes, but Piper had no feelings in her eyes. They were glassy, icy, stoned.

We had let her down. Alcohol spoke for us that evening. Why would someone do this to her? We didn't lie about her whereabouts to hide our shame and guilt. We lied because that's what we believed.

CHAPTER 20

VENUS STORM'S 21ST PARTY

I wasn't really feeling Storm's 21st birthday party. Every year was such a big fuss, she was such a spoilt brat, and I'm sure she felt privileged because of her light complexion.

I never really seemed to feel that much energy from them when it was my birthday. But I didn't really have any other friends, so I hung on to this lot because Giselle was a shade or two, maybe three shades lighter than me, but she wasn't as pale as the rest of them, and I suppose Jazz was a bit darker but not as dark as Giselle. So, I guess I kind of blended in somewhere. Anyway, no one else wanted me.

Piper and Storm possessed the diamond that attracted men, with their curviness and naturally blond streaky hair.

Storm was always a bit abrupt in her attitude and made cruel comments about me. Well, at least it felt like that anyway.

I didn't want to leave the group, there were some good things about it, like River she was so cute, and she was the only child that called me aunty. I loved her. I disagreed that she called Jazz her mum, I thought it was unfair, but River was bright. I told her one day she should stop, she replied it was up to her sister, not me.

I had followed these guys around for so long it was not worth the breakup. I even allowed them to let me in on some dark secret and lose my educational rights. My mum whipped me with a leather strap, then made out with me to apologise. At the time, I enjoyed it. Other times, I wanted it to stop, but she always talked me around. By the time I was twenty, she had disappeared, no note, no goodbye, nothing. In a way, I was relieved, even though I missed her. One thing the girls were right about was that it was wrong. On the other hand, my mum was right. I was just too dark to be loved.

I liked Piper. She was always nice to me, always went out of her way to check in on me, and ensured that I was fully included in everything. Lately, she wasn't really that friendly and seemed to be practising avoidance with me. I guess it was because I kissed her lips like they all did with one another. Not all the time, but just when they are going through stuff. Well, Piper was upset about something. She wasn't crying, she never cried, but she was upset. So, I cupped her face in my hands like they do to each other, and I planted a firm kiss on her lips, you know, to let her know it was ok. Since then, she hadn't really spoken to me appropriately.

Ok, I may have lingered there a bit too long, and she may have struggled a bit to push me off. I might have subconsciously whispered in her ear that I was wet for her.

Her reaction was gruelling. She was somewhat mortified. I did apologise. Maybe it's because everyone was watching. Rasi wasn't impressed either. He just shook his head at me, pulled Piper to one side, and said he was taking her home.

I tried my best to dress the same, perform the sassiness and behave like them. But I wasn't like them. You see, I didn't even like men. So, when I say l liked Piper, I, well, I really like her, like how friends shouldn't like their friends. I guess she didn't feel the same. I was embarrassed by her reaction. I just wanted her to see what it felt like to be hurt. So, when Marlon asked me to set it up to just scare her, I didn't think he was going to take it so far. I didn't know he would end up murdered.

My outfit for the party was a crushed velvet dark blue dress that I nearly had to paint on; it was so tight. I put my hair in an updo, and I was ready to go, not before taking out a gift from my cupboard that someone had already given me last year, a soap set with a tea candle. I wrapped it up and signed the tag on it,

"To Storm, my lovely friend, I love you so much, lots of love, Venus." I know everyone had gone all out, but I didn't really feel that she deserved my money. Even if I was sleeping with her man.

I shoved it into my handbag and made my way out the door.

When I arrived at Storm's house, it was quite clear they had all arranged to meet there and get dressed and help set up. In fact, they had been there all day. They even had breakfast. Before my pathetic attempt to bed Piper, she usually would have called me, kept me informed, but I'd seriously messed up. This bitch really needed to get over herself. It was just a kiss. She had plenty of them already from the number of men she'd been with. Knowing full well how Rasi felt about her, she should be ashamed of herself. I would have bedded him myself, but he only had eyes for Piper.

The week before the party, I'd caught Piper talking about me and the kissing incident, saying that she didn't know what came over me and she couldn't look at me the same again. I heard Storm laugh and giggle that I needed a good man. Piper had responded by saying or maybe two and that I'd made her feel sick. Jazz thought I was just confused, but I heard them laughing at me, and it made me mad.

I wanted to speak to someone about my own feelings, but I was just one big joke to them. Well, I was about to have the last laugh.

I arrived at the house. They were already drinking and having fun without me. I tried not to appear jealous and joined in, but Storm gave me her skanky arse looking down on my stare, or that's how it felt. Why was I even here stressing myself, anyway? I'd see it through to the end, as much I complained about them, I did like their company.

The party was in full swing. I really didn't mean to hurt anyone; I was just angry and a bit scared. Marlon knew my secret. He said he would tell everyone if I didn't help him out, and he had pictures of me. So, I went along with his offer. I didn't realise what he was talking about. I thought he meant to keep a lookout, like when Storm had sex with Ryan whilst they watched, for money. I didn't know what he was going to do.

I was the first upstairs, just after Piper went up to put clean towels in the bathroom. Like I said, I liked Piper. I signalled to Marlon to go in, but he had four others with him. Corey was one of them. I tried to stop them, but Marlon reminded me of the video he had. So, I backed down.

So, I did as I had promised, and I naively became their lookout.

Marlon had deliberately forgotten to get enough brandy, knowing full well he would ask Storm to ask

Rasi to get some more. Then, once he was out of the way, they would have a word with her. Rasi never let Piper out of his sights, ever, so this was the only way.

I lied to the girls that I had not seen Piper, but they lied too. They said they had seen her, and they hadn't. I was fed up with Giselle and her fake praying. I didn't even believe in God. I had an image of the Devil tattooed on my belly. I felt comfort from that. I know I sound confused.

I felt sorry for Piper; indeed, I did, but I hope she realised this reflected her behaviour. I sat at home that night and burnt orange incense sticks. I prayed for each one of them as I placed my hands against my stomach and bowed my head to the image on my wall. Followed by the chant, "HUM RENGAY SHINGA HUM".

CHAPTER 21

RASI STORM'S 21ST PARTY-

Exhilaration wasn't the word I would utilize to describe how I was feeling

I was besotted with Piper, everything about her, the way she smelled, her sultry delicately comely round ass in her jeans, the way she commanded a room. Piper was mesmerising, and she knew it, but for some reason, she always had me hanging on, and I would always follow along like some lost puppy.

I knew, deep down, she was in love with me, but she was an adolescent. She needed space to grow and find herself. So yes, I knew she slept around. I turned a blind eye, as she hadn't authentically concurred to be my personal girlfriend. Yet, I was the one she would always call when she needed to verbalize or needed anything. Except for money, she would never take a penny from me.

She would always offer to pay if she invited me out. I never let her. I'm an archaic type of guy. We would go to the movies, to her family home have lots of one-on-one time together, yet she would never plenarily commit, and it was driving me crazy.

Piper and her friends had even worked a divest bar for a few months, on a Saturday followed by one day in the week. But I quickly put a stop to that. I never understood why they felt they had to work like this; I agree like they verbally expressed it was expeditious money.

I pulled on my white shirt and dark blue jeans, my upbringing betokened that I should always be well dressed where ever I presented, but well dressed for these puerile girls could designate me an old man. I needed Piper to want me. Tonight, I would not sanction her to flirt in front of my eyes or slip away with some man. Tonight, she was mine. It was time I stepped in and showed her I was no longer her game.

I arrived at the party with Ryan, Blue, and Pier. Unfortunately, we got to the house just as the girls were establishing the stacks of drinks.

Ryan had vanished as customary, but I mentally conceived I knew he was up to no good with Marlon and Corey.

I didn't care what he was doing so long as the girls were not in any peril.

Storm came bouncing in like a wild puppy ready to play.

"Heeeeey," she teased.

I bowed to her and held my arm out. "Madame,

your carriage awaits."

She took hold of my arm, hitched her dress just above the knee, and replied, "Why sir, thank you."

We played around singing *I'll Do Anything For You* from Oliver twist's play, making up our own version.

"*I'll do anything, for you dear anything, for you mean everything to me.*"

"*Would you wipe my nose?*" Storm giggled.

"*Anything.*"

"*Wash in between my toes?*"

"*Anything.*"

"*Kiss away my tears?*"

"*Anything.*"

"*Tell me the colour of Piper's underwear?*"

"*You can think again.*"

I enjoyed that evening with the girls. Piper stood watching, canvassing us in her sultry pink two-piece. She relished the relationship I maintained with the girls. I relished all their company. I adored Storm when she was in this mood and not attempting to bed everyone's boyfriend. As she had made her suggestions with me, I gently declined in order not to make a sizably voluminous fuss. Storm knew she had overstepped the mark with me once too often. She never tried it again after my cordial word, but we could still have a laugh and be solitary together. She knew where she stood, and it wasn't with me.

Jazz was always in control and enjoyed giving dictations. If she wasn't in charge, it wasn't transpiring. I liked her when she was stern, but I could be too.

I loved her daughter River. She was exceptionally delicately comely and very sapient for her adolescent age.

Giselle pretended to be a pussy feline, no chance. Give her an option, the time, and she would let you know what was what. I got on with all of them genuinely well. They were like my little sisters. I had grown very fond of them all, and I doted their company. Venus, on the other hand, I never authentically trusted her. Something just didn't rest right. I was never sure what it was, but I suspected she was up to no good. I just wish I had realised sooner what she was up to.

It was 1.55am when Storm realised they were out of brandy. I offered to go to the shops to buy more. Storm explained where her uncle's off-licence was. I don't believe I was gone that long, maybe twenty minutes, ok, 30 minutes, but I had to drive around as it wasn't facile to find. I had never authentically been to an off-licence before. My drinks were always brought into the house, albeit I didn't drink anyway.

The twins came with me, and I must verbally express that we struggled to find good quality drinks. Storm's uncle, who we had met a few times but never been to his shop, had managed to convince us that what he had on his shelves was good quality brandy. In my head, I didn't concur. But we went with it nonetheless.

We had supplied a range of wines, but these young girls did not enjoy wine, and genuinely, I should have known that. But it was a 21st, and I wanted to ascertain they had the best.

We chose a range of spirits and returned to the house, blissful and elated. The twins were teasing me about Piper and the length of time it took to become her boyfriend.

We went in straight past the living room and into the kitchen to unload the drinks. The twins decided to stay in the kitchen and handle the bar.

As I approached the front room, I could spot the girls laughing, dancing, joking around.

I scanned the room for Piper, but she wasn't there. I glanced back into the kitchen before I headed into the living room to be greeted by the tipsy bundle of girls, who automatically roped me into a dance. I moved with them for a few seconds before I shouted to Jazz above the music.

"Where are Sweets?"

"She was here a minute ago; I think she went to the toilet."

I questioned Storm, "Have you seen sweets?"

336

"Oh, don't worry about her. She just popped in to get a drink. Dance with us. She'll be back in a bit, Mr lover-lover." They all laughed.

I waited a few minutes, but something wasn't resting right with me. I turned to Giselle. "When was the last time you saw Sweets?"

"Erm, to be honest, come to think of it, I don't think I've seen her since you went to the shops. But I have seen her around, I think."

That was when I realised they hadn't stuck to their pact of searching for one another if they were missing for more than three minutes. So, what happened to the three-minute rule? Alcohol and music took precedence.

I swing out of the room real fast with Giselle on my heels. I took the stairs three at a time, panic racing through me. What if she wasn't well and had collapsed?

I knew I could panic fast when it came to Piper, but my gut instinct alarmed me intensely.

The door to Storm's bedroom was ajar, and the light sparkled out the bottom. As I stood in front of it, an overwhelming feeling began to ride my nerves. Finally, I grabbed the gold doorknob and pushed it open.

The sight in front of me was unnerving, uninviting, and wild.

My feet barely carried me to the blood-drenched bed, where her bottom half of clothing is missing. With an animalistic cry, I ripped the jacket from my back and covered her. Then, I grabbed at the sheets already on the bed to wrap around her.

Her eyes were lifeless, but she was breathing. There were no punctures, which indicated she had not been hurt by a sharp object.

"Sweets, Sweets," I cried, "tell me what happened. 'I'm calling an ambulance." I reached for my phone as her weary-sounding voice stopped me.

"No," was the whisper. "Please don't, I beg you."

I checked her over, then held her in my arms, tightly rocking her body.

"Who did this?"

Her return was, "I don't know."

Suddenly the other girls were standing at the door screaming and wailing. How could they have been so careless? How could they have left her? How could they have been so foolish?

I ordered them to leave, but Piper was stern with her objection to my request. We lay there in dull moments deciding what to do. Piper had control. Ambulance or police were not what she wants. The bleeding was a worry and needed to be checked.

I picked her up and carried her into the shower. I removed my t-shirt and trousers, and I climbed in with her to wash her down. I knew I was washing away the evidence, but it is what she requested.

Shortly after, I took her and the girls to my house, except Storm and Venus. They needed to stay at home to clear away the evidence. It was the longest drive to Knightsbridge I had ever encountered. We met the doctor at my house, who stood eagerly waiting to check her over. A very discreet family doctor. Once he was done, I observed the three friends as they slept huddle around Piper on my bed.

CHAPTER 22

FALLEN EMPIRE, PIPER, STORMS 21ST PARTY

This is my version of events, a chapter I don't wish to tell, but I will. It's also the longest chapter in this chapter of my life.

There was only one way to deal with this. Would I run or stay? My view was supposed to be one of beauty. But all I felt now was fear. As I stand at the edge of the bridge, teasing my toes over the side, there was always something about heights that disturbed me. Now I could feel the power of its uneasiness. I spread my arms as I reluctantly move a little closer; the breeze is tap dancing around me. I push against its force to not throw me over. Then, finally, I'm in control; I will decide when it's time to let go.

I gate-crashed into my parents' dysfunctional lives on earth early one morning. I was supposed to be their soother, entangle them together to maintain rich love. What a joke. They were never available to even be together.

Have you ever thought that maybe you came down the wrong pathway during birth?

Like when you're gushing down a water tube at a theme park, the adrenaline is so immense you slip and slide around and almost catapult over the side.

Then you slowly drown in the intense pressure of the waves hugging you, squeezing you, making you pass out into this bright light. You wonder if, during the underwater transition, something played a joke on you and swished you in through another gate, but it's too late you've already ended up in the wrong hands.

This chapter is my dark chapter, the night our empire fell apart.

Have you ever heard it said that unconscious fear-related memories can remain totally hidden from your conscious mind? Yet, those memories still could dramatically affect everyday behaviour and emotions?

You see, everyone has a Black Sea gushing through their heads. It's that dark place where you empty rubbish, and it swims around for years until the barriers break, and the contamination from the thick fluid begins to leak into your body and soul.

My uncle taught me that you will drown in your own head if you don't find a way to swim. That's where I learnt the valuable skill of blacking out.

Have you ever buried a lousy memory so deep that the constant banging to let it out just becomes a part of your pain? I have.

I'm going to tell you a secret.

I hope you are stable and sitting comfortably. As I find this chapter quite tricky but essential to write. I will be quick, I promise not to go into too much detail for my sake and yours, but you will have to read between the lines. If you choose to be judgmental after the events you have read about me, close this book, and burn it now.

Are you sitting comfortably?

You see, I knew about the events before they happened.

It was the night of Storm's 21st birthday party.

Yes, Princess Storm would be 21, the last of the bunch to reach such a pinnacle milestone.

Life can change so dramatically in an instant. So, I won't bore you with the previous arrangements like how we were excited and deciding what we should wear, decorating the house, sending invitations. But most importantly, how Storm's parents had given us free rein over the house.

We were happy. That's the bottom line. Music was flowing, as were the drinks and weed.

We had our moment together before everyone arrived as we always did. Said a prayer together, held hands, and promised we would look out for one another, as we always did. Giselle will tell you we didn't pray, but that's a lie.

It was our ritual wherever we went. We all knew the timing for disappearing. If one of us was missing longer than three minutes, we were coming in, as we always did.

But tonight was different; we made a different vow. We prayed, but we didn't need to look for each other. This we had never done before.

We were in a safe place. We were in Storm's house, and we knew it like the back of our hands. So why would we need to look for each other there?

Why would we need to check if someone didn't return in 3 minutes? We were safe, or so we thought!

How wrong were we, how destructively wrong were we? We changed our vows, and it cost us our friendship. We dared to dance with the devil, and he took us on a waltz.

Rasi found me lying quietly on the large low double bed. I hear my stance was somewhat shocking, provoking, uninviting. It screamed havoc.

Something made him instantly remove his jacket and lay it over my limp body covered in blood.

I heard his cries; they were breathless and stifling as though he was in a nightmare, unable to scream.

There were other voices, screaming, headless bodies running around. Then, finally, there was a deafening screech. At the time, I couldn't work out if it was a voice or a car screeching. I really don't know.

A door slammed a key locking. Then I was in his arms rocking, sobbing, apologising.

I felt safe, wrapped up in his arms. The only man on this earth to ever be allowed to question me about anything. I never meant to hurt him. Honestly, I didn't. But I ran away from life that night. The same night I ran away from my faith and my beliefs.

You see, I just couldn't keep my mouth shut when it came to Marlon. I hated him. I also overheard him telling his friends what he was going to do to me. And how. He warned me a few times that night to watch out. Had I taken him seriously, I would be living a happy life right now, married to Rasi.

I volunteered to go upstairs to replace more towels in the bathroom so people could dry their hands, or whatever it was that some white boys were doing in the toilet after three of them had emerged from it!

"Where did Storm find these people?" I pinned myself to the wall and turned my head to the side to let them pass as they stumbled out giggling apologetically, scraggy long curly hair, musty smelling. The only three white boys in the house enjoying a bit of blackness were pretty cool and harmless.

I hurried them along before going in after them to put clean towels in.

I then returned to Storm's room to lock her on-suite bathroom door (the only black girl I knew with an on-suite), where I had collected the towels. As I turned to leave, the five of them stood there, not the white boys, Storm's violent boyfriend, Marlon, and Giselle's evil-looking boyfriend Corey, then there was Rasi's friend, Ryan, and two others I didn't recognise.

They hated me. They always had. Because I was the mouthy one, I wouldn't let them get away with shit.

Now I was on my own, in confrontation, but my friends would come looking very soon, I prayed.

My ability to blackout was failing me, and our vow to come looking had taken a rest for the night. The last friend in the group closed the bedroom door behind him, not locking it, just shutting it with a gangster stare. I knew I was finished.

Yes, I did see them approach me. Yes, I felt my body dragged along the floor, and yes, I felt myself slammed into the hard bed. Yes, I felt the bottom half of my clothing being ripped from me, and yes, I was pinned down like a caged animal. But my ability to blackout kicked in just after the first sharp pain.

I promised you that I would not go into too much detail for my sake and yours, so I'm going to leave it there and leave the rest to your imagination.

There were no sounds of police sirens, no sounds of ambulances, no parents informed, because it was my choice. My friends respected my wishes, but life got complicated after that night, extremely dark and brutal.

Imagine you knew all night what was going to happen to you. Imagine you already knew they were coming because you heard your friend set it all up. I didn't stand a chance. I heard Venus and Giselle arrange it all. But I laughed because I just didn't believe they were capable.

Storm's boyfriend Marlon was found murdered in his home the next day, after her birthday. I promise you I didn't do it.

Yes, of course, I had a motive, but I'm not a murderer. Well, not deliberately anyway. Remember I already told you that ''I'm an opportunist? But unfortunately, this wasn't one of those times.

Do I know who done it? That's a good question. None of us knows who done it. Someone has been watching us. We were framed. However, one of us had to take the blame.

I know that one of us would serve a lengthy time for a murder we didn't commit. We could have saved each other, but for our own selfish reasons, we chose not to.

Why am I telling you this? Because it's part of my story, It's the part that tore us down.

CHAPTER 23

THE SERPENTS AND THE DOGS - PIPER

I'm not sure if I have ever sat in a police station before. I thought I was supposed to feel petrified and nervous. Instead, I felt shivery, hungry, and eager to act. Or were those nerves? The room I sat in was clinical smelling, painted all white. Why do people paint rooms white when they are trying to renew them? I could still smell the faint smell of paint, giving me a headache and irritating my throat. A window rested above my head. I stared up at it in the hope I could force it open with my mind.

This was the last place I wanted to be, stuck in a white room that smelled as though they had previously been burning incense, either to make me talk or to drown out the smell of the last victim.

"Piper Monterac." My head stood to attention to its name. "You do not have to say anything that you do not wish, but it may harm your defence if you do not mention when questioned something which you later rely on in court. Therefore, anything you do or say may be given in evidence.

"May I remind you that speaking to us is voluntary, and as such, if you wish to remain silent or answer no comment, you may do so. The recording may be used in the court of law for evidence should you plead not guilty to the offence.

"Name?" the officer demanded.

"Piper," I answer warily, unsure of the role I need to play just yet, as I didn't have a script to read or a character reference to adhere to.

"Surname?"

"Monterac."

"Age?"

"Twenty-one"

"Miss Monterac, as you are aware, a young man also presents at a party you attended two nights ago was found dead. We would like to establish how this came to be. The quicker you co-operate, the sooner you get to leave. Do I make myself clear?"

I nod to her question.

"Can I call you Piper?"

"Yes, of course." I'm courteous in my response.

"Piper, were you at the 21st birthday party of Miss Storm Underwood?"

"Yes, I was."

"What time did the party begin?" the officer

questioned.

"It was scheduled to begin at 8pm."

"What time did you arrive?"

"Around 8am." The officer eyed me suspiciously. "I was helping out, so I was there all day."

"Tell me about the party, Piper."

"It was a party fit for a princess. There were lots of people, more than Storm's parents had agreed to, lots of food, drink, and dancing."

"Was there anyone that you didn't recognise? Anyone you thought looked suspicious?" I thought about Storm's other friends and how random-looking they were. They had no connection with anyone.

"There were lots of people I knew and lots I didn't. Everyone seemed ok. Marlon had a few suspect-looking friends." I make sure Marlon's friends are already suspects and at the forefront of their minds.

"What was Marlon's mood like that night?"

"I don't really know; I didn't see much of him. Yes, he was there with his usual crowd and a couple of others I didn't recognise, lording it up. But, apart from that, I didn't take much notice of him."

"You said he was 'lording it up.' What do you mean?"

"I mean, he was doing his usual act. Acting as if he was in charge like everyone owed him something."

"I get the impression, Piper, that you were not very

fond of the deceased, Marlon?"

"I'm not going to lie; no, I didn't like his attitude."

"What time did the argument happen at the party?"

"I don't know about any argument."

"Really, Piper, you didn't see Marlon arguing with his friends? Apparently, it escalated into the garden. The neighbour called in regarding a disturbance. And you didn't hear that?"

I think back to being sprawled out across the bed, being mauled like an animal. I did hear the screaming and baritone voices after they left me half-dead. To be honest, I thought it was my friends screaming after finding me. Perhaps it wasn't.

"No, I didn't hear a thing. It was noisy. There were people everywhere."

"What time did the party end?"

"I left the party early as I wasn't feeling very well."

"Time?"

"11.07pm."

"That's very precise."

"I remember checking my watch to see if I could hold out any longer. I couldn't, so I called for a friend to take me home."

"Might that friend be one named Mr Rasi Malawi?"

"That's correct."

The officers sneaked a peek at one another. As soon as they heard his name, Rasi already prepared me they would try to bother me, but they knew better than to take it too far. I was already in the clear, but they wanted me to slip up. They had to go through the motions to have it on paper to prove they had questioned me. But they had no supporting arguments. Rasi and his dad had studied all our behaviours in preparation for our questioning. He and his dad prayed with us for two days. They knew they were coming for us. Every interrogation, we had already answered. They despised the fact I knew Rasi, but they would try anyway.

"Can I ask how you know Mr Malawi?"

"Why? Is he a suspect?"

"No, just out of interest."

"He's an acquaintance of a friend of mine."

"A boyfriend?"

"Of mine? No."

"Are you sleeping with him?"

"Why, would you like to?"

The officer instantly grew so angry she snapped the pencil in her hand into two clean pieces.

"Sorry, Officer, did I hit a nerve?"

She didn't answer, but she did retaliate. "Tell me about your family life, Piper. What was life like for you, growing up?"

Officer Collins face was immaculate, her makeup was flawless, and her hair was smooth, pulled back in a slick bun, not a strand out of place, she wore a pale pink lipstick that looked freshly done, and I couldn't make out if she was wearing false eyelashes or not.

Her features were chiselled, but she wasn't bad-looking for a white woman. On the other hand, her colleague was much younger looking than she was, with the natural beauty of youth. She looked like an over-excited puppy; she kept smiling at me every time I spoke. Perhaps she was in training.

I pictured myself as a child before answering her unnecessary question. Even though I knew It was coming.

I pictured myself yearning for my mum at my uncle's funeral. Witnessing my cousin sprawled across the floor in the middle of a seance with chicken blood draped over her, whilst some nutty spiritual healer spoke in tongues, being pinned down by the witches of Eastwick. I thought about him and his groping hands, with the stench of cornflakes on his stale breath. I thought about how I was never accepted as a child, my own father not wanting me but giving me everything I asked for. Then, being dumped in some private school, assigned to a cult of racists. I touched my arms and flinched at my own touch as I reminded myself of the scars caused by believing I was not worthy.

"Mm, I had a good childhood," I answered. "I went to a private school, I had the best of both worlds, and

I was a privileged child, both parents at home, holidays three times a year, a dog, a cat, and two fish."

"Piper, isn't your mum die?"

"Yes," I answered as if I had suddenly lost the plot. My head shook like a crazy woman.

"Didn't you attend your mum's funeral last year?"

"That was my aunty, but I referred to her as my mum."

Officer Collins turned her sheet of paper over and took a deep sigh. She glanced at the other officer sitting next to her, who looked as though she might combust and turned back to me.

"Piper, you only see one mum, right?"

"I don't see my real mum if that's what you mean. She is also dead. She died when I was two."

"Ok." Officer Collins appeared sensitive.

"What's this got to do with anything"?

"Nothing," she mumbled, "just something I read."

The officer looked as though she had just had a light bulb moment.

"What did you read?" I questioned.

"Oh, it's nothing. I was thinking of someone else." She smiled at me warmly, and a little bit confused and moved quickly on to the next question. *Crazy cow*, I thought.

"Why were you excluded from Whittingdon High?" Officer Collins' expression was serious, like a don't-mess-with-me expression.

"Because they were racist. They blamed us for everything, even when we were not involved."

"But why did they exclude you?"

"I just told you, they wanted us out, so they made up a lie."

"What was the lie, Piper?"

"One of us was pregnant by a teacher."

"Were you pregnant, Piper, by the headmistress' husband?"

I laughed out loud. "Officer Collins, you need to research properly. That girl jumped off the school building and took her own life."

"Pushed, I heard she was pushed. You had been at the school for seven months, you and your friends."

"Are you accusing us of murder?"

"Just seems Piper, that everywhere you and your friends go, trouble just seems to follow. Did you push her Piper, then bury her dead baby?"

"You are unbelievable."

"Maybe, Piper, but we are watching you, or is it, Paige? Wasn't that your real name before your uncle changed it."

I need to talk to myself and take control. I needed Paige to appear, just for a second.

But Piper took over.

"Paige was my cousin. She drowned in a river."

"Oh, how convenient, Piper. Yet another death, people just keep dying around you."

"Yes, some of us lead unfortunate lives."

"Piper—" she eyed me intently, "—I'm going to ask you a question, and I need the truth. You see, depending on how you answer, this could be a game-changer for you." Officer Collins cleared her throat. "Did something happen to you at the party, Piper? Something that would make you angry and lead you to seek revenge?"

I dug my nails into my wrist under the table and began pulling at my skin. I stared inspector Collin's dead in the eye.

"Like what?" I quizzed her.

"Like, did something happen to you? Did anyone hurt you?"

"Hurt me how?"

"Like physically."

I dug my nails in harder to my wrist. "Nothing happened to me. No one hurt me. I'm starting to wonder if you have the right person or, better yet, the right party."

"So, nothing happened to you on the night of the 15th of September at Storm's party".

"Unless I missed something, I went home early. But, like I said before, I was unwell, too much dairy, so I left with Rasi."

"Did you have a motive to murder Marlon?"

"No."

"Who did?"

"Lots of people wanted Marlon dead. Even his cat wanted him dead." The young officer giggled. Officer Collins turned to her in disgust.

"Did you want him dead?"

"Look, Officer, Marlon wanted himself dead. He often spoke about getting out of the gang life. He was stuck. Storm said she was worried about him because he spoke about suicide a lot."

"Are you sure he didn't hurt you, Piper? And you killed him by accident? Let us help you."

"Marlon didn't hurt me. I'm not sure why you think that. I wouldn't wish anyone dead, but I would look in Venus' direction if you mean did any of us kill him. Marlon had something on her. She was scared, petrified."

"Piper, Is there any reason anyone would invent or lie about Marlon hurting you?"

"Perhaps to turn the light from them. What's he supposed to have done to me?"

Again, the two officers looked puzzled, and I could feel Officer Collins coming in for the kill. I could feel her assessing my behaviour. Rasi warned me she was trained in that area. Time to get my acting head-on and forget about the pain I was still managing from two nights ago.

"Piper, we have been informed," her voice was very soft now, "that a brutal attack was witnessed at the party. We were also informed that the victim was removed by her friends. Piper, was this you?"

Her eyes are pleading with me as if she feels my pain. As if she is telling me not to let them get away with it. But I can't commit to trusting her, Rasi has warned me. They don't have a solid suspect; I could end up doing time for being a victim.

I want to burst out and cry and tell her it was me. I want her to hug me and not blame me, tell me it's going to be okay. I won't lie, Officer Collins was a brilliant actor, but I had the edge on her. I adjusted my bum on the chair, crossed my leg to release some of the excruciating pain I was still feeling. I leaned into Officer Collins with direct eye contact, just like Mrs Whittaker used to do to us. I creased my brow at her, and in my mind's eye, I placed myself on the stage, standing in the first position.

"Someone is lying to you. THAT is a bad lie to tell. Do you think, Officer, if I was brutally attacked, as you put it, I would be sitting here talking to you. Now I don't know who wants to get off the hook so desperately, but I guarantee you that I would tell you if it was me. Because I wouldn't allow the bastards to get away."

"Even if it stuck you with a motive to be the murderer, Piper?"

"Even if it would send me to hell and back, Miss Collins."

Our heads were so close now and eyes piercing, both our breaths could be heard steaming in the silence of the room.

Officer Collins was the first to withdraw.

"Ok, Piper. If you say so." She didn't take her eyes off me.

"Are my friends ok, Officer?"

"Why do you ask, Piper?"

"You just got me thinking. After I went home, did something happen to one of them?"

"Something happened to one of you Piper, we just need to find out who's not telling the truth."

Officer Collins removed a pink floral scarf from a zip-proof bag and laid it on the table in front of me.

"Is this your scarf Piper?"

"No, I've never seen that in my life." Marlon had brought it for Storm as one of her presents.

"Is it Storm's scarf?"

"How would I know."

"She liked scarves, didn't she? Didn't Marlon buy this for her birthday?"

"I'm not sure on everything he got her. Why?"

"This scarf Storm was found at the scene. It was

used to strangle Marlon. One of you is very strong."

"Oh," was all I could respond with.

"Your bag was packed. Where were you going? Were you running?"

"No, I was going to visit my uncle in Canada. It was already arranged a while back. So, I would visit him for a couple weeks in September after Storm's birthday."

Officer Collins appeared beaten; she requested a break but not before asking.

"Piper, who killed Marlon?"

I sat back in my chair, and I thought to myself, *Someone is not sticking to the plan. Who told them I was attacked? Which one of my friends sitting in the other rooms have finally cracked? Or which one is the mole.*

"I really don't know, Officer," was my final answer.

CHAPTER 24

THE FOX AND THE MOLE - JAZZ

I sat in the small cold room waiting to be questioned. The Sargent walked in with another officer, and they introduced themselves before taking a seat. I pulled my cardigan around my shoulders. The room was dark and musty smelling, the younger skinny sergeant pulled a cord above his head, the old heater blew out some burnt smelling dust followed by some heat that hovered above my head like a black cloud, before dropping sprinkles of fumes upon me, I coughed through the mist and fanned it out of my eyes.

"Can I call you Jazz?" the larger of two policemen asked.

Bloody cheeky, I thought, *it's Miss Bailey.*

"Yes, of course, that's fine."

"We will be recording this call, you do not have to say anything that you do not wish to, but it may harm your defence if you do not mention something when questioned, which you later rely on in court. Anything you do say may be given in evidence."

He spoke as if he was tired of repeating that

360

sentence. As if he had recited it a million times that day. He then turned to me to say, "Got that?"

I nodded my head. "Sorry I didn't hear you," he replied sarcastically

"Yes, I've got it."

I was made aware that all our interviews had begun simultaneously to prevent any type of conspiracy. Furthermore, Rasi had provided each of us with the best lawyer's money we could buy, should we need it.

"Full name," officer Hendon demanded.

"Jazz Bailey."

The skinny officer didn't really have much to say. The larger one, whose surname was Hendon, seemed to talk more.

"Jazz, what do you do in your spare time?"

What kind of a foolish question was that? I thought to myself.

"I skip."

Officer Hendon looked at me quizzically. "Skip?"

"Yes, in the gym, I skip in the gym." I could see he was not very tolerant and had realised quickly I was going to be a pain.

"What else do you do, apart from skipping?"

"I play the piano, read, and I enjoying cooking," I responded energetically.

He scratched his bald patch before shaking his head and mumbling something under his breath that I couldn't understand.

"We are led to believe that the death of, one, Mr Marlon Clarke was due to an argument a couple of nights before during a birthday party at his girlfriend's house. A Miss Storm Basildon. Is this correct?"

"Is what correct, sir? That the party was a couple of nights ago or that there was an argument?"

Hendon did not appear amused. "Miss Bailey, do not play with me. Was there an argument at the party?"

"No, there was not an argument."

"So, you didn't see or hear an argument."

"With whom, Officer?" he looked at me as if I was pissing him off.

"With Storm and her boyfriend."

"They never had an argument; she was with us most of the night."

"Did you witness anything between them, anything unusual?"

"No more than the usual. They were like any other boyfriend and girlfriend."

"Jazz, did Storm have any reason to want to murder her boyfriend?"

"Who doesn't want to murder their boyfriend from time to time? That doesn't mean you would actually do it."

Officer Hendon stared at me for a while before

moving to his next question.

"Did you like Marlon?"

"I guess he was ok. He wasn't really around much".

"We are led to believe that he and Storm were extremely volatile towards one another."

"Not that I know of."

"So, you never saw any bruising on your friend?"

"No, Officer."

"How well did you know your friend, Jazz?"

"Very well, we've been friends since we were eleven."

"Is that when you met at Whittingdon high, the school you lost your places at?"

"Yes." *Damn*, I thought, *he's going in deep.*

"What was the secret, Jazz, that you held that helped you lose your place?"

"No secret, someone made up a story about us."

"That one of you was pregnant by a teacher?"

"Yes."

"Are you saying it's not true?"

"Yes."

"How old is your daughter Jazz?"

"What's she got to do with anything?"

"She's not your daughter, though, is she?"

"No, she's my little sister."

"Why does she call you mum?"

"Because my mum thought it would be comforting

for her, so she didn't feel lonely."

"Don't you think it's an odd request for a dying mother to ask her 15-year-old daughter to let her little sister call her mum?"

"No, not really."

"Why wasn't this request also made for your brother?"

"I don't know, Officer, maybe because he's autistic and couldn't cope with the name change."

The officer barely made eye contact as I spoke. Instead, he took a swig of his cold coffee and sighed heavily.

"You're the child of the one they refer to like Shakespeare, correct?"

"Yes, sir," I reply. I allow a fake tear to leave my eye. Hendon hands me a tissue as we both play out our roles.

"I apologise if your father's name upsets you. But I'm just wondering if perhaps you may have adopted some of his tendencies."

"My dad was not a murderer, neither am I."

"He was a drug lord, though, wasn't he?"

"And?"

"Obviously, he still protects you from the inside. Could he have set up Marlon's exit because he hurt your friends?"

"What my father chooses to do from the inside is

no concern of mine."

"Would you tell us if he did?"

"Like I said, my dads' actions are no concern of mine, which is why he is in there, and I am out here."

"But if you needed protection, you would only have to say the word."

I stared Hendon down, enough to make him flinch. He loosened his top button as his neck turned a shade of red, followed by beads of sweat. He pulled an off-coloured hankie from his back pocket and wiped his neck and brow.

"What time did Piper leave the party?"

"She wasn't feeling well, maybe around eleven."

"Can anyone else vouch for this?"

"Yes, lots of people saw her go. Rasi picked her up."

"Is that Mr Malawi?" He appeared surprised.

"Yes, sir."

"Have you ever met Piper's cousin, Paige?"

"Yes, of course, a couple of times, a timid girl."

"Face to face, did you see her face to face."

"Yes, sir, why?"

"Were you present when Paige drowned in the river?"

"I had only just arrived, there was lots of commotion, but her body was never found."

"Do you think Piper is capable of murder?"

"Piper? No way, she gets upset if someone steps on

an ant."

"Which one of your friends is capable of murder?"

"I wouldn't pin this on any of them. There were a lot of people there that night. It could have been anyone. Marlon also had a lot of enemies. But, being in a gang, it was bound to happen sooner or later."

"Miss Bailey, did you want Marlon dead?"

"Look, I didn't like the guy, but I wouldn't want him dead."

"Who do you think killed Marlon?"

"I don't know, officer."

"Who had a motive? Is there anyone else who could shed some light on the incident?"

"Well, if anyone had a motive, it would be Venus. He had some dirt on her. She was doing things with her mum, you know, things you shouldn't be doing. Marlon saw her and took some photos, he blackmailed her with them, he was going to show everyone, if she didn't sleep with him."

"Someone was brutally attacked at Storm's party. Who was it?"

"If that happened, it would have been Venus. But I didn't hear of a brutal attack. Did Venus tell you that story? She's very good at inventing things. If you don't know her, you will believe every word she says. Maybe she knows who killed Marlon and is trying to delete herself from the scene."

"Trouble seems to follow you girls, who pushed the young lady from the building at Whittingdon High?"

"That happened, long before we were residents there."

"Thank you, Miss Bailey. We will take a short break." Officer Hendon appeared exasperated.

"Would you say that Piper is a pathological liar or any of your friends for that matter?"

"No, that's a bit drastic."

"Jazz, do you recognise this scarf?" He pulled a scarf from a sealed see-through bag. "No, Officer. I've never seen that scarf."

Someone had been watching us. Someone knew too much about us.

I guess it's like I always said, there was a mole amongst us.

CHAPTER 25

LIAR LIAR- VENUS

Who's right, who's wrong. They believe in God, I think, I don't.

So, who's helping me? Do I really need an invisible force to guide me? I didn't know, so I began to pray.

When my door was knocked, and the police were grazing my path like a million cows, I buckled at the entrance as they held me up and asked me to come to the station for questioning. I wanted to run. I grabbed at anything and everything I could get my hands on, no time to check if I had left any evidence behind, evidence that may incriminate me. I shovelled it under the bed as I shouted, "Just grabbing my jacket." Frantically making sure I did not leave anything important behind. I feel the curtains twitching as I voluntarily enter the car. I arrive at the station, then it suddenly dawns on me I have left the most crucial evidence behind, evidence that proves I had a motif.

"Venus, really", the two officers glanced a look at each other. I guess my name was kind of unusual.

"You and your friends have extremely unusual

names".

He shook his head in disapproval as if the uniqueness of our names bothered him.

"Venus", his tongue, strutted my name.

"What was your relationship with Marlon."

"He was a very good friend of mine".

"How close was he to you".

"Very close".

"Were you his lover".

"No".

"Did you want to be"?

"No".

"We are led to believe you were sleeping with him".

"No, he's not my type".

"What is your type then, Venus".

"I don't have a particular type".

"No, of course, you don't, you just enjoy sleeping with your mum, is this true".

My pits begin to sweat, I can't keep still in my chair, I'm finding it hard to breathe.

Suddenly my mouth is dry.

"Touch a nerve, Venus".

"I don't know what you are talking about. That's absurd, how dare you".

"Well, is it true or not"

"No comment".

"Marlon had photos of you, didn't he with your

mum? He was blackmailing you. He told you he was going to show the world if you didn't do as he asked".

"No comment".

"Let us help you Venus, how many times did your mum abuse you".

"She wasn't abusing me", I answer through splutter and tears

"How long had she been grooming you".

I can't answer. I just cry and cry until the pain in my chest has eased to a numbing.

"My intentions are not to arm you, Venus, but it's a pretty good motive to have, don't you think?

I nod in agreement. "But I didn't do it", I insist.

"Perhaps that may be true, but someone did, and someone needs to pay".

"Who was Marlon arguing with on the night of the party".

"Marlon was always arguing with someone, he's a hood rat, he was always beating Storm, maybe it's her come back. He and storm were always arguing, it was nothing new".

"What time did you arrive at the party, Venus."

"I got there around 6.30 pm. I had to work".

"At the strip club".

"Yes, at the sleazy strip club".

"You didn't enjoy it then".

"No, the girls said it was an easy way to earn some

quick cash, but they left me by myself on my first night because princess Storm had her party". I'm sure the officer detected the bitter jealousy in my tone. "I didn't know what to expect; I can't dance like them, especially Piper, so I got laughed off the stage. They threw orange peels and nuts at me. But I told them I had a good time".

"Life has thrown you some real lemonades, hasn't it, Venus".

"I guess so". I hang my head in shame.

"Is there anything you would like to tell us, Venus", the officer's voice is gentle and soothing?

"Yes, I would like to tell the truth".

"When you're ready, Venus, just talk to us, but first, do you recognise this scarf".

"Yes, it's the scarf that Marlon brought Storm for her birthday". The Officer scribbles something on the notepad in front of him.

I took a deep breath and decide not to stick to the plan. These girls had gotten away with so much it was time for them to pay.

"I didn't kill Marlon, but I wanted to. I wanted him dead, so he didn't reveal my secrets, but someone beat me to it. I think Storm murdered him; she was always going to; she wanted to get him back for murdering Marcus. She told me Marlon put his hand over his mouth to shut him up; he didn't mean to kill him; it was a freak accident.

But she didn't have the heart to tell on him because he was so hurt. Marcus wasn't Marlon's son; he was Corey's, Giselle's boyfriend. he was going to tell Giselle her man had a baby with her best friend, he put himself in grave danger. Storm is lethal; she is not to be messed with. So, Marlon threatened to kill Storm first.

I heard him tell Storm he would get her friend and hurt her. He waited until Storm's birthday to get at Piper because she was mouthy, and she knew everything. Storm could have killed him before, but she didn't want to spoil her birthday. When storm found out what Marlon had done to Piper, she was mad, outraged; Marlon was basically finished. Two days later, I hear he is dead. That's the bottom line of it".

"What exactly did Marlon do to Piper".

"He and four of his friends, well, they waited for her, and they attacked her like wild animals".

"Was it reported"?

"No, Rasi sorted Everything out".

"Do you have any proof or a witness to back you"?

"All of us are witnesses; it just depends how much you are prepared to reveal".

"But who actually knows about Piper because they all deny it, including piper".

"They're lying; Rasi covered everything up, he even prepped storm. But he only cares about piper, he doesn't care about us, I hate him".

"Why do you feel so strongly about him".

"Rasi has everything; he can do anything; he can make people disappear".

"Have you got proof of this"?

"Oh, come on, this is Rasi, who would tamper with him."

The officers glare at each other; they don't waste any time changing the subject.

"Tell us about Whittingdon High".

"It makes me sad, they made me lose my space, they bullied me into doing things I didn't want to".

"Such as".

"Hiding secrets, dark secrets".

"Baby secrets".

"Yes".

"Who was pregnant."

"Piper was pregnant, by whom I don't know, she never revealed that but I heard it was Rasi's baby. But because he was ten years her senior and he wasn't fully Jamaican, she hid it from him".

"Venus, what happened to the baby".

"They buried the body in the school grounds. Piper, Jazz, Storm, Giselle and Mrs Whittaker, the principal. But that's not the biggest secret they have.

There's more, much more than that. A dark secret that Piper doesn't know about".

"Do you have Proof, Venus" "No, it's what I was told"?

"By whom"

"I don't know, someone told me one night, as I walking home. They told me not to turn around, or they would kill me. They didn't show their face to me. They revealed all the girl's secrets">

"Was it a male voice or female".

"I'm not sure; the voice was disguised."

The officers noted everything I said, I know they thought I was crazy, but I was telling the truth.

I know what I had done was unsafe, but what other choice did I have. It was hard to explain to anyone why I continued in their presence; I wasn't scared of them, but in some stupid way, they protected me; I felt safe with them, I knew where I stood.

They were not my real friends, but we were in a long-standing relationship, yes it was toxic, but strangely I enjoyed their company.

The officers lean in as I reveal the secret the girls are hiding. I felt bad after, but I had suffered enough at their hands and disrespecting my skin colour. I had grown to like them, but it was not enough for me to protect them. I was not going down for something I didn't do.

Later I would pay for my betrayal. However, I wasn't the mole.

CHAPTER 26

THE MAGPIE AND THE FOOL - GISELLE

I couldn't breathe. My head was throbbing. I couldn't decide it was from the stress of the police station or the unsteady level of alcohol I had partaken in last night. It was probably a combination of both. I had been told repeatedly that the most important steps were the first and the last. It was something that I carried within me in everything I did, but then Piper and Jazz showed up and disrupted everything. Did I think I was living an ordinary life? I was so mistaken it's difficult to even explain.

The mere fact that you exist makes you extraordinary. I was unique, but it wasn't in a positive way. I tried to latch on to God, but I was hanging with a bunch of sinners, accomplices to their dark lives. I prayed for Piper for what she had endured that night, I knew Storm blamed her, but no one deserved that, not even Piper. If it meant I would have to selfishly tell the truth to relieve myself from ending up in demon valleys such as prison, I would say to them Piper had a motive

"You do not have to say anything that you do not wish, but it may harm your defence if you do not mention when questioned something which you later rely on in court. Anything you do say may be given in evidence.

"May I remind you that speaking to us is voluntary, and as such, if you wish to remain silent or answer no comment, you may do so. The recording may be used in the court of law for evidence should you plead not guilty to the offence.

"Do you understand?"

"Yes."

"Name?"

"Giselle."

"Real name?"

"That is my real name."

"Ooh, we have a swan in the room. Let's see if she can swim."

I held a stern face at the officer, probably trying to attract his white counterpart and keep his job. He was kind of cute, though, with his shiny bald head.

"Let's cut to the chase, young lady. What time did Piper leave the party?"

I was getting restless with the number of questions being fired my way. I wondered how everyone else was coping.

"She left around 11pm. She wasn't feeling great, so

Rasi drove her home."

"Rasi?"

"Oh yes, he's our friend."

"Was he at the party?"

"Yes, he was. He goes everywhere with us."

"Really?" The officer looked surprised.

"His name did not appear on our list for questioning. Are you sure he was there?"

"Positive."

"Your friends seem to think differently."

"Oh, they would. They lie about everything. Don't listen to a word they say."

Officer Bernard glanced at his colleague sitting next to him. They shared an advanced grin as if I was mad.

"What was the argument about, between Marlon and Storm?"

"Oh, they always argue, but it wasn't between them. It was Marlon and his friends. I was having a really good time, it was a 21st birthday, and if there was an argument, it would have been because Marlon started it. So, I'm not sure what it was about."

"What time did you leave?"

"I was there until 4 am. I helped to tidy up."

"Did any of your friends have a motive to harm Marlon?"

"Why would any of us have a motif? Yes, he was an arsehole, but he didn't deserve to die."

I prayed to God to forgive me for the lies I had just told.

"So, he could have had lots of enemies then?"

"Maybe, I don't really know."

"But you didn't like him?"

"Not really."

"Enough to want him dead?"

"Oh no, I wouldn't wish anyone dead. I'm a Christian."

The inspector sat with squinted eyes and peered over the top of his glasses at me. I could feel my eyes squinting as they did when I was not telling the whole truth.

"What do you do for a job?"

"I've just finished college and going on to further education."

"What are you studying?" He never looked up when he asked these questions but carried on writing. The older officer sitting next to him never took her eyes off me. She observed my actions to suss me out and catch me lying. I just needed to breathe, act like a fool, and stick to the plan.

"I'm studying law." I grinned energetically, but my answer was ignored.

"Did Marlon have another girl at the party?"

"Marlon had lots of girls at Storm's party. He was such a cheat, always sleeping around. But then again, so was Storm. She loved the men."

"What is Storm like as a person?"

"She's my friend, and I love her, but she can be violent, aggressive, erratic, spontaneous. Kind and helpful, very flirty. She would sleep with your boyfriend if she got the chance. I bet she's sleeping with the policeman she's with right now."

The officer coughs and looks at me in surprise.

"Do you think Storm is capable of murder?"

"I wouldn't put it past her. She's very hot-headed, shoots first, and asks questions after." My laugh was disturbing.

"Giselle, did you ever hear Storm say she wanted Marlon dead?"

"Sometimes she joked about killing him herself, but don't we all? I do know she looked into hiring someone to do it for her, but she never went ahead with it."

I asked for a glass of water as my throat was so dry from all the talking. The officer stopped the recording before he left the room. When he returned, I was in conversation with the other officer. He was not impressed.

"Giselle, who helped you murder Marlon?"

"No one, I didn't kill him."

"Can anyone vouch for your whereabouts at the time of Marlon's death"?

"I was at church." I knew that Sadie, the girl I had

befriended in church, would back me, or I would tell the pastor she smokes weed out the back with the Sunday school teachers. We had all befriended a weak friend at some point in our lives. It was something we had planned, just in case we needed an alibi. We arranged to make friends with someone not in the group, who could be easily blackmailed at the drop of a hat. Sadie was a dizzy white girl who was petrified of her strict dad. I had seen Sadie with whiplash marks on the tops of her legs. Her dad beat her regularly to make sure he kept her in check.

"What's the name of your church?"

"Clapham."

"Sorry?" the officer questioned.

"I mean, it's in Clapham. It's called Garden Roots." At least that was the truth.

"Thank you. We will check it out later. Do you have a surname for Sadie?"

"Sadie White"

We knew everything about our add-on friends, from what they ate to who they slept with, their favourite foods, and the worst person in their life."

"Did Storm suffocate her baby?"

"She might have, but the post mortem said cot death." I knew she didn't do it full well, but right now was every man for himself, and I promise you, I was not going down. They all thought I would break easily.

I had played stupid for long enough; it was time to unleash Giselle.

"Did she drown Piper's cousin Paige?"

"Well, we were all going swimming in the lake. When we arrived, Storm was already looking for her. Storm is a strong swimmer, so she was diving to the bottom, but it was too late she couldn't find her. Piper was hysterical. She kept sending Storm back down. When the diving team arrived, they couldn't find her either."

"Do you believe Paige actually existed?"

"Of course, she did. I saw her."

"Up close? Were her and Piper ever in the same room?"

"Come to think of it, I don't believe they ever were. Perhaps Paige murdered Marlon."

The officer appeared confused as if I had missed the point. "Do you think any of your friends are capable of murder?"

"All of them are capable; they are a force to be reckoned with. If they did it, they wouldn't tell me. They look at me as being very religious. I would make them hand themselves in."

"Don't you have your own secret?"

"Such as Officer?"

He cleared his throat as the female officer began to fidget in her chair. "What happened in the fire at your house, the one when you were a little girl?"

"Sir, I have no idea what you are talking about."

"Your mother conducted a house fire to get away from your abusive father. Your identity was changed to protect you, wasn't it Giselle, or is it Georgina?"

"Georgina was my cousin; you leave her out of this," I spoke before thinking to reveal I was that child in the fire.

"What was your name before it was Giselle?"

"Kendra, my name was Kendra. Unfortunately, my mother did not start that fire."

"But Kendra died in that fire, didn't she, Giselle?"

"No, my cousin Georgina died in that fire."

"Is that what your lying mother told you. Your aunty was blind, so your mum thought she couldn't tell if her own child was dead or alive. So, your mother swapped you to ease the pain of her own child dying".

My head began to swirl. I couldn't believe what I was hearing. My palms were sweating so much I could bring them out. Could this be true? Was my mum lying to me all these years? Was I Georgina, was my aunty really my mum? It was strange how she insisted on calling me Georgina when we were alone. Strange how I knew the words to songs I'd never even heard; odd, my mum wouldn't allow me to have blood tests. The penny dropped. It wasn't quite yet time to panic.

There was still time to salvage the situation. At

least, that was what I was telling myself.

The reality was that it was time to panic. I continued to delude myself into believing I was right. One of us was going down. Now I was not so sure if it would be me.

My lawyer sat next to me, demanding I did not have to answer, but I saw this on TV. You reply, "No comment" too often, and next thing you know, they are reading you your rights.

"Please, I need some air," I requested. The officer was staring at me as if he realised he'd gone too far.

I bolted from the room into the mild breeze and fell to my knees sobbing. How did they know all of this? Who had been talking? Only my friends knew my life story, but the part about Georgina? That was ludicrous. Or was it.

There was a mole in the house.

CHAPTER 27

SHATTERED GLASS- STORM

I felt bewildered before I even sat down. All eyes were on me. Marlon was my boyfriend, which meant I was the perfect suspect by default. It's odd how your body drives a severe cold through you when you're under pressure. The tired room with a stale tobacco smell was warm, although I was trembling. I wasn't behaving as if I stood a chance. I prayed silently to beg for forgiveness, to escape from being caught up in this whirlwind. Getting involved with my friends, if that's what you could call them.

Don't get me wrong, I loved Piper. Only God knows how sorry I felt for her. Is it wrong to say she may have brought this upon herself? Why did Piper always have to be so mouthy with Marlon, constantly goading him and upsetting him?

Everyone knew he had a temper; she couldn't help herself. So here we were again shielding her. Only this time, I wasn't just being refused a coffee in the café, thrown out of a wine bar, getting into a fight, or sleeping with a guy whose girlfriend had upset me. I wasn't losing my place in a racist independent school; I was losing my calling in life. Did anyone think about that? Did anyone stop to think that I didn't want to be a party to any of this?

Marlon tried with her, but she hated him. I wasn't sure why. Suppose I just told the truth and we all went down together, did time together? Oh no, not Piper. She got herself raped. Now I had to lie to save her. I was prepped by Rasi to get her off the hook, but what about me? I couldn't even remember what he told me to say to ensure I didn't go down.

"May I remind you that speaking to us is voluntary, and as such, if you wish to remain silent or answer no comment, you may do so. The recording may be used in the court of law for evidence should you plead not guilty to the offence. I also remind you that you have waivered your rights to a solicitor."

"Right, let's move on."

"Storm Basildon, real name?" the well-painted stern-faced officer asked. She was going to try my last nerve.

"That is my real name," I spoke slowly, "Storm Basildon."

She cleared her throat and looked at me sarcastically before adding. "Well, you have created a bit of a storm, haven't you?"

Was that supposed to be a joke? Because it really

wasn't funny.

"I guess so," I answered abruptly.

"Storm, how long have you known the deceased?"

"Seven years."

"Describe the nature of your relationship to him."

"I was his girlfriend and mother of his now-deceased child," I added that bit in to stop them, putting me through any more grief.

"What was your relationship with his best friend Corey, Giselle's boyfriend?"

"We were close, more than friends, I guess."

"So, you were having an affair with him?"

"I guess so." I just wanted them to arrest me now.

"Did Giselle know you were sleeping with her boyfriend?"

"No, she thought Piper was."

"And was she? Was Piper sleeping with Corey?"

"No, Piper hated him and Marlon."

"Did anyone know about your relationship with Corey?"

"Yes, I told Piper, and she told Jazz."

"Who was baby Marcus' real dad?"

I stall for a few seconds before answering. No point in lying; I'm already a prime suspect.

"Corey," I whisper

"Sorry, I didn't hear you; you will need to speak up."

"I said, Corey, he was Marcus's dad."

"Did Marlon know?"

"No, he would have killed me."

"So, you killed him first." The officer stares me down, waiting for an answer, waiting for me to say I did it. But I didn't. I really didn't do it.

"No, I loved Marlon. I would never hurt him."

"Even though your relationship was hostile? We have reason to believe that Marlon was quite physical with you, violent, in fact.

"We had our moments, but I gave as good as I got."

"Did you murder your boyfriend Storm?"

"No, I promise you I didn't."

"Tell me about your party, Storm. How did the evening play out for you?"

"It was a great evening. I thought so, anyway. All my closest friends and family were there, a few faces I didn't recognise, people who came as a friend of someone else. Great music, all my favourites, nice food my mum and aunties made before they left us. Obviously, lots of alcohol."

"So, it's fair to say you could possibly have been intoxicated to not notice if something sinister took place."

"Maybe for the others, but I don't drink, so I was fully aware of what was going on."

"How was Marlon's mood that night?"

"Usual, he was in good spirits."

"What would that look like, Storm?"

"Well, the usual happy go lucky, Marlon."

"Would you say your relationship with Marlon was hostile? Because according to your friends, you were both quite violent towards one another."

"Wow, who told you that? Marlon was so loving. Why would someone speak like that?" I managed to squeeze a tear from my eye, hanging my head in despair.

Officer Ferguson handed me a tissue. He waited for me to stop sniffling before he continued his interrogation.

"Do you know why someone would say something so untrue about you?"

"To get themselves off the hook."

"Did Marlon have another girlfriend at the party?"

"No?"

"Really, we were informed that Piper was seen with her hands around a girl's throat because she was seeing Marlon."

"Not that I know of."

"Is Piper Violent, Storm?"

"No, she hates violence, and I know this session will be bothering her immensely?"

"Did anyone see you and Marlon together?"

"Yes, lots of people. I was so upset with Marlon he

kept on disappearing."

"Was there physical contact between yourself and Marlon?"

"In what way?"

"Was he aggressive?"

"I just told you, Marlon was loving." Listen to me lying. I wanted to tell them how I wanted to kill him for every bruise or broken bone he caused me, for every near-death scenario, for my baby, but I couldn't because it was the Piper show.

"How did you feel when you heard he was dead."

"Devastated, I still am. He was the love of my life. ''I'm heartbroken, and being questioned like this is not helping. I've had little time to grieve."

"What did you do, in response?"

"Well, obviously, I cried and smashed a few things." I smoked a spliff. First, I couldn't believe he was gone. Then I was happy he was gone. I had no interest in Marlon after Marcus died. After that, I was numb to everyone. So, sitting here discussing his death, I was cold to it all. I was still grieving for my baby he killed.

"Who did you tell first about Marlon's death."

"I think I told my mum."

"How did she respond."

"She was upset. She liked Marlon." I allowed a tear to dance down my cheek. My parents hated Marlon; I wouldn't be surprised if they ordered his death themselves. Maybe I should have said they did it.

"Then who did you tell?"

"I told Piper."

"How was her reaction?"

Should I tell them she offered to help me hide the body, that her empathetic response was, "Good riddance to bad rubbish?" Or that she said she wished she had done it herself? Which one of those statements would put her behind bars? I had recorded all my friends' responses in case I needed them. But my Dictaphone had mysteriously gone missing. Piper was clever. I believed she cottoned on and disposed of it.

"She was shocked."

"Did any of your friends have a motive to want Marlon dead?"

"Only, Venus. He was blackmailing her."

"What about Piper? Didn't he brutally attack her at your party?"

"These lies just keep getting worse," I quickly lied.

"Whilst we are on the subject of lying, Storm, the scarf that was found around Marlon's neck was apparently the same scarf he had bought you."

"Which scarf was that?"

Officer Ferguson pushed a photo in front of me of a baby pink scarf with gold stars. I loved that scarf. It was my favourite. I would spray it with my favourite perfume and wear it on mild summer nights. The girls often teased me and said I looked like a granny.

"I've never seen that scarf in my life."

"Your friends seem to think that it is yours. They said you never left home without it."

I didn't mean to lie, but I didn't kill Marlon, and I didn't want to go down for something I didn't do. We had rehearsed this with Rasi. My friends wouldn't give out that information. What were they playing at?

"Did Marlon ever hit you?"

"No, he wasn't violent."

"Do you know who might have done this?"

"Marlon had a lot of enemies, but I wasn't one of them."

"Where were you when Marlon was murdered?"

"I stayed at my sister's house; it was her birthday."

"Can your sister vouch for this?"

"Of course, she can."

Officer Ferguson scribbled something on a piece of paper, then turned back to me.

"How well do you know your friends?"

"I thought I knew them really well?"

"Are you doubting their actions?"

"I don't know now."

My heart was pounding. All the evidence was pointing at me. I felt like ''I was fighting for my life whilst someone was letting me down. Officer Ferguson's white beard suddenly began to look greasy.

He kept stroking his dry white hand over it. His hazel eyes bordered on tired. ''I wasn't sure if he felt sorry for me or was just defeated. I got the impression he already knew he would arrest me later for the murder of my boyfriend.

"Storm, who helped you murder Marlon?"

"I didn't do it," I grabbed back a cry.

"Do you have any other witnesses?"

"No," I choked at his question.

"Is there anyone else we should talk to regarding the night of the party"

"I don't know." ''I was too petrified to talk, so I asked for my lawyer.

Officer Ferguson was a chubby police officer, clean-cut, and quite good-looking.

His white shirt is a bit creased but clean. His eyebrows appear reasonably groomed, and his fingernails were cut short and clean. He smelled a bit musty as if he has been on the job all night. His breath was stale from the numerous amounts of coffee. I reckoned he was a bit OCD, as he kept lining up his pencils whilst speaking to me.

"You and your friends have a lot of trouble hanging over your heads. Firstly, there is the mysterious secret that had all you expelled from Whittingdon high. Then the premature death of the young pregnant girl who was pushed from the school building. The disappearance of Piper's cousin, Paige. The death of your own son and the truth about whether you suffer from domestic violence. The scarf you claim is not yours. The list goes on and now this. In every event, Storm, you have been present or nearby. It really is not looking good for you. We have a valuable witness who claims she knows you very well, she can identify you at every event, and she has proof you were involved in all these events. You're a great liar, Storm, but your times up, you have been found out. We have hospital evidence of bruises on your body caused by Marlon. We had photos of you on the roof when the young girl was pushed, and we also have video footage of you leaving Marlon's house the morning he was murdered. And last, your blood was found on the scarf that was used to strangle Marlon.

"What do you have to say for yourself, Storm? Can you explain any of this?"

I knew as soon as the officer stood up, I wasn't going home. I sat and cried genuine tears, heart-wrenching tears. I cried for everyone I knew. How did this happen to me? I didn't do any of it, did my friends set me up? Piper was right. There was a mole amongst us. But I would serve time first before I found out who.

Ten years the judge slammed me with. I would serve the total amount. My mum collapsed In the courtroom in her wheelchair, with my dad holding her up. My sister looked at me in disgust as my brother held his head in his hands and bawled. Jazz mouthed to me to hold my head up. Giselle was hysterical. Piper, well, she was Piper, never cried, but she blew me a kiss.' 'I'm sure I saw a tear roll down her pretty face as she mouthed a thank you. I was doing most of her time for all the things they had accused me of. But Piper had suffered enough. In some respects, she was already doing time.

That didn't change the fact that someone was watching us.

Despite every event we had been party to, we didn't murder Marlon.

So, who did? We had been framed.

CHAPTER 28

THE CALLIGRAPHER

There are different types of secrets, the ones where you want to surprise someone at a birthday party; and those that will ruin your life. I knew the group had held on to plenty of secrets throughout their time on this earth.

They believed they had lived through the storm. So, they held on to the worst type of secrets. Too late to tell anyone, so they would prefer to let it gnaw away at them. Then again, telling someone could end up getting you killed.

I watched them closely over the years, the five friends, as they attempted to impress every soul in the room with their talent and intelligence. Of course, there was no doubt that they were clever, but they had a yearning to prove it. I wondered if they would be so quick to prove that you could not believe a word they said. Would they be so quick to prove their unforgiving lies, deceit, and murderous acts? The fact that they were the most intelligent and beautiful women in the room could easily have been deduced, but they didn't really pay much attention to one another. They only cared about themselves. Their lives had been filled with bitterness and anguish. They hung out together as no one else would put up with the false images they portrayed to one another.

We had been studying the group for years now. We turned up at every event they were at, served food as waiters, chauffeured them to places, babysat their children, went to the same parties, even sat next to them in the cinema. I even made Storm's 21st birthday cake.

Their self-indulgence didn't allow them to notice us. I think Piper may have been curious once about one of us, but it didn't last long, and she was the observant one. I watched them for so long I became obsessed. They had been unable to build solid relationships with anyone because the people they embraced were not people they had things in common with, but people they didn't ever want to be like.

When I first met the person in charge, I was in awe. I wanted to be like her. She trained me well.

We worked out very quickly that Piper was the ring leader. As much as she played the victim, she did it to her advantage because her friends would always protect her. Along the way, we had to help them out, such as getting rid of Marlon. I had great pleasure ending his journey; he deserved it. I just wish we had arrived sooner.

At times it was tough love. We spent most of our lives hiding in and out of theirs. The years were long and slow, we wanted to kill their pleasure, but we had to wait. Patience soon became a natural skill I developed. What would their reaction be? Would they reach the finish line humbly, or would we pay for this? I did know their time was up.

Over time they had forgotten who they were. So instead, they believed their own stories.

I'd been practising the art of calligraphy writing for years. It's a visual art related to reporting. However, executing this varied style of lettering takes time and patience.

I was now a qualified expert. Performing it with ease was no arduous task for me. Scriptwriting for companies became my favourite skill. I owned a creative ability to switch between my two forms of writing. Calligraphy was only used when I didn't want anyone to recognise me.

I was confident and in my own world when writing, but today was different.

I needed to make sure my calligraphy was at its best; I needed to ensure that not a soul would catch on.

My hand shook as I wrote precisely and evenly. I screwed the first paper up and tossed it onto the floor. Come on, I told myself; you can do this.

I rubbed my left hand with the other and picked the pen up; a knock on the door disturbed me. "Who is it?" My response was abrupt.

"Room service," came the quick jumpy voice.

"I didn't order anything." I waited for the reply

"We have you down for ordering breakfast, Madame."

Shit, I think to myself. Yes, I made an order of breakfast to my room for fear of being seen in the restaurant. But suddenly, I'm no longer hungry.

"Err, I'm so sorry," I say from the other side of the door, "would you mind if I changed my mind? I'm not feeling too great."

"Oh, sorry to hear. That's fine, Madame, but there will still be a charge, I'm afraid."

"Ok, thank you."

"Will that be everything?" I was sure I'd just told this man I wasn't feeling great; what else could he possibly do for me?

"Yes, that will be all, thank you."

I kept my ear to the door as I listened to his feet rub against the carpet as he walked away; why don't people pick their feet up when they walk? A real pet peeve of mine.

I returned to the desk and stared down at the paper; I continued writing my note to the six friends. The short break answering the door had calmed my nerves;

I swiftly glided the pen across the paper and wrote each one of them the same script.

I placed each note into its own white silky envelope and stick a circular black and white logo onto the top righthand corner. I dipped my finger into the glass of water on my desk and glided it over the sticky opening of the envelope. I sealed it shut. I then carefully dropped all six into an empty section of my handbag and prepare myself to leave, but not before thinking of her. I could still see her beautiful face and hear her voice now.

"It's a beautiful and elegant instrument to possess," she was breathless as she spoke whilst she swished her hand in the air, demonstrating how to form the flicks and curves. She had always been a great teacher with the highest standards; everything she performed was flamboyant yet graceful. Without her outstanding teaching, my calligraphy writing would not have been so on point. So, I had a lot to thank her for.

She often told me she regretted not perfecting this creative flair when she had written to the principal about the girls in Whittington High.

I was eager to reveal the truth about their lives to all their family and friends, but the timing is wrong, and it would be too risky. The truth always makes things easier, but not for these girls. Instead, the truth would fracture the group over again.

As I left the hotel room, I walked down the steps from the train station in a bit of a hurry, knowing the secrets in my briefcase must be secured as quickly as possible. Bounding down the steps, I turned suddenly as I heard someone behind me. I panicked in my quickness and stumbled over a can that some lazy git refused to throw in the bin.

A deep chill fills my body as I encounter a pair of white trainers placed deliberately on the stairs. How did I miss them? That was not possible.

Someone was there.

My palms began to sweat as I gripped the briefcase tightly and pulled it into my chest. A shadow passes over mine in the dim sunlight, but I don't dare turn around. I freeze, unable to breathe. I whispered a faint, "Who's there?" No answer.

I could hear her voice in my head saying, "Don't get caught. We must be careful. If they have a chance to lie, then it's all over. So, every timing must be precise."

I conjured up the courage. I slip along down the alleyway without turning around. I never knew if someone had seen me or if I had imagined it.

PAULETTE INGRAM SYNOPSIS

There are different types of secrets; and different styles of lies. Piper held on to plenty of them throughout her dysfunctional life. But these were not the lies you told when planning a surprise birthday party; these were the worst kind of lies that would eat away at your insides. Lies that would get you killed if you told anyone.

Piper battled to grow up amid the turbulence inflicted upon her in her own home as a young girl. Then, her cousin Paige's erratic behaviour turns vicious, leading Piper to direct a genre of survival techniques. From compulsive lying to an accidental murderer, Piper is drawn into always covering for her cousin's irrational thinking.

Piper also has her five friends to contend with; they share each other's deepest darkest secrets. They make a pact that nothing and no one can come between them. But can Piper trust them? Can they trust each other?

The arrival of an anonymous letter on the principal's desk leads to their dismissal from Whittingdon High secondary school. An independent, state of the arts secondary school for the privileged white middle-class children.

As a series of events unfolds around them, the friends find themselves swimming deeper and deeper in the darkness; their lies and deceit become uncontrollable. Finally, a body is found after one of the friends hosts her 21st birthday party.

Piper and her friends are now the suspects; as the girls turn against one another to protect themselves, one of them must pay the price for the brutal murder. As a result, the girl's relationship is jeopardised and ends abruptly.

But who has been watching them? Who knows about all their vicious lies? Who knows the most critical secret they hold so close to their hearts? A secret they would take to the grave.

SERVICES

SILENT RIVER BOOK CLUB

Silentriver2010@gmail.com

PAULETTE OWUSU PHOTOGRAPHY

Specialising in photography for parents and carers of children with disabilities,

Children

Families

Portrait

Candid shots

Landscape

Products

Funerals

Backdrop photography

headshots

www.pauletteowusu.co.uk

create on the floor backdrops.

SOCIAL MEDIA

FB:@POP1PHOTOGRAPHY

INSTA:pop_classic_photography

YOUTUBE

Paulette Owusu

Pophotography69

I AM ECHO

Co-owner @iamecho

Confidence and fashion platform ltd

Confidence course for children and adults. Teaching confidence through the art of cat walking, event organisers, providing a platform for up-and-coming artists and designers.

Providing confidence workshops in school and online.

www.iamecho.co.uk

FB:iamechofashionplatform

Insta:iamechofashionshows

Youtube:I AM ECHO Confidence and Fashion ltd

PAULETTE INGRAM BIOGRAPHY

Paulette Ingram, better known as Paulette Owusu, is gifted with a range of skills and talents. She is a new author and writer of Silent River, her first trilogy of three short stories. The other two books in this series, soon to be released, are Silent River Runs Deep and River Deep.

Paulette is also one of the many Co-Authors in the global achiever's book, 2021 summit

Silent River was birthed twelve years ago as a fiction story. But Paulette felt the incentive to complete it during the first COVID 19 lockdown in March 2020.

Her vivid imagination takes you to places that enable you to explore the power of the mind and question your own capabilities and relationships.

Paulette says, "Most people can find a piece of them in Silent River."

Her greatest accomplishment is setting up her photography business, specialising in creating her on-the-floor backdrops where she crafts material into amazing scenes to enable children with disabilities to be placed in a world of pure imagination. The backdrops allow the child to appear in various motions and much more. Paulette's Photography gives parents and carers of children with disabilities a sense of resilience, power, and strength. Paulette says she wants to raise awareness of children with disabilities by highlighting their differences, to open conversation points.

Paulette was born and raised in southeast London. She is a behaviour learning mentor for children and young adults who have social or emotional problems that affect their learning. She is a mother of two young men who are also gifted in the art criteria.

Paulette is also co-owner of a company called I AM ECHO, teaching children and adults how to build confidence through the art of runway training. She is also a runway coach and was trained at the Laurie Small School of modelling.

Her other skills involve writing poetry, writing songs, and singing. She has recently taken up sewing, creating body creams, designing clothes out of newspapers, t-shirts and working with youngsters in the community.

In addition, she enjoys long walks and going to the theatre. Paulette is also writing children's picture books and creating story boxes for children with disabilities.

Printed in Great Britain
by Amazon